The Bible in/and Popular Culture
A Creative Encounter

Society of Biblical Literature

Semeia Studies

Number 65
The Bible in/and Popular Culture
A Creative Enounter

edited by
Philip Culbertson and Elaine M. Wainwright

THE BIBLE IN/AND POPULAR CULTURE
A CREATIVE ENCOUNTER

Edited by

Philip Culbertson and Elaine M. Wainwright

Society of Biblical Literature
Atlanta

THE BIBLE IN/AND POPULAR CULTURE
A CREATIVE ENCOUNTER

Library of Congress Cataloging-in-Publication Data

The Bible in/and popular culture : creative encounter / edited by Elaine M. Wainwright and Philip Culbertson.
    p. cm. — (Society of Biblical Literature semeia studies ; 65)
    Includes bibliographical references and index.
    ISBN 978-1-58983-493-4 (paper binding : alk. paper) — ISBN 978-1-58983-494-1 (electronic library copy)
    1. Bible—Influence. 2. Popular culture—Religious aspects. 3. Arts and religion. I. Wainwright, Elaine Mary, 1948- II. Culbertson, Philip Leroy, 1944- III. Title: Bible in popular culture. IV. Title: Bible and popular culture.
    BS538.7.B525 2010
    220.09182'109045—dc22
2010016749

CONTENTS

Acknowledgments

This volume of essays had its origin in a course, The Bible in Popular Culture, co-taught at the University of Auckland by the editors. Philip and I wish to thank all of our students in 2006 and 2007 whose engagement with the course material and undertaking of creative assignments stretched our knowledge and imagination considerably. Emily Colgan and Jayson Rhodes, postgraduate students who tutored in the course, brought both new resources and creative insights and we are grateful for their ongoing engagement with us in exploring the intersection between the Bible and popular culture.

My special thanks go to Dr. Philip Culbertson, who has undertaken the major part of the editorial task even though he is no longer formally engaged in tertiary education. His attention to detail and his relentless following through on all aspects of the editorial role have brought this volume to a very satisfactory conclusion.

INTRODUCTION

Elaine M. Wainwright

> I wonder ... whether we Bible scholars shall be brave enough to focus on the Bible's heritage in our culture.... [T]he gain of doing cultural/biblical studies so-called, outside organized religion especially, may be enormous. Who knows, this way the Bible may continue to exist as a book for life, an identity cultural marker. Redefining it as a cultural commodity which, yes, also happens to be a religious book may save the Bible from popular oblivion. And it may save us Bible scholars from socio-political insignificance too—while allowing for great fun, of the serious and the light-headed types, in the process. (Brenner 2000, 11)

These words of Athalya Brenner in her foreword to *Culture, Entertainment and the Bible* (2000) provided a significant challenge to biblical scholars—an invitation to a reading of the Bible outside "organized religion," a reading of the Bible as "cultural/biblical studies." Her challenge remains valid today, almost a decade later, even though many such readings have been undertaken in the interim, and so her words provide a fitting opening to this collection of essays in which biblical scholars engage with the Bible in/as popular culture in ways that are both serious and fun.

That biblical scholars are engaging with popular culture is evident in the almost four-hundred-page volume *Teaching the Bible through Popular Culture and the Arts*, published in 2007, in which Mark Roncace and Patrick Gray engage not only a number of biblical scholars with experience in this nexus of Bible and popular culture but also a range of popular media and the arts: music, film, art, literature, and other media such as comics and television shows. Roncace and Gray provide a compendium of resources for those teaching biblical studies in today's classrooms. What they do not provide, however, is a theoretical engagement with the very nexus itself—the Bible in/as/and popular culture—also an essential tool for those who teach in this area. One of the surprising aspects of this is that, given the penchant in biblical studies for hermeneutical and methodological issues, there is as yet no systematic study of the interrelationship between the Bible and popular culture.

Such a lacuna does not exist in theology and religious studies. Just by way of example, two books appeared in 2005 addressing theology and popular culture. In *The Blackwell Guide to Theology and Popular Culture*, Kelton Cobb engaged with theories of popular culture in dialogue with a theological framework as the foundation from which to analyze a range of popular media and their conveying of theological meaning. Gordon Lynch, on the other hand, in his *Understanding Theology and Popular Culture*, also published by Blackwell, drew more heavily on cultural theorists, such as Adorno, Bourdieu, Barthes, and Certeau, as well as a three-pronged framework of author-focused, text-based, and audience-centered approaches familiar to biblical scholars, to examine the theology/popular-culture nexus. In the following year, 2006, Adam Possamai published his *Religion and Popular Culture: A Hyper-Real Testament*.

The title of Roland Boer's 1999 book, *Knockin' on Heaven's Door: The Bible and Popular Culture*, promised just such an analysis in relation to biblical studies. He, however, makes clear the very explicit and limited dimensions of his work when he says in the introduction:

> My effort in this book does not seek biblical dimensions in contemporary cultural products as such, nor does it restrict itself to the application of cultural theories to the Bible, nor is it interested in explicit representations of the Bible in contemporary culture. Rather it juxtaposes biblical and other cultural texts and it does so from the perspective of dialectical Marxism. (Boer 1999, 1–2)

The need for a more general theoretical framework/s remained.

What biblical scholars have done is to turn their attention to the representation of biblical figures, biblical themes, even biblical genres in popular culture, with the most explicit attention being directed to the Bible and film (see, by way of example, from a wide range of titles: Aichele and Walsh 2002; Reinhartz 2003, 2007; Runions 2003; Shepherd 2008; and the many books examining Mel Gibson's *The Passion of the Christ*, such as Corley and Webb 2004; Beal and Linafelt 2006; and Fredriksen 2006). That this aspect of the Bible-and-popular-culture nexus has developed or is developing significant theoretical frameworks of analysis is evident in the words of Christopher Fuller in his review of the most recent publication, *Images of the Word: Hollywood's Bible and Beyond* (Shepherd 2008):

> Whereas past studies have tended to focus on story at the expense of visual analysis, these essays demonstrate that the study of the Bible and film has matured into … a beautiful friendship. The greater awareness of film history,

the inclusion of foreign films, more concentrated attention on cinematic sty-
listics, and a better grasp of film scholarship recommend this collection to
anyone who is interested in this field. (Fuller 2009)

Fuller does not, however, allow biblical scholars engaging with film studies to
rest on their laurels but challenges them to further engagement between biblical
studies and film studies, so that "the names Eisenstein, Bazin, and Mulvey are
as familiar to biblical scholars as Wellhausen, Bultmann, and Käsemann" (Fuller
2009). How much more so the challenge in relation to other media.

This volume of essays arose out of an awareness that, as Roncace and Gray
have demonstrated, biblical scholars are engaging not only film but a range of
media within popular culture to assist in their teaching of biblical studies and also
out of an awareness that popular culture is a significant arena of contemporary
biblical interpretation. As indicated already, there has been much less attention
paid to media beyond film and even less theorizing, so that Fuller's challenge to
biblical scholars working with other media would be much stronger. Some of the
authors in this volume have begun this task in their recent publications (Gilmour
2004, 2005, 2009; McEntire 2006; Clanton 2009), especially in relation to music.
There are, however, other media that still require significant attention, such as
graphic novels, comics, fiction, and television shows. In these areas, theorizing is
just beginning. This volume will not be able to provide a comprehensive theoretical framework/s for the engagement with the Bible in popular culture. Each essay
will, however, give attention not only to the ways that a range of media engage
biblical texts, characters, themes, and genres but also to the ways that authors
begin to analyze the biblical material through the lens of selected theorists of biblical hermeneutics, popular culture, and its media modes in all their diversity.

Michael J. Gilmour's opening essay, "Some Novel Remarks about Popular
Culture and Religion: Salman Rushdie and the Adaptation of Sacred Texts," draws
attention to a mode of reading with which biblical scholars are familiar, namely,
intertextuality. Generally, however, such scholars are looking back to the ways
in which earlier biblical texts, those of the prophets for instance, are drawn into
later texts such as the gospels. Intertextuality, however, also provides a theoretical
framework for examining how traces of biblical texts function within contemporary literary and visual arts, music, and other multimedia. It is a process that
could be said to characterize the entire field of the Bible in popular culture. To
demonstrate this, Gilmour draws on a wonderful image from Salman Rushdie,
namely, an ocean or a sea of stories swirling around in myriads of intersecting
currents to which Rushdie's title *Haroun and the Sea of Stories* alludes. Gilmour
dips into this swirl of currents as he examines the way that the biblical figure of
Satan/the devil/Lucifer morphs through Milton's *Paradise Lost* into Rushdie's *The
Satanic Verses*. He does not stop, however, with literary analyses but draws on the

postcolonial theory of Homi Bhabha to determine the sociocultural function of Rushdie's work.

The omnipresence of the biblical stories and images in ongoing human meaning-making through various media is evident in Mark McEntire's "Red Dirt God: Divine Silence and the Search for Transcendent Beauty in the Music of Emmylou Harris." Like Gilmour, McEntire examines the imagery of falling from the heavens in the first lyric of Emmylou Harris's album *Red Dirt Girl*. For McEntire, the narrative category of characterization provides a mode for examining the God of the biblical narrative who, he suggests, becomes more and more hidden as the narrative unfolds. This notion of a God who "lurks in the background" provides McEntire with a frame for encountering the elusiveness of God across the songs on Harris's album. The invitation to listeners is to enter into the pain of "the long loneliness of the world." Music, like story, swirls in that ocean that Rushdie envisaged and invites its listeners into the serious type of fun that Brenner predicted for biblical scholars in engaging with Harris's album and McEntire's analysis of it.

Intertextuality could be said to characterize Dan W. Clanton Jr.'s exploration, "'Here, There, and Everywhere': Images of Jesus in American Popular Culture." He does not limit himself to one medium, such as literature or music, but rather ranges across media to demonstrate his two categories of the current appropriation of Jesus within American popular culture, namely the "biblical/devotional Christ" and the "Jesus in Elseworlds." His theoretical approach is that of reception history, raising for readers the question of the relationship between intertextuality and reception history in seeking to understand the current swirling of a central biblical character such as Jesus within the ocean of popular culture. From Clanton's study, the Jesus of popular culture is not elusive or hidden in the way that McEntire suggests for the God of the biblical narrative and Emmylou Harris's lyrics. Rather, through examining selected movies, fiction, and music, especially country and bluegrass, Clanton suggests that the popular/devotional Jesus is a model to be emulated and a focus of faith, while the Jesus in Elseworlds challenges readers/viewers/listeners to examine their own views of Jesus. He concludes that Jesus functions mythically within American culture, thereby opening up at the end of his essay another rich field of scholarly exploration—the nature and function of myth within popular culture.

The reception of a biblical character in popular culture is also the concern of Philip Culbertson, in "'Tis a Pity She's (Still) a Whore: Popular Music's Ambivalent Resistance to the Reclamation of Mary Magdalene," as he turns the lens of Freud and Jung onto the image of Mary Magdalene among the youth who engage with this culture and participate in courses examining the Bible in popular culture. Culbertson grapples with the complex hermeneutical issue of the radical change in the characterization of Mary Magdalene over centuries, culminating in her portrayal across a broad range of popular lyrics that he places into four categories. This in itself raises significant questions for further exploration. As a psychotherapist and a practical theologian, Culbertson then speculates on the "gains" to today's young women of the sexualized Mary Magdalene of popular culture, using the theories of Freud and Jung that he has explored briefly, together with a notion of *reverse hermeneutics* and an engagement with contemporary studies of youth culture. It must surely have been fun to explore the "ninety-two topical songs in the pop repertoire" and Culbertson's essay gives readers a brief glimpse of these. His essay, however, raises and begins to explore more serious issues in relation to the Bible in/as popular culture, while alerting his readers to much more remaining to be done.

Reading Jim Perkinson's article, "Spittin', Cursin', and Outin': Hip-Hop Apocalypse in the Imperial Necropolis," is indeed "fun"—both lighthearted and serious. He undertakes an innovative turn in relation to the Bible-and-popular-culture nexus, refracting the Bible and hip-hop into one another and exploring the spaces in between. He analyzes the "hip-hop hermeneutic of Holy Writ" with a rhythm and a beat in his prose that echoes that of the music and musicians he is analyzing. He throws down a challenge to biblical interpreters through the words, phrases, and rhythms of the hip-hop artists—"a use of words to infuse the surge of percussive memories of refusing the grave." Having drawn his readers into his style and his empire-disturbing analysis, he provides examples of the very refraction that he is proposing between specific biblical texts and hip-hop artists and their lyrics. While the reading of this article may be fun, as one enters into the rhythm of its language, its content and its challenge are much more disturbing.

As Perkinson leaves his readers with questions, Noel Leo Erskine begins with one: "The Bible and Reggae: Liberation or Subjugation?" He asks whether the Bible, especially as it was used in Bob Marley's reggae, contributed to liberation or subjugation in Jamaica. Biblical themes, images, and terminology are refracted through Rastafarianism, Erskine argues, to inform Marley's lyrics that, in their turn, awaken Jamaica's poor to their subjugation in a colonial context. Erskine uses the category of history, or the "larger story," in a number of ways in his essay: tracing the history of Marley with that of reggae and Rastafarianism, plotting the effect of Marley's reggae in raising the hopes of Jamaica's poor, placing the history of those poor within biblical history, and demonstrating how Marley's lyrics ignited the people's leaving of Babylon. Such histories are shown to be at the service of liberation. With a final brief glance at reggae and Marley's ideas about and imaging of women, Erskine suggests that liberation movements are never finished, as they often contain aspects of the Babylon they seek to leave behind.

As Erskine moves readers from the cultural consumers of American pop culture to the streets of Jamaica's poor, Tex Sample returns them to the United States of America, but into the lives of working-class Americans, in "'Help Me Make It Through the Night': Narrating Class and Country Music in the Theology of Paul." This is the context for his listening to two songs of Kris Kristofferson, "Help Me Make it Through the Night" and "Me and Bobby McGee," which he reads against the practices of inequality and oral culture that characterize the lives of the working class among whom the songs are popular. He weaves into his reading a brief engagement with Bakhtin, Certeau, and other theorists to argue that the popularity of Kristofferson's songs points to practices of resistance. In a move, however, that contrasts significantly with the intertextuality of Michael Gilmour or the reception-history approach of Dan Clanton, Sample brings the reception of Kristofferson's lyrics to a "narrating" of them into the theology of Paul. He has demonstrated that the interrelationships between the Bible and popular culture are multidimensional. An interpreter may begin with popular culture to develop a reading lens for the Bible or may use the biblical text as lens for reading popular culture. Nuanced forms of both approaches are evident in this volume. As a result, a range of theorists can be used as dialogue partners in the analysis of the relationship between the Bible and popular culture's refraction of it.

Sample, like most other authors in this volume, has drawn a variety of sociological studies and cultural theories into his study, suggesting that the theory that facilitates an analysis of the Bible-and-popular-culture nexus will be as varied as the media, the artists, and the genres being studied. Roland Boer, in "Jesus of the Moon: Nick Cave's Christology," demonstrates this through his dialogue with Nick Cave's "Jesus of the Moon" as a vehicle for studying Cave's turn to Jesus. Boer leads his readers through Atalli's study of noise and Gracyk's analysis of rock music, while listening to the hint of Adorno's music criticism, to understand Cave's early music as backdrop to the question of how his turn to quieter music relates to his turn to Jesus. This is an overturning of the way the question is usually posed, according to Boer. At appropriate points in his analysis of one song, "Brompton Oratory," Boer plays three theorists—Alan Bloom, Camille Paglia, and Theodore Gracyk—against one another in order to demonstrate his claim that Cave's Christology is heretical, in that it belongs to his own unique interpretation. For Boer, critical theory as a vehicle for analyzing an aspect of popular culture, namely the music of Nick Cave, and in particular, his song "Brompton Oratory," becomes the focus of his study, with only a hint of its relationship to the biblical Jesus. This is to move beyond intertextuality and reception history, or their reverse, to a more explicit study of popular culture that refracts a biblical character and a study of that refraction in dialogue with those theorists of such culture. Boer has demonstrated once again that serious and light-headed fun can be combined when engaging popular culture with the Bible in hand.

In a significant shift of the focal medium, Terry Ray Clark, in "Prophetic Voices in Graphic Novels: The 'Comic and Tragic Vision' of Apocalyptic Rhetoric in *Kingdom Come* and *Watchmen*," turns his attention to two graphic novels, as the title indicates, in dialogue with Ostwalt's theory of secularization and sacred texts. Ostwalt regrets modern biblical studies' devaluation of the potential metaphorical and mythical effects of biblical narratives in addressing questions of ultimate human concern. Clark uses this theory together with O'Leary's categories of the cosmic and the tragic developed out of his dialogue with Kenneth Burke. He examines how apocalyptic literature can have an effect that might be comic or tragic. Within the tragic frame, there is a recognition that human history will end tragically and can be saved from this end only by divine intervention. Within the comic frame, focus is on human potential. Clark's analysis of the two graphic novels cited above within the analytic frame that he develops reveals that they can function in a comic mode to address the question of humanity's survival in the face of potential self-destruction. His study, like many others in the volume, has provided a model that both students and other scholars might use for other analyses or that demonstrate the range of theories that might lead to the generation of new models.

The same could be said of Steve Taylor's engagement with a New Zealand animated cartoon, *bro'Town*, which until recently aired on prime-time television, in his article, "Reading 'Pop-Wise': The Very Fine Art of 'Making Do' When Reading the Bible in *bro'Town*." Taylor draws into his analysis South African biblical scholar Gerald West's hermeneutic of "reading otherwise," or reading with ordinary readers, suggesting that *bro'Town* belongs to such a type of reading. It is Certeau, however, who provides Taylor with the name he gives to his approach: a hermeneutics of "making do." He sees such a hermeneutic functioning in *bro'Town*'s use of the Bible. The reader is foregrounded in the undertaking of readings that are "culturally enmeshed" within the Pacific Island culture of migrants from the Pacific to New Zealand. Such readings in their turn function as a critique of the way that the Bible is read traditionally in the new context of New Zealand society. At the same time, however, through the cartoon's characterization of God and of Jesus, a new theology is being woven. Taylor has demonstrated that cultural and hermeneutical theory can aid interpretation, but creative engagement with the new media as a site for interpreting biblical and theological themes and issues requires attention to the metaphoric effect of the medium.

The volume closes with Tina Pippin's "Daemons and Angels: The End of the World according to Philip Pullman," in which she undertakes a refraction not unlike that of Jim Perkinson. For Pippin, rather than the refraction being the Bible and hip-hop, it is that of biblical apocalypse/s and Pullman's apocalyptic trilogy, *His Dark Materials.* The refraction process multiplies, however, as other apocalyptic texts and experiences, such as C. S. Lewis's Chronicles of Narnia, Tolkien's *The Lord of the Rings,* and the Tribulation Trail at Mount Vernon Baptist church in Stockbridge, Georgia, are drawn into it. Finally, it is turned back on the empire not of Domitian's first-century Rome but of the United States of America in the contemporary era. Pippin does not turn to any metatheory but remains with the refraction throughout in a way that takes her readers on a journey through and between many apocalyptic visions and worlds. The journey indeed is fun; the outcome of the journey is, however, more serious.

Cultural theorists such as Certeau, to name the one most cited in this volume, are becoming familiar to biblical scholars, even if not as familiar as Bultmann and Käsemann. The significance of hermeneutical or theoretical frameworks or approaches for the analysis of a broad range of relationships between the Bible and popular culture is also being underscored. The surprising lesson from this volume is, however, the possibility that one comprehensive theoretical framework for the nexus of the Bible and popular culture may not be possible. The media are too diverse and the possible approaches too numerous to try to engage the topic within a single framework. What this collection of essays has provided, however, is a range of approaches to the Bible and different media within popular culture using different hermeneutical perspectives, different theoretical frameworks and theories. This will enrich the repertoire of theoretical analyses available to biblical scholars as both scholars and teachers. The essays also provide an excellent range of focused approaches that could be taken up by students and directed to different biblical characters, themes, or texts and to different media. The fruits of this endeavor have the potential to be rich indeed as students and teachers have great fun—of the serious and the light-headed type—as they engage the Bible in popular culture.

WORKS CITED

Aichele, George, and Richard Walsh, eds. 2002. *Screening Scripture: Intertextual Connections between Scripture and Film.* Harrisburg, Pa.: Trinity.

Beal, Timothy, and Tod Linafelt, eds. 2006. *Mel Gibson's Bible: Religion, Popular Culture, and "The Passion of the Christ."* Chicago: University of Chicago Press.

Boer, Roland.1999. *Knockin' on Heaven's Door: The Bible and Popular Culture.* Biblical Limits. London: Routledge.

Brenner, Athalya. 2000. Introduction. Pages 7–12 in *Culture, Entertainment and the Bible.* Edited by George Aichele. JSOTSup 309. Sheffield: Sheffield Academic Press.

Clanton, Dan W., Jr. 2009. *Daring, Disreputable, and Devout: Interpreting the Bible's Women in the Arts and Music.* New York: Continuum.

Cobb, Kelton. 2005. *The Blackwell Guide to Theology and Popular Culture*. Malden, Mass.: Wiley-Blackwell.

Corley, Kathleen, and Robert Webb, eds. 2004. *Jesus and Mel Gibson's "The Passion of the Christ."* New York: Continuum.

Fredriksen, Paula, ed. 2006. *On "The Passion of the Christ": Exploring the Issues Raised by the Controversial Movie*. Berkeley and Los Angeles: University of California Press.

Fuller, Christopher. 2009. Review of David Shepherd, ed., *Images of the Word: Hollywood's Bible and Beyond. Review of Biblical Literature*, June. Online: http://www.bookreviews.org/pdf/6913_7490.pdf.

Gilmour, Michael J. 2004. *Tangled Up in the Bible: Bob Dylan and Scripture*. New York: Continuum.

———. 2009. *Gods and Guitars: Seeking the Sacred in Post-1960s Popular Music*. Waco, Tex.: Baylor University Press.

———, ed. 2005. *Call Me the Seeker: Listening to Religion in Popular Music*. New York: Continuum.

Lynch, Gordon. 2005. *Understanding Theology and Popular Culture*. Oxford: Blackwell.

McEntire, Mark H. 2006. *Raising Cain, Fleeing Egypt, and Fighting Philistines: The Old Testament in Popular Music*. Macon, Ga.: Smyth & Helwys.

Possamai, Adam. 2006. *Religion and Popular Culture: A Hyper-Real Testament*. New York: Peter Lang.

Reinhartz, Adele. 2003. *Scripture on the Silver Screen*. Louisville: Westminster John Knox.

———. 2007. *Jesus of Hollywood*. New York: Oxford University Press.

Roncace, Mark, and Patrick Gray, eds. 2007. *Teaching the Bible through Popular Culture and the Arts*. SBLRBS 53. Atlanta: Society of Biblical Literature.

Runions, Erin. 2003. *How Hysterical: Identification and Resistance in the Bible and Film*. New York: Palgrave Macmillan.

Shepherd, David, ed. 2008. *Images of the Word: Hollywood's Bible and Beyond*. SemeiaSt 54. Atlanta: Society of Biblical Literature.

TEXTS AND THEIR AFTERLIVES IN LITERATURE: A FRAME

Some Novel Remarks about Popular Culture and Religion: Salman Rushdie and the Adaptation of Sacred Texts

Michael J. Gilmour

Linda Hutcheon defines adaptation as "repetition without replication" (2006, xvi; see also 4, 7, 149, 173, 176), "repetition with difference" (142), "derivation that is not derivative" (9), paraphrase, and translation (17). She adds that residual traces of an earlier text in a later one provide degrees of pleasure. The mixture of repetition with variation offers the satisfaction of familiarity and the delight of discovery as audiences and readers recognize ways that artists reshape sources for new settings (173). As she puts it, we enjoy adaptations because they blend "the comfort of ritual … with the piquancy of surprise" (4). These are useful observations as we consider adaptations of the Bible in later cultural artifacts.

Canonical writings lend themselves to this kind of repetition and paraphrase, according to Robert Alter. He defines canon as a "transhistorical textual community" involving received writings on the one hand and readers appealing to those texts for meaning and authority on the other, but this dynamic does not limit their elasticity. In the case of the biblical canon, even among communities of traditional believers the Bible "has been imagined to endorse as a matter of divine revelation rationalism, sensualism, determinism, free will, and a good deal else." The concept of canon lacks fixity, he argues; there is no "singular, authoritative meaning, however much the established spokesmen for the canon at any given moment may claim that is the case" (Alter 2000, 5). From this, Alter goes on to observe that creative writers using the Bible are similarly flexible:

> Modern writers merely push to the next step this process of extending the range of meanings of the textual community in which they participate when they use the biblical canon [referring here to the specific writers he examines] to express vitalistic pantheism, or an individual fate of hapless victimhood, or a vision of cosmic pitilessness, or a notion of eternal recurrence. (5–6)

He further argues that the imaginative response to the Bible by "writers in a wide variety of languages bears witness to a power of canonicity that is not limited to doctrine or strictly contingent on belief in the inspired character of the texts invoked" (60).

Theoreticians are not the only ones who reflect on the complexities, subtleties, and ubiquity of literary influence. Salman Rushdie imagines all the stories of the world as waters swirling around a vast sea, "a thousand thousand thousand and one different currents," he adds, with a nod to Scheherazade and the *Arabian Nights'* tales, "each one a different colour, weaving in and out of one another like a liquid tapestry of breathtaking complexity." This ocean of stories already told, and those yet to be told, is "in fact the biggest library in the universe" (Rushdie 1990, 72). This instructive image from his novel *Haroun and the Sea of Stories* illustrates why, even though artists continually adapt earlier materials (Hutcheon), including canonical stories (Alter), attempts to track the Christian Bible's influence on popular culture and the arts are always partial and selective. A thousand colored currents, crisscrossing and mingling with one another, will perpetually create new combinations, and while biblical stories, themes, and imagery are frequently part of the mix, they do not stand alone in this intertextual soup. We cannot drink all the colored currents composing this ocean but we can, like Haroun Khalifa, who floats along the surface of Rushdie's magical ocean, dip a golden cup into the waters and take the occasional sip (Rushdie 1990, 72). Even a small taste permits some insights into the qualities of this ocean as a whole. Said differently, exploring particular instances of influence helps readers appreciate aspects of the phenomenon as a whole, reminding us that all stories are intertextual in nature—byproducts and rewritings of, and contributions to, other stories.

For what follows, I dip a cup into one specific story to observe ways that a biblically rooted image morphs into something very unlike itself as it appears in its canonical setting. Rushdie's *The Satanic Verses* is an unusual choice for this particular exercise, to be sure, since most readers associate this novel with creative reflections on the Qur'an and Islamic theology, but this is precisely one of the points I wish to make. As stories migrate from one context to another—from sacred text to the popular media and the arts—they inevitably bump into other stories. In the example that follows, Rushdie stirs what amounts to a footnote in the Judeo-Christian Bible with other religious and mythological material, and, as his liquid metaphor suggests, these story waters mingle to produce something entirely new.

I focus on Rushdie's rewriting of the story of Lucifer's fall, a myth originating in the biblical text and adapted by, and widely disseminated in English through, such imaginative works as John Milton's *Paradise Lost* (1667). The name Lucifer is Latin and so obviously does not originate in the Hebrew and Greek Scriptures.

The adjective *lucifer* means "light bringing," combining the feminine noun *lux* (light, brightness) with the verb *ferō* (to bear, carry), and is used substantivally to render the Hebrew phrase "son of dawn" in Isa 14:12: "How you are fallen from heaven, O Day Star, son of Dawn!" Though the wider context of this verse refers to an earthly ruler ("you will take up this taunt against the king of Babylon," Isa 14:4; see also Ezek 28:11–19), Christian readers, especially since the publication of John Milton's *Paradise Lost*, regularly assume that the Isaiah passage refers to the fall of the angel Lucifer. The name Lucifer is therefore synonymous with the Hebrew *satan* (Satan; accuser) and the Greek *diabolos* (devil).

Several biblical passages inform the popular imagination concerning the Lucifer/Satan/Devil figure. He is the adversary in the book of Job, the satan who questions the protagonist's integrity before God (1:6–2:7), and in the New Testament he tempts the fasting Jesus (Matt 4:1–11; Mark 1:12–13; Luke 4:1–13). In the Christian Scriptures, the term devil (*diabolos*) is interchangeable with the transliterated satan (e.g., Matt 4:1 vs. Matt 4:10). The devil's fall from heaven is mentioned in Rev 12:9: "The great dragon was thrown down, that ancient serpent, who is called the Devil and Satan, the deceiver of the whole world—he was thrown down to earth, and his angels were thrown down with him." In Luke 10:18, Jesus watches "Satan fall from heaven like a flash of lightning."

A radical adaptation of this myth in Rushdie's novel illustrates some of the ideas mentioned above. We find that mix of familiarity and surprise noted by Hutcheon in this retelling of a well-known story. We see the elasticity of the biblical canon Alter describes, as a story rooted in Scripture becomes a disturbing statement about systemic injustices, resulting in yet another example of a modern creative writer pushing "to the next step this process of extending the range of meanings"—in Rushdie's world, the fallen, devilish angel is a victim, not a villain.

BIBLICAL CONTENT IN SALMAN RUSHDIE'S
THE SATANIC VERSES (1988)

In the tradition of such diverse storytellers as Ovid and Franz Kafka, Salman Rushdie often imagines the plight of characters who transform into nonhuman creatures. The most obvious illustration appears in *The Satanic Verses*, in which an individual named Saladin Chamcha changes into a goatlike devil. There are, in fact, two major, interrelated stories of transformation in this novel. One describes the alteration of the human Gibreel Farishta into the archangel Gibreel/Gabriel. In his transformed state, Gibreel transcends time and space and is simultaneously a spectator and a participant in events happening in both modern London and the world of the sixth- and seventh-century prophet Mahound/Mohammed.

Much of Rushdie's sharpest religious critique involves the angelic Gibreel. For instance, Gibreel's mobility and constantly changing perspective suggest flaws in the processes of communicating the divine word, because this character alternates between so many roles, including auditor, prophet/speaker, divine source, and stand-in for the deaf masses (Cavanaugh 2004, 395). Furthermore, Gibreel makes dubious contributions to Mahound's new religion because of the ambiguities of his prophetic role; Gibreel tends to "reduce prophecy to prescription" and serves as both prophet and fulfiller of prophecy in a tyrannical way (Cavanaugh 2004, 403). While Gibreel's story is a central one to the novel and closely tied to Saladin Chamcha's story (see below), I focus here on the latter because of its more explicit adaptation of a biblical precursor.

The transformation of the Indian migrant Saladin Chamcha into a monstrous devil begins in the opening pages of Rushdie's *The Satanic Verses*, which describe its two principal characters—Saladin Chamcha and Gibreel Farishta—falling from the sky to the shores of England after their plane explodes. Farishta interprets the miracle of a second chance at life as a rebirth, a "second period of gestation" (Rushdie 1988, 85). As he puts it, "Born again, Spoono, you and me" (11), "To be born again … first you have to die" (3; these are the opening words of the novel, which appear again on p. 86; cf. John 3:3). Birthing imagery is explicit in the moments following the explosion of the jumbo jet *Bostan*, Flight AI-420. Chamcha falls headfirst, the "recommended position for babies entering the birth canal" (5). At the very moment the bomb is detonated, the narrator observes that this is "not death: birth" (89). In the days before the explosion, when Gibreel and Saladin are hostages aboard the *Bostan*, Gibreel names a long list of stories and mythologies involving different kinds of metamorphoses or "eccentric reincarnation theories" (85). Each represents a form of rebirth: phoenix-from-ashes, the resurrection of Christ, the transmigration of the soul at death, the soul of the Dalai Lama in the body of a newborn baby, and the metamorphosis of Jupiter into a bull (imitating Vishnu). Gibreel also comments on Hindu beliefs concerning the progress of humans through successive cycles of life, "now as cockroaches, now as kings, toward the bliss of no-more-returns" (86). Collectively, these stories anticipate the metamorphoses of the novel's two principal characters. Since Gibreel draws most of his examples of transformation from religious myths, it is appropriate that he and his friend become the embodiment of religious figures, resembling, in particular, ones from Judaism, Christianity, and Islam (i.e., the archangel Gabriel and the fallen angel Lucifer).

The explosion and birth that propel the narrative defy conventional notions of time and space, suggested not least by the biblical language of "falling stars" (4; cf. Isa 34:4, cited by Jesus in Mark 13:24–25). There is a pun involved in Rushdie's imagery, since both men were actors, celebrities, and therefore "falling stars" in a literal sense; but there is more. The narrator of *The Satanic Verses* speaks of "a big bang.... A universal beginning, a miniature echo of the birth of time" (4). Such language appears to anticipate the angelic presence in the novel (the transformed Gibreel) because it alludes to the divine speaker in the book of Job, who indicates that angels ("morning stars") attended the creation of the universe (38:4–7).

There is also a devilish presence in the story, a satanic narrator lurking in the pages of this novel (Rushdie 1988, 4, 95–97, 114, 137).[1] To give but one example, there is a moment when Gibreel Farishta, transformed into the angel Gibreel, finds another entity speaking through him to the prophet Mahound:

> The dragging again the dragging and now the miracle starts in his my our guts, he is straining with all his might at something, forcing something, and Gibreel begins to feel that strength that force, here it is *at my own jaw* working it, opening shutting; and the power, starting within Mahound, reaching up to *my vocal cords* and the voice comes. *Not my voice* I'd never know such words I'm no classy speaker never was never will be but this isn't my voice it's a Voice. (114)

The scene suggests the machinations of a puppeteer controlling characters in the novel, including the angelic Gibreel. He and Saladin are in some sense possessed during their rebirth, following the universal beginning represented by the exploding plane. While falling, these characters experience trans/mutation (5), they tumble into Alice's Wonderland (7), and they experience, as seen, "birth" (9; see also 137). As they undergo these transformations, both men become intertwined, both literally, as they hold on to each other while dropping from the sky, and more profoundly at the moment when their "transmutation began": "Gibreelsaladin Farishtachamcha, condemned to this endless but also ending angelicdevilish fall" (5).[2] This blending of names and the nature of their possessions/rebirths introduces the inevitability of their combined fates in a way that recalls the close ties and ongoing battles between the fallen and the loyal angels of the biblical and Miltonian stories (see table below).

There is a further allusion to this angelic battle in the description of a Christian fundamentalist early in the novel, a fellow passenger on the doomed *Bostan*. This American creationist appears to represent the archangel Michael, often described in military terms in the Bible (e.g., in Dan 12:1, Michael is "the great

---

1. Saladin Chamcha might appear physically devilish, but he is still distinct from this satanic narrator. The relationship is one of possession. Saladin is not himself satanic.

2. Saladin and Gibreel's close connection is evident in other ways as well. For instance, later in the story readers learn that Gibreel Farishta's legendary bad breath (13) is sweetened and his halitosis inherited by Saladin Chamcha (137).

prince, the protector of your people"; in Jude 9, he battles Satan). The particular battle this passenger wages is against Darwinism. Indeed, he finds the name "Mr. Darwin" as distasteful as "any other forktail fiend, Beelzebub, Asmodeus or Lucifer himself" (77). He also has "a pair of Chinese dragons" that are "writhed and intertwined" on his shirt, which seems to echo the battles between Michael and Satan described in Revelation and Jude as well as the closely linked Saladin Chamcha and Gibreel Farishta. Gibreel eventually takes this passenger's seat beside Saladin (81), thus bringing together the angelic and satanic characters who, soon after, battle in the sky just as the archangel and the devil do in the Apocalypse of John (see Rev 12:7).

The satanic figure taking hold of Saladin Chamcha makes his presence known early on in the novel, asking the reader "Who am I? Who else is there?" (4), language echoing the Rolling Stones' song "Sympathy for the Devil" (1968): "Pleased to meet you, can you guess my name?"[3] As Chamcha falls, he feels "his heart being gripped by a force so implacable that he understood it was impossible for him to die." After his "feet were once more firmly planted on the ground," he is overtaken by "a will to live" (1988, 9; note the echo of Rev 12:18). This possession transforms Chamcha and he quickly loses all sense of independence. He feels like a bystander watching his metamorphosis, as his blood changes to iron, his flesh to steel. Soon this "will to live" conquers him so completely, it "could work his mouth, his fingers, whatever it chose, and once it was sure of its dominion it spread outward from his body and grabbed Gibreel Farishta by the balls" (9).

The story of Saladin Chamcha, a star (celebrity) falling from the sky to earth like the morning star (angel) Lucifer, with physical attributes traditionally linked to the devil (horns, hooves, tail), echoes biblical, literary, and popular discourses dealing with Christian notions of the great enemy of God. The following table highlights some of the links between Rushdie's novel, the Christian Bible, and John Milton's *Paradise Lost*,[4] to illustrate the point.

---

3. This connection is plausible given Rushdie's love of rock and roll music generally (Rushdie 1999) and the Rolling Stones specifically. For his glowing review of a Rolling Stones performance, see Rushdie 2002, 87–91.

4. Rushdie's novel *The Moor's Last Sigh* (1996) also draws connections between characters in the story and Milton's *Paradise Lost*. When the narrator Moraes (Moor) Zogoiby tells his story, he aligns himself with Milton's Satan through various allusions, describing himself as the offspring of a daemonic woman and therefore "a modern Lucifer" (5). Moor tells his readers, "Mine is the story of the fall from grace of a high-born cross-breed ... my banishment from what I had every right to think of as my natural life" (5). Tales about his great grandparents are "the first of my story's four sequestered, serpented, Edenic-infernal private universes" (15).

The Satanic Verses	Paradise Lost	The Christian Bible
"Out of thin air: a big bang, followed by falling stars. . . . Who am I? Who else is there?" (4; the satanic narrator, see above)	"'Art thou that traitor angel ... / [Who] Drew after him the third part of Heaven's sons" (2.688, 692)	"the morning stars sang together" (Job 38:7; often interpreted as angels) "a great red dragon [i.e., Satan] .... His tail swept down a third of the stars of heaven and threw them to the earth" (Rev 12:3–4)
"Saladin nosedived" (5) "When Mr. Saladin Chamcha fell out of the clouds over the English Channel he felt his heart being gripped by a force so implacable that he understood it was impossible for him to die" (9; i.e., satanic possession) "You think *they* fell a long way? In the matter of tumbles, I yield pride of place to no personage, whether mortal or im-. From clouds to ashes, down the chimney you might say, from heaven-light to hellfire" (137)	"[Satan was] Hurled headlong flaming from th' ethereal sky" (1.45) "toward the coast of earth beneath" (3.739) "Tartarus ... opens wide / His fiery chaos to receive their fall" (6.54–55)	"there was no longer any place for [Satan and his angels] in heaven. The great dragon was thrown down, that ancient serpent, who is called the Devil and Satan, the deceiver of the whole world—he was thrown down to the earth, and his angels were thrown down with him" (Rev 12:8–9)
"[Chamcha's] feet were once more firmly planted on the ground" (9)	"on the beach / Of that inflamèd sea, he stood and called / His legions" (1.299–301)	"the dragon [i.e., Satan] took his stand on the sand of the seashore" (Rev 12:18)
"its [i.e., the satanic narrator's] dominion" (9)	"Satan exalted sat ... / His proud imaginations thus displayed. / 'Powers and Dominions, deities of heaven, / ... though oppressed and fall'n,	"the devil led [Jesus] up and showed him in an instant all the kingdoms of the world. And the devil

	/ I give not heav'n for lost'" (2.5, 10–11, 13–14)	said to him, 'To you I will give their glory and all authority; for it has been given over to me'" (Luke 4:5–6)
"it had conquered him totally [i.e., the satanic possession] … and [it] grabbed Gibreel Farishta by the balls" (9) "'a humble foot soldier, sir, in the army of Guard Almighty.' … '[T]o do battle with the most pernicious devilment ever got folks' brains by the balls'" (77)	"Go Michael of celestial armies prince, / And thou in military prowess next / Gabriel, lead forth to battle these my sons / Invincible, lead forth my armèd saints / By thousands and millions ranged for fight; / Equal in number to that godless crew" (6.44–50) [Angel and Satan fight in the same way in *The Satanic Verses*; cf. 4.1006: "Satan, I know thy strength, and thou know'st mine" (Gabriel speaking)]	"war broke out in heaven; Michael and his angels fought against the dragon. The dragon and his angels fought back" (Rev 12:7)

These echoes of the Bible and Milton do not stand alone in the novel. Rushdie integrates the narrative of Lucifer's fall with other religious mythologies, such as the Qur'anic story of Iblis's disobedience, and literary villains like Shakespeare's Iago from *Othello* (see esp. Clark 2001, ch. 6). The stories whirl in and out of one another like so many currents in Rushdie's magical ocean. So what does he do with this biblical imagery as it mingles with so many other diverse influences? At this point, I explore how Rushdie politicizes his adaptation of a biblical story (Satan's fall) in this setting, allowing it to function as a vehicle for commentary on racism and the plight of immigrants.

RECONTEXTUALIZING A BIBLICAL STORY FOR THE PURPOSE OF SOCIAL COMMENTARY

Significantly, the demonic possession occurs as Saladin Chamcha moves from East to West, from India to England. Early in the story, Rushdie links Saladin Chamcha's identification with and affections for England with his struggle to escape India and especially his father's attempts to preserve both the past and the traditional family ways. Like other migrants, Saladin's true self/identity remains hidden beneath disguises when he moves to England (Rushdie 1988, 49), as he attempts to deny his familial and ethnic inheritance. His father recognizes this, calling him a "demon up from hell," language that anticipates the literal transformation he will undergo later in the novel. The father's language here equates the desire to westernize or integrate with the demonic, and to a degree this parallels those in England who demonize Saladin—and all immigrants—as invading outsiders. Saladin becomes a devilish figure when he migrates, during his encounters with Westerners. At the same time, he is already devilish in the eyes of his Indian father, who condemns his son for moving to London in the first place. Saladin is a borderland character, trapped at the interstices of two very different worlds.

Among other things, Saladin Chamcha's metamorphosis into a fallen devil points to the consequences of racism and systemic abuse. For the most part, it is during his migration from India to the United Kingdom that Chamcha's remarkable transformation from a human being into a devilish animal occurs, a nightmare that commences with the appearance of "two new, goaty, unarguable horns" (Rushdie 1988, 145). One scene illustrating Saladin Chamcha's profound sense of displacement as an immigrant from India trying to fit in to his new London home occurs in the back of a police van shortly after his fall from the *Bostan* to the shores of England, as three immigration and five police officers brutalize and humiliate him (162–69). The fact that a new immigrant arriving to the West experiences this abuse/transformation while under the control of white, Western authority figures implies a sharp criticism of British society. Chamcha is not British in their eyes and therefore he is "other," treated like, and therefore transformed into, an animal. The brutal treatment and racist slurs directed at Chamcha during his captivity coincide with his physical transformation into a devilish goat.

It is telling that some of the police officers' remarks distinguish cleanliness from filth. This is a recurring trope in discourse relating immigration experience, according to Katarzyna Marciniak. Those crossing borders represent a threat to the establishment, often represented as contamination or the entry of filth into an otherwise clean space (Marciniak 2006, 39–41, 92, 94). Rushdie literalizes this notion. When the frightened Chamcha shits himself ("a large number of soft, pellety objects had appeared on the floor") during interrogation, the guards respond with further derision:

> "Animal," Stein cursed him as he administered a series of kicks, and Bruno joined in: "You're all the same. Can't expect animals to observe civilized standards. Eh?" And Novak took up the thread: "We're talking about fucking personal hygiene here, you little fuck." (Rushdie 1988, 164)

If we read this short speech as a kind of colonial discourse and therefore as more than mere trash talk, a significant rhetorical strategy is discernible. Homi Bhabha describes colonial discourse as an apparatus that both recognizes and disavows racial, cultural, and historical differences" (1994, 100). Strategically, it serves to create space for subjugated people by producing knowledge through which "surveillance is exercised and a complex form of pleasure / unpleasure is incited" (100–101). This knowledge involves stereotyping both colonizer and colonized, but in such a way that the two are positioned antithetically to one another. The police-van scene in *The Satanic Verses* involves repetition of familiar tropes concerning migrants—they are dirty, undignified, and somehow less than human—and functions for those abusing Saladin as a rhetorical means of distinguishing themselves as insiders from Saladin as an outsider. Chamcha becomes a symbol of the migrant experience, at once despised by the English and ridiculed as an Anglophile by other migrants and those back in India, like his father.

A second episode illustrating Saladin Chamcha's liminal status occurs in the Shaandaar Café. This location is, according to Richard J. Lane, a "nightmarish urban space" that is also "a vision of a dystopian London … focused on the migrant cultures that live out their 'indeterminate' identities of belonging and not-belonging through their ongoing redefinition of the situations that they have found themselves in" (2006, 89). Lane is describing here the café and rooming house where the now-monstrous Saladin sequesters himself in an effort to hide his disfigurations. The Shaandaar Café is a ghetto where immigrants from India, Pakistan, and Bangladesh—"variegated, transient and particoloured inhabitants" (Rushdie 1988, 251)—who cannot assimilate into their new environment find refuge with other, similarly marginalized, dislocated souls. Though he finds temporary shelter here, Saladin insists he does not belong in such a ghetto because, unlike the other residents who do not assimilate well into British society, the Anglophile Saladin embraces the culture and language of the United Kingdom.

Saladin Chamcha is, Shailja Sharma observes, the ideal immigrant; he is upwardly mobile, without accent, wealthy, and thoroughly assimilated (2001, 607–8). Once the transformation into a devil occurs, he "tries his best to retain the vestiges of his bowler-hatted, English self with his tweedy-voiced wife, but fails" (608). The Anglophile Saladin's metamorphosis is complete when he ends up at the Shaandaar Café, the antithesis of everything he holds dear. Leftist Muhammad Sufyan owns the café and his establishment is a haven for working-class Asians and illegal immigrants. Chamcha rejects identification with this group ("I'm not your kind. You're not my people" [Rushdie 1988, 253]), thus setting up two "opposing models of integration in a foreign country" (Sharma 2001, 608). On the one hand, Chamcha is "a determinedly apolitical, upper-class man who wants to be adopted as part of Britain," and on the other, Sufyan is an "exploiter of fellow immigrants … whose sense of community unites in his victimhood and resistance with people of his 'own kind'" (608). British society rejects and ghettoizes Chamcha. Bhabha observes that when Saladin is at the

Shaandaar Café in his transformed, mythic-animal state, his symbolic role is evident: "Chamcha … has turned into a Goat and has crawled back to the ghetto, to his despised migrant compatriots…. He has become the 'borderline' figure of a massive historical displacement—postcolonial migration" (1994, 320).

Saladin Chamcha's story illustrates a widespread pattern in Rushdie's work, namely, his use of bestial imagery at intersections between cultures and in contexts involving violence. Marina Warner argues that "tales of metamorphosis often arose in spaces (temporal, geographical, and mental) that were crossroads, cross-cultural zones, points of interchange on the intricate connective tissue of communications between cultures" (2002, 17). These stories can serve numerous functions, such as promising change, providing a rationale for the oppression of others, indicating progress, or articulating traumas.

Though *The Satanic Verses* deals with biblical and religious subject matter, and despite the hysteria following its publication and the infamous fatwa calling for the author's death, this novel is not concerned primarily with Islam or the biblical and Miltonian story of Lucifer's fall. Indeed, according to Rushdie himself, the "central theme [of *The Satanic Verses*] is that of metamorphosis" (2002, 68). Saladin finds himself at the interstices between two worlds as he tries to escape India for the West. His eccentric father recognizes the confusion over Saladin's identity that results: "I have your soul kept safe, my son, here in this walnut tree. The devil has only your body" (1988, 48). The first half of this statement points to a failed metamorphosis; like so many others, Saladin is unable to integrate completely into his new world because the British will never accept him fully as one of their own. The second half of this statement prepares readers for the very real metamorphosis that the migrant Saladin will undergo later in the story. Rather than becoming British, Saladin is humiliated, beaten, and rejected. His father's reference to the devil having Saladin's body not only anticipates the literal transformation of the actor into a goat—the goat traditionally a symbol of the devil's incarnation—it also points to the vulnerability of migrants more generally. As is often the case in Rushdie's novels, he introduces hostility and monstrous/bestial imagery at a moment of encounter with otherness.

SOME CLOSING THOUGHTS

According to Roger Y. Clark, a constant in Rushdie's finest work is "a questioning of fundamental truths as they have been formulated by the great religions and myths of the past" (2001, 18). Rushdie's explorations into the nature of the universe "lead him to juxtapose one cosmic system with another, and to question the balance within any one system" (18). Like the individual currents in the sea of stories, narratives—even canonical, biblical narratives—do not stand alone and consequently do not gain preeminence over others. Clearly, there is an element of subversion in Rushdie's fiction, directed specifically at religious extremism. We see this in his depiction of "the bearded and turbaned Imam" who dreams of revolution in *The Satanic Verses* (1988, 211–12). We see it also in the Cultmaster Khattam-Shud, the villain in *Haroun and the Sea of Stories*, who wants to silence all storytelling and dialogue and believes "The world is for Controlling" (1990, 161).[5] By flooding his stories with a seemingly endless mix of voices, reflecting religious and cultural diversity—Judeo-Christian, Islamic, Hindu; Indian, Middle Eastern, Western; high and low art—Rushdie seeks to prevent the dominance of any one worldview.

This blending of voices inevitably occurs in other artistic productions, including the variety of media subsumed under the umbrella term popular culture. Here, too, biblical influence is ubiquitous (see, e.g., Roncace and Gray 2007) but always one voice among many, mingling with other stories in ways recalling the intertwining of Gibreel and Saladin in *The Satanic Verses* or the rushing story currents in *Haroun and the Sea of Stories*. As we see in the example just considered, artists repeat but do not replicate (Hutcheon 2006, xvi), extend the range of meanings of canonical writings, and take advantage of their enormous flexibility (Alter 2000, 5–6).

WORKS CITED

Alter, Robert. 2000. *Canon and Creativity: Modern Writing and the Authority of Scripture*. New Haven: Yale University Press.

Bhabha, Homi. 1994. *The Location of Culture*. London: Routledge.

Cavanaugh, Christine. 2004. Auguries of Power: Prophecy and Violence in *The Satanic Verses*. Studies in the Novel 36: 393–404.

Clark, Roger Y. 2001. *Stranger Gods: Salman Rushdie's Other Worlds*. Montreal: McGill-Queens University Press.

Gilmour, Michael J. 2009. Teaching Biblical Hermeneutics through Salman Rushdie's *Haroun and the Sea of Stories*. Teaching Theology and Religion 12: 151–61.

Gorra, Michael. 1997. *After Empire: Scott, Naipaul, Rushdie*. Chicago: University of Chicago Press.

---

5. Rushdie almost certainly has Iran's Ayatollah Khomeini in mind with both characters. Khomeini's infamous 1989 fatwa calling for the author's death obviously followed the release of *The Satanic Verses*. Rushdie wrote *Haroun and the Sea of Stories* in response to this crisis. For reflections on the fatwa and its consequences, see, e.g., Gorra 1997, 149–56. For connections between *Haroun and the Sea of Stories* and Rushdie's response to religious totalitarianism, see Gilmour 2009.

Hutcheon, Linda. 2006. *A Theory of Adaptation*. New York: Routledge.

Lane, Richard J. 2006. *The Postcolonial Novel*. Themes in 20th Century Literature and Culture. Cambridge, Eng.: Polity.

Marciniak, Katarzyna. 2006. *Alienhood: Citizenship, Exile, and the Logic of Difference*. Minneapolis: University of Minnesota Press.

Roncace, Mark, and Patrick Gray, eds. 2007. *Teaching the Bible through Popular Culture and the Arts*. SBLRBS 53. Atlanta: Society of Biblical Literature.

Rushdie, Salman. 1988. *The Satanic Verses*. New York: Picador.

———. 1990. *Haroun and the Sea of Stories*. London: Granta.

———. 1996. *The Moor's Last Sigh*. Toronto: Vintage.

———. 1999. *The Ground beneath Her Feet*. Toronto: Vintage.

———. 2002. *Step Across This Line: Collected Nonfiction, 1992–2002*. Toronto: Knopf.

Sharma, Shailja. 2001. Salman Rushdie: The Ambivalence of Migrancy. *Twentieth-Century Literature* 47: 596–618.

Warner, Marina. 2002. *Fantastic Metamorphoses, Other World: Ways of Telling the Self*. Oxford: Oxford University Press.

Texts and Their Afterlives in Music and Other Multimedia

Red Dirt God: Divine Silence and the Search for Transcendent Beauty in the Music of Emmylou Harris

Mark McEntire

Recent interpretations of the Hebrew Bible have begun to focus upon the development of God as a narrative character in the biblical story. Initial interest in characters as a component of narrative criticism typically led to the examination of human characters, but eventually these methods of analyzing character development were applied to God. This emphasis may find its fullest expression in treatments such as *God: A Biography,* by Jack Miles, and *The Disappearance of God: A Divine Mystery,* by Richard Elliott Friedman. On a narrower scale, the development of the divine character is the focal point in a work such as *The Character of God in the Book of Genesis: A Narrative Appraisal,* by W. Lee Humphreys. All of these works recognize a trajectory in the divine character development that ends by depicting God as what Humphreys and others have called an "agent," an invisible force working behind the scenes, acting in the world only indirectly (Humphreys 2001, 241). This kind of development does not occur in a straight line. It has largely been accomplished at the end of the book of Genesis and can be observed in the Joseph narratives, in which God's role is so stunningly reduced compared to the divine role earlier in the book. This trend is temporarily reversed, however, in dramatic fashion in the book of Exodus, where God becomes a "full-fledged character" again. The diminishment of God as a narrative character then resumes as the biblical story line continues.

In the modern world, there is a vast array of media by which we can transmit narratives containing a divine character—written literature (prose, poetry, and drama), visual art (painting and sculpture), film, music, and theatre. Individual media can also be creatively combined in forms such as music videos, graphic novels, and performance art. These individual and combined media all have their inherent advantages and limitations. The complex kind of character development we find in the Bible and in other large works of literature is difficult to accomplish in a narrative vehicle like popular music. When the divine character appears in a popular song, there is little time to produce more than a snapshot of this character. One way this difficulty can be overcome is in a sequence of songs, such as might be found on an entire album. After establishing the general narrative pattern of divine character development in the Hebrew Bible, this essay will explore the development of the divine character in the 2000 album by Emmylou Harris, called *Red Dirt Girl*. In a sequence of songs, Harris depicts the divine character as a mysterious, hidden force, and she explores and questions the nature of this force through the experience of the human characters she presents in her songs. An examination of divine character development in the Hebrew Bible will reveal a being at the end of the canon who may be compared in fruitful ways with the divine presence in Harris's music.

THE DEVELOPMENT OF THE DIVINE CHARACTER WITHIN THE BIBLICAL NARRATIVE

At the beginning of the Bible, God is a highly visible, speaking character who carries on ordinary conversations with Adam, Eve, Cain, Noah, Abraham, Sarah, Hagar, Isaac, Rebekah, and Jacob. A shift begins to take place, however, with Jacob, who also has a divine encounter in a dream in Gen 28:10–17. This new development takes control by the end of the book of Genesis, where the main character, Joseph, has no direct contact with God whatsoever but only receives symbolic dreams (Miles 1995, 78–79). The movement reverses in the book of Exodus, where Moses has frequent direct conversation with God, a pattern that continues all the way to Moses' death at the end of Deuteronomy, but a large element of this story is the uniqueness of Moses, who mediates between God and Israel because of the inability of the latter to have direct access to the former. Perhaps the most poignant text in this regard is Exod 20:18–21, where, after the divine gift of the Decalogue, the Israelites say to Moses, "You speak with us and we will listen, but God shall not speak with us lest we die." In a more recent work, Jerome M. Segal has made similar observations about the relationship between Joseph and God, but Segal moves in a somewhat different direction in his conclusion that this withdrawal of God provides room for the "moral transformation" of Joseph, who does not need God's direct action. Joseph becomes a more complete moral agent in the story and, thus, a representative who acts for God (Segal 2007, 22–28).

This narrative pattern in which God withdraws from direct involvement in the realm of human activity within the entire Hebrew Bible has been examined more specifically by Richard Elliott Friedman in *The Disappearance of God: A Divine Mystery*. Friedman points to the invisibility of God in the later narrative books of the Bible, such as Ezra and Esther (1995, 9–13). This is not necessarily a negative quality for Friedman. Among other things, the withdrawal of God from the human sphere may display "divine parental wisdom" and represent a "rich source of interpretation" (114). Miles raises a haunting possibility with the question he poses to the end of the canon: "Does God lose interest?" (1995, 397–408). This question leads Miles to consider the possibility that the Tanak is a tragedy, a conclusion he only barely avoids. While the book of Job represents a threat to God's existence as a narrative character, that character is rescued in books such as the Song of Songs, Ecclesiastes, Esther, Daniel, and Ruth not by a reassertion of narrative vigor but by a steady maintenance of divine silence in the midst of faithful human characters. In Miles's words, "Thus the otherwise deathly silence of the Lord God is covered over by the rising bustle and hum of real life" (1995, 405). Harold Bloom describes this process as the "self-exile" of God (2005, 200–216).[1] The freedom of creation requires space, which God must choose to give it. The Tanak, in the view of Friedman, Miles, Bloom, and others, tells the story of this divine retreat from the world.

The examination of God as a narrative character became a framework for doing biblical theology in Walter Brueggemann's 1997 work, *Theology of the Old Testament: Testimony, Dispute, Advocacy*. Brueggemann carefully identified disputing voices in the Old Testament and he presented these voices in the hypothetical context of an adversarial courtroom, paying careful attention to the grammar used to speak of God. Isolating examples of God as the subject of verbs, God described by adjectives, and God named by nouns is the starting point for asking who the character called God in the Bible is. Brueggemann has recognized and stated, with astonishing clarity, that in the Jewish and Christian traditions, God is a character constructed by utterance that comes to us in literature and that biblical theology "must pay close attention to the shape, character, and details of the utterance, for it is in, with, and under the utterance that we have the God of Israel, and nowhere else" (1997, 122). The delineation and evaluation of contemporary religious experience is simply not the task of biblical theology. This is not to deny the importance of religious experience, but the religious experience of the past is that against which we measure our own, and literature became the way to transmit this experience of the past. Thus, literary canons became normative in

---

1. Bloom builds this idea on the Kabbalistic notion of *zimzum*, developed by Isaac Luria in the sixteenth century. This term refers to an act of divine withdrawal or self-emptying by which God creates the space necessary for the world to exist. The act of creation requires a deliberate retreat of God's presence (2005, 205–12).

Judaism and Christianity. In Brueggemann's theology, the active, full-fledged God character is "Israel's Core Testimony," as biblical literature describes a God who creates, makes promises, delivers, commands, and leads (1997, 145–212). The God who is merely an agent is found in what Brueggemann classifies as "Israel's Countertestimony." This God is described as hidden, ambiguous, contradictory, and unreliable (1997, 317–406). A theological appropriation of the Old Testament literature differs from a purely narrative appropriation in its need to put all texts on level ground. Thus, the final portrait of God in Brueggemann's forensic model is found in the tension between testimonies, rather than at the end of a process of narrative development. Miles and Friedman have both argued effectively that the invisible God found at the end of the Hebrew Bible reflects the religious experience of the postexilic community, which shaped the canon (Miles 1995, 304–5). Thus, the character named God in the Bible was all along becoming the God whom this community encountered or, more accurately, did not encounter, at least not directly. This trajectory of character development is disrupted, of course, in the Christian Old Testament by the rearranging of the books in the canon. The God of whom the prophets speak at the end of the Christian Old Testament is different from the God of Ezra–Nehemiah.

It is difficult not to notice that institutional religion and overtly religious art forms give more attention to the full-fledged God character. This may be in part because this character makes for a better story. Try to imagine a film about the return of the exiles to Jerusalem in the late sixth century B.C.E., under the leadership of Zerubbabel, Jeshua, Ezra, Haggai, Nehemiah, and Zechariah, that has the power and appeal of Cecil B. DeMille's movie, *The Ten Commandments*.[2] On the other hand, it may be that art forms that portray God as merely an agent are not often recognized as overtly religious. Their religious aspects, like the God they portray, lurk within the background, veiled behind subtle imagery and oblique references to religious traditions. Such ambiguity is not the usual content of organized religion, which tends to avoid the kind of countertestimony described by Brueggemann and others.[3] Careful attention to the songs on Harris's *Red Dirt Girl* will reveal a divine presence that surfaces from time to time and that matches this subtle, ambiguous being who appears toward the end of the canon.

---

2. The appeal of Demille's film is a complex phenomenon, which also has much to do with the political, social, and cultural context into which it was released. For a careful consideration of these aspects, see the analysis of Melanie J. Wright (2003, 89–127).

3. For a prime example of this, see William Holladay's documentation of the censoring of the Psalms in the church's guidelines for their use, from the Liturgy of the Hours in the Middle Ages up to modern lectionaries (1993, 304–15).

The Divine Presence in the Songs of *Red Dirt Girl*

The opening song of Emmylou Harris's album *Red Dirt Girl*, "The Pearl," establishes an otherworldly setting at the beginning with references to dragons and an "ancient war." Religion enters this context about a third of the way into the song, as the plaintive voice, which represents a beleaguered and wandering group, sings:

> Our path is worn, our feet are poorly shod.
> We lift up our prayer against the odds,
> and fear the silence is the voice of God.

The characterization of a hidden God is a threat to those who hope for more direct divine assistance. The overriding sense of the song is negative, and the listener may wonder why the refrain keeps returning to "We cry Allelujah." Why are these people praising God? A countervoice comes only in the final stanza, depicting the feelings of confusion and loneliness of human life but pointing to an ultimate payoff, "until we behold the pain become the pearl." Those who long for purpose find it only at the end of a long process, like an oyster producing a pearl through a lifetime of painful irritation. This is the characterization of God found at the end of the narrative line of the Hebrew Bible, the God who leaves humans alone to try to read the divine presence and purpose into their circumstances.[4] This silent God presented in the first song will be the one who inhabits the entire album, and the fear that the experience of silence is the only representation of the divine presence in the world will haunt its most poignant human characters.

The second song is called "Michelangelo" and is sung in the voice of a person who has a dream about the great artist. This may be the most cryptic song on the album, its details murky like a dream. It is difficult to hear the line "You were digging up the bodies buried long ago" sung to the greatest sculptor of biblical figures without picturing Michelangelo's Moses, David, and various pietàs. The singer longs to help the artist in his moments of suffering and loneliness and to prevent the tragedy that befalls him. Nevertheless, the singer recognizes that the artist's pain is the source of his brilliant work:

---

4. This may be the predicament of the reader, who reaches Ezra-Nehemiah and finds a different mode of storytelling. In the words of Meir Sternberg, the narration in these books is "empirical" rather than "inspirational." The narrators are "limited" rather than omniscient. This shift in the style of narration appears, not accidentally, in the only narrative books to use first-person narration. One could never imagine the authors of Exodus, Joshua, or First Samuel using "I" or "we." These other books are narrated from an omniscient, almost godlike perspective (Sternberg 1985, 86–87).

> Last night I dreamed about you
> I dreamed that you were weeping
> And your tears poured out like diamonds.

This observation, of course, is consistent with the image of the oyster and the pearl in the previous song, presenting pain that produces a precious object.

In the fourth song, "Tragedy," Harris overtly raises ultimate questions with the opening line:

> Some say it's destiny, whether triumph or tragedy,
> But I believe we cast our nets out on the sea,
> and nothing we get comes for free.

The unnamed person whom the singer addresses in the song is a tragic figure who resists intimate relationship and the emotion it brings. The story of the singer and the addressee is beyond redemption and nearly over. This song serves as an introduction to the upcoming sequence, and it becomes apparent only in the next three intensely personal songs that Harris is exploring the uneven, often heartbreaking nature of life. She does so from three different perspectives— friend, mother, and daughter. In two of these three cases, the person about whom, or to whom, she is singing is dead. The song closes with "You made me believe in tragedy" and fades slowly into silence only after a sequence of plaintive groans.[5] Some things are just beyond fixing. The resulting agony of these personal stories might again be understood as the sand in the oyster from "The Pearl," and in the songs that follow, the portraits that result are the works of art generated by the singer's pain, like Michelangelo's sculptures.

The album receives its name from the fifth song, in which the singer tells the painful story of herself and a childhood friend in Alabama named Lillian, "Two red-dirt girls in a red-dirt town." Lillian dreams of escaping from her confining surroundings to a place where she can "make a joyful sound."[6] This echo of a biblical phrase is the closest this song gets to overt religion, which is odd for a story that takes place in the depths of the Bible Belt. Lillian's life spins out of control when her older brother is killed in the Vietnam War, her father becomes abusive, and she gets pregnant. Lillian gets married, continues to have more children, and her dream of escape fades into the distance:

---

5. Careful listeners may recognize the voices of Patti Scialfa and Bruce Springsteen in the background of this song. The presence of these two voices, which have sung so many songs of struggle and tragedy, adds another dimension of meaning to this recording.

6. Almost surely a reference to Ps 100:1.

Nobody knows when she started her skid,
She was only twenty-seven and she had five kids.
Coulda' been the whiskey, coulda' been the pills,
coulda' been the dream she was trying to kill.

In the end, Lillian is buried "without a sound in the red-dirt ground." The hope-lessness of the song is overwhelming, and the silence of Lillian's death recalls the silent voice of God lamented in the first song of the album. This time there is no sense of something valuable emerging from the painful, tragic experience described in the song.

The sixth song, "My Baby Needs a Shepherd," is sung in the voice of a mother, concerned about the welfare of her daughter. As the song progresses, the singer moves through a list of metaphors for divine guidance in each subsequent stanza:

My baby needs a shepherd, she's lost out on a hill....
My baby needs an angel, she never learned to fly....
My baby needs a pilot, she has no magic wand.

These metaphors seem to fail and fall away in turn, until the final stanza begins with "My baby needs a mother, to love her till the end." A painful refrain inter-venes between the stanzas, changing slightly each time, until it produces the line:

Toora loora loora lo, to the cradle comes the crow.
Toora loora loora li, my kingdom for a lullaby.

There is a realization here that the painful circumstances of life cannot be avoided or erased by the parade of divine metaphors. The love of the mother, which is what the song determines the child needs in the end, is not a guide or an overt companion but an invisible, even unknown presence. The child will have to make her own way in the world, which creates a darkness of separation even from the parent who "loves her till the end."[7] The singer returns again to the theme of silence, realizing that what she thought were the cries of the daughter were "just the wind."

---

7. This tension between the mother's hope for a painless life and the harsh reality of ex-istence is a pervasive theme in the strain of country music that has probably most influenced Harris, that embodied by Hank Williams. See the discussion of this theme in the work of David Fillingim (2003, 63–65).

Harris has confirmed in numerous places that the seventh song on this album, "Bang the Drum Slowly," is about her father.[8] The man addressed by the singer appears to have flown airplanes in a war and to be a farmer by trade. The song is filled with regrets about all of the things the singer did not ask this man—"I meant to ask you how to fix that car," "about the war," "how you lived what you believed," and "how to plow that field." The repeated chorus, which contains the title line, also misquotes Gen 3:19: instead of the familiar "For you are dust, and unto dust you shall return," she sings, "To dust be returning, from dust we began." Aside from the paraphrasing, this line reverses the birth-to-death movement of the couplet in Genesis.[9] The misquoting seems quite intentional, as the singer longs to have him back in order to pose all of the unasked questions. As the song nears its end, the singer offers this tribute:

> The songs of my life will still be sung,
> by the light of the moon you hung.

This godlike figure is a stand-in for the hidden God,[10] but even he seems too often to be a silent presence, as the song acknowledges so many things left unsaid.

After this sequence of relational songs and their painful contemplations of life and death is complete, a very different tone is struck by the eighth song. Not only does it sound strikingly different but its title and frequently repeated refrain are the French saying, "j'ai fait tout." The completion of this phrase in the chorus is "ce que j'ai pu." Literally, the phrase means something like "I did everything that I could." This song seems to look back on the previous three, and at the end of this trail of strained and difficult relational portraits, the singer longs for the grace that comes with the acknowledgement that everyone involved did their best. This idea runs directly into the theme of human limitation. The more common religious response to such limitation, a plea for divine assistance and deliverance, is not present in any overt way.

---

8. The title phrase has a long history. In 1956, Mark Harris wrote a novel by this title about a fictional baseball team, and it was made into a movie starring Robert DeNiro in 1973. In the book, one of the characters sings a song of uncertain origin typically called "The Streets of Laredo," which contains this phrase. One of the major characters in the book, the one played by DeNiro in the film, dies from a tragic illness.

9. See my discussion of this song among other popular songs that make reference to Genesis (McEntire 2006, 5–6).

10. This mature, moral agent reflects the description of Joseph in the book of Genesis, as described above and developed in the recent work of Segal (2007, 22–28).

The final song on *Red Dirt Girl*, "The Boy from Tupelo," is more than just an obligatory tribute to Elvis Presley. The song opens with a stunning reversal of the familiar line from the children's gospel song "Jesus Loves Me," as Harris laments:

> You don't love me this I know
> Don't need a Bible to tell me so

The song is obviously about a disappointing romance, and Elvis is at the top of a long list of images of things that have gone away. The singer plans to vanish like Elvis, the buffalo, and the five-and-dime store. Nevertheless, the connection of this failed love with an elusive divine love brings back the theme of a silent, hidden God with which the album opens.

The Elusive Divine Presence in Scripture and Song

Emmylou Harris's exploration of divine elusiveness on *Red Dirt Girl* has some interesting similarities to the work of singer-songwriter Nick Cave, which has been the subject of significant consideration by scholars interested in the interaction between theology and popular music. Cave's expression of this idea on his 1997 album *The Boatman's Call* was the subject of an article called "Faith, Doubt, and the Imagination: Nick Cave and the Divine-Human Encounter," by Anna Kessler. Cave took a more overt approach by opening *The Boatman's Call* with the statement "I do not believe in an interventionist God" (Kessler 2005, 79–81).[11] Kessler finds in Cave's music an "inward turn" toward an "interactive" rather than interventionist God. God's presence in the world emerges in our acts of imagination, in which "we allow God to speak through us by giving [God] a voice that would otherwise be silenced" (90–92). This sounds much like Miles's understanding of the latter portions of the Tanak, in which God's direct presence, or its disappearance, is "covered over by the rising bustle and hum of real life." It is only humans who act in the world, while God's presence is limited to the dreamworlds of Joseph and Daniel and the prayer lives of Ezra and Nehemiah, and God's lack of any presence is so striking in the Hebrew version of the book of Esther that its Greek translators and editors felt compelled to add lengthy prayers spoken by the main characters.

---

11. The songwriting of Nick Cave, along with that of P. J. Harvey, has also been explored by J. R. C. Cousland. Cousland's essay moves in a different direction from Kessler's, focusing on the grotesque in the music of both of these artists, but draws similar conclusions about how they use divine absence to point toward transcendent beauty (2005, 130–31).

Red Dirt Girl follows a similar path as it introduces this haunting divine silence and then dives into the pain and struggle of human existence that fills the resulting space. In the penultimate song, "The Hour of Gold," the singer describes marriage as "a hard and holy road." The entire song speaks of things being wounded, broken, and torn. In the end, though, the singer proclaims the reward of such determined love in divine terms:

> But the world will be my witness when they excavate my heart,
> And find the image of your face imprinted there like some Shroud of Turin.

This image is once again like the pearl, the thing of beauty created from a life of pain. In the larger narrative of this album, the divine character does not grow toward silence and absence. This, rather, is the starting place. The progress that is made is on the part of the singer and the listeners, if they choose to go along, who must learn to live with this silence, to engage it as an act of faith, and not succumb to the temptation to fill that silence with the easy words of the denial of pain.

The veiled God to whom the Hebrew Bible leads its readers likely reflects the religious experience of those who produced the books at the end of the canon and those who shaped it. The canon pushes stories and images of an active, visible God into the distant past, and these stories and images characterize the religious experience of ancient heroes. Biblical theologians have begun to pay careful attention to this trajectory of divine character development. Meanwhile, the religious experience of contemporary persons is typically closer to that described at the end of the canon. Attending to this kind of experience requires acts of great imagination. Popular music, which may portray an experience of divine silence or absence more openly than overtly religious music, may provide the nourishment to sustain this kind of experience.

Works Cited

Bloom, Harold. 2005. *Jesus and Yahweh: The Names Divine*. New York: Riverhead.

Brueggemann, Walter. 1997. *Theology of the Old Testament: Testimony, Dispute, Advocacy*. Minneapolis: Fortress.

Cousland, J. R. C. 2005. God the Bad, and the Ugly: The *Vi(t)a Negativa* of Nick Cave and P. J. Harvey. Pages 129–57 in *Call Me the Seeker: Listening to Religion in Popular Music*. Edited by Michael J. Gilmour. New York: Continuum.

Fillingim, David. 2003. *Redneck Liberation: Country Music as Theology*. Macon, Ga.: Mercer University Press.

Friedman, Richard Elliott. 1995. *The Disappearance of God: A Divine Mystery*. Boston: Little, Brown.

Holladay, William L. 1993. *The Psalms through Three Thousand Years: Prayerbook of a Cloud of Witnesses*. Minneapolis: Fortress.

Humphreys, W. Lee. 2001. *The Character of God in the Book of Genesis: A Narrative Appraisal*. Louisville: Westminster John Knox.

Kessler, Anna. 2005. Faith, Doubt, and Imagination: Nick Cave on the Divine-Human Encounter. Pages 79–94 in *Call Me the Seeker: Listening to Religion in Popular Music*. Edited by Michael J. Gilmour. New York: Continuum.

McEntire, Mark. 2006. *Raising Cain, Fleeing Egypt, and Fighting Philistines: The Old Testament in Popular Music*. Macon, Ga.: Smyth & Helwys.

Miles, Jack. 1995. *God: A Biography*. New York: Vintage.

Segal, Jerome M. 2007. *Joseph's Bones: Understanding the Struggle between God and Man in the Bible*. New York: Riverhead.

Sternberg, Meir. 1985. *The Poetics of Biblical Narrative: Ideological Literature and the Drama of Reading*. Bloomington: Indiana University Press.

Wright, Melanie J. 2003. *Moses in America: The Cultural Uses of Biblical Narrative*. Oxford: Oxford University Press.

"Here, There, and Everywhere": Images of Jesus in American Popular Culture

Dan W. Clanton Jr.

Let's begin our exploration of Jesus in American popular culture with three examples. First, Reuben Wentworth—the protagonist in Henry Ward Beecher's 1867 novel *Norwood*—claims unashamedly, "My Savior is everywhere—in the book and out of the book. I see Him in nature, in human life, in my own experience as well in the recorded fragments of His own history. I live in a Bible. But it is an unbound book!" (quoted in Prothero 2003, 70–71). Second, in a 1997 episode of the multiple Emmy Award–winning series *NYPD Blue*, police detective Andy Sipowicz has a dream/vision in which he visits with his murdered son in a diner.[1] During the conversation, Andy is rude (as he is wont to be) to another patron, after which his son informs him, "That's Jesus Christ, Dad. Congratulations on pissing off Jesus." Finally, and most recently, in December 2008 hundreds of members of the Praise Chapel Christian Fellowship in Kansas City dressed as Jesus and went about their daily routines, such as working and shopping, in order to protest what they felt was the removal of Jesus from all things related to Christmas (Hollingsworth 2008).

What do these examples have in common? They all display a remarkable openness here in America to reimagining, refashioning, or resituating Jesus. Beecher's "unbound book" now includes Jesuses in genres as various as film, television, art, music, literature, comics and graphic novels, online videos, and pieces of material culture such as bumper stickers, magnets, and T-shirts. This article will probe the malleability and the multifarious images of Jesus in American popular culture through the lens of reception history. This avenue of inquiry—the theoretical basis for the Blackwell Bible Commentaries—centers on the "premise

---

1. The episode is entitled "Taillight's Last Gleaming" (season 4; originally aired February 18, 1997).

that how people have interpreted, and been influenced by, a sacred text like the Bible is often as interesting and historically important as what it originally meant" (Guidelines for Authors). Basing my approach on this series, as well as the work of other scholars such as Yvonne Sherwood and John Sawyer, I will explore two main trends in recent popular-cultural products that either resituate or reimagine Jesus. My examination will necessarily be selective, as it would be neither feasible nor desirable to track all the references to Jesus in American popular culture. First, I will focus on "The Biblical/Devotional Christ" and discuss the ways in which fiction, music, film, and cultural events such as Passion plays attempt to retell the story/ies of Jesus primarily for devotional purposes. Second, I will discuss film, television, comics, and graphic novels under the heading of "Jesus in Elseworlds." The term Elseworlds is taken from the DC Comics Elseworlds imprint, which bears the tagline, "In *Elseworlds*, heroes are taken from their usual settings and put into strange times and places—some that have existed, and others that can't, couldn't or shouldn't exist. The result is stories that make characters who are as familiar as yesterday seem as fresh as tomorrow." By discussing animated television shows such as *South Park* and comics such as *Battle Pope* and *Loaded Bible: Jesus vs. Vampires*, I will examine how Jesus is altered and adapted to new and sometimes bizarre settings. I will conclude by trying to determine what, if anything, can be gleaned from the multiple and often strangely ambiguous representations of Jesus that proliferate like loaves and fish in our popular culture.

Reception History

Before examining our two trends, we need to be clear as to why and how we will discuss them. The former is easier than the latter, as many scholars now have embraced the usefulness of interpretive renderings of biblical literature in understanding a given passage or book. John Riches writes,

> The language, metaphors, and concepts of the Bible permeate our culture in endless kinds of ways: from the turn of phrase which may add a twist to a scene, through the exploitation of major biblical metaphors and concepts which may shape a work as a whole, however they are received or reworked (or indeed rejected), to works which reflect on the role of the Bible itself. (2000, 113)

Lamenting the pervasive ignorance of biblical literature among people today, Riches is skeptical that we can engage our culture, let alone the Bible, in any meaningful way.[2] After discussing the handmaids in Margaret Atwood's *The Handmaid's Tale*, who know only what they are told and nothing else, Riches notes:

> To the extent that we are not even aware of those themes and motifs from the Bible which hold us and condition our social mores, our position may be even worse. If we do not know what it is that holds us, how can we criticize, let alone recover the biblical elements in our culture? The way to a deeper appreciation and critique of our cultural heritage is barred. So too is the way to a more liberating and redemptive use of the Bible. (116)

If we do not engage the interpretive tradition of the Bible, then we cannot under-stand our culture, nor can we appreciate the disproportionate impact these later renderings have had and continue to have on the way in which readers consume the Bible. John Sawyer claims as much when he writes, "the afterlife of the Bible has been infinitely more influential, in every way—theologically, politically, cul-turally, and aesthetically—than its ancient near-eastern prehistory" (2004, 11).

Our second question (how do we do reception history?) is a bit more com-plicated and can be answered in two ways. The first way is to talk about theory, and discussions of this sort usually focus on philosophers such as Hans Georg Gadamer and theorists such as Hans Robert Jauss and Wolfgang Iser.[3] The basic assumption that underlies reception theory has to do with the issue of "textual determinacy," that is, where does meaning reside in reading: in the text, in the reader, or in the process of reading itself? By and large, reception theory holds that meaning is not found in the text. The text, in and of itself, has no meaning, so the reader creates a meaning that will most likely be different from the mean-ings created by other readers of the same text. In this way, multiple meanings are not only possible, but all of them can be seen as valid given the assumptions and contexts of a reader's "interpretive community," the sum total of the traditions, methods, and approaches to texts that enable the reader to read a certain way and that validate the reader's interpretation. For example, if one reads the bibli-cal text as an Orthodox Jew, one approaches the text with certain assumptions that are different than the assumptions held by an evangelical Christian. The way in which our Jewish and Christian readers read the text would differ as well, as would the meanings they create from their encounter. Finally, their traditions would validate certain meanings as acceptable but would probably reject some

---

2. For this issue, see also Alter 1992, 195–96.

3. For more advanced discussions of the theory behind reception history, see Holub 1984; Luz 2006; and Parris 2009.

meanings as falling outside the parameters of their historical identity or religious experience. Reception history encourages scholars to take seriously these meanings as well as those created and transmitted through other genres such as art, film, music, and so on, so that we can track the ways in which the Bible has been used to create important and influential meanings for real people throughout history. By doing so, we hope to regain a better sense of our own history, as Ulrich Luz notes:

> The history over centuries the Bible has had with us, during which it formed and shaped our culture and our churches, has become unknown for most so-called "educated" people of today. We do not know any more where we come from! . . . But without knowing what we owe to history and why we have become what we are—spiritually, ecclesiastically, culturally ... no consciousness of our interrelation with history and our indebtedness to history ... is possible. The study of reception history of eminent texts like the biblical texts is an important help to regain this consciousness and to clarify our own relation to the texts of the past we study. (2006, 125–26)

Though these discussions are interesting and indeed necessary, for the neophyte it is more useful to focus on the second way to answer the question, that is, what is the practical or hands-on way to do reception history? Here we should distinguish reception history from the type of inquiry in which biblical scholars like James L. Kugel engage.[4] Kugel examines Jewish and Christian scriptural interpretations to identify what he calls "exegetical motifs," that is, commonly held answers or resolutions to biblical ambiguities. He then tracks the genealogy of these motifs through other, later interpretations in order to illuminate how the Bible has been read. Reception history, too, collects interpretations and renderings of biblical literature, but unlike Kugel's work, reception historians do not confine themselves to scriptural commentary. Rather, as Luz notes,

> The study of reception history includes non-scholarly interpretations of the Bible in prayers, hymns and all kinds of pious literature. It includes also literature: poems, novels etc. Beyond this, the interpretation of the Bible in visual arts, music, dance, private or political activities, wars and peace, ethics, institutions and institutional texts, suffering and martyrdom is the object of studies of reception history. (2006, 129–30)

The goal of being so inclusive, according to Luz, is to remind "theologians that they are not the only, and not the most important, persons who interpret

---

4. See, e.g., Kugel 1994, 1999, 2006.

the Bible" (130). As such, reception historians amass data and examples from
numerous genres and discourses to show how the Bible has been interpreted by
different people/communities in different times for different purposes. On the
one hand, the examinations that result might be arranged diachronically, that
is, one may analyze interpretations as they appear chronologically, or one may
address renderings by the order of the biblical book one is investigating, as the
Blackwell Bible Commentaries do.[5] On the other hand, sometimes examinations
are arranged thematically, as in what follows; in other words, groups or clusters
of interpretations may be discussed in order to reveal what they imply about a
biblical story, book, or character. In general, the hope of reception historians is
that through examining these renderings, we can make sense of at least some of
the ways the Bible has functioned in our culture as well as how flesh-and-blood
interpreters have made sense of their world by interpreting the Bible. Reception
historians try not just to elucidate the malleability of biblical literature but rather
to divulge the reciprocal relationship between individual and corporate identity
and interpretations of the Bible.

The Biblical/Devotional Christ

Many images of Jesus found in popular culture exhibit a religiously devotional
or didactic purpose: they attempt to retell the story of, or stories about, Jesus in
order to reinforce or inculcate piety or an increased religiosity. As I have argued
elsewhere, the popular nature of these interpretations does not nullify their religious content; rather, this aspect allows them to be more readily engaged by
consumers as well as more accessible (Clanton 2007a). No genre of popular culture has embraced this type of representation more than film. As early as 1905,
with the release of Ferdinand Zecca's *The Life and Passion of Jesus Christ*, film-
makers have used (and sometimes abused) the stories of Jesus in order to inspire
audiences to adopt a more fervent religiosity.[6] In America, this religiosity is most
clearly seen in two films: Cecil B. DeMille's *The King of Kings* (1927) and Mel
Gibson's 2004 blockbuster, *The Passion of the Christ*. The former—with its rever-
ent and almost childlike portrayal of Jesus—was easily the most influential and
most viewed Jesus film until the 1960s, when Jesus films once again came into
vogue.[7] DeMille was adamant that not only the audience but also his cast adopt

---

5. A good example of this diachronic emphasis can be found in Schniedewind 1999.

6. For surveys of the history of Jesus in film, see Stern, Jefford, and DeBona 1999 and Tatum
1997.

7. I say "childlike" deliberately: one of DeMille's most effective techniques in this film is to

a reverential attitude toward the source material and even insisted that his actors refrain from immoral behavior (Birchard 2004, 222). An indication of just how important DeMille thought his film was, not only to believers but to all humanity, can be found in a 1927 essay printed in *Theatre* magazine. DeMille claims in this essay,

> The fundamental truths brought out through the ministry of Jesus cannot be confined to belief, race, nationality, or social position. Whether he believes that Jesus was a divine being who descended to humanity or a human being who rose to divinity, it is not after all tremendously important in view of the fact that His ideals apply to all of us. (1927, 32)

This means, according to DeMille, that in the wake of World War I all peoples, regardless of their religious traditions, should come together around the teachings of Jesus presented in his film in order to achieve a better and brighter future. So, DeMille wants not only the faithful but everyone to demonstrate an increased piety based on his cinematic rendering of Jesus.

When we turn to Mel Gibson's *Passion*, the audience shrinks decidedly. It seems clear that Gibson's goal is to inspire reverence for the suffering that Christ underwent and, in so doing, to increase the audience's gratitude for that sacrifice, which should then translate into a heightened religiosity. However, even though Gibson claimed that his main audience was "the unchurched," both his production company and the massive number of evangelical Christian viewers who catapulted the film to a staggering take of over six-hundred million dollars worldwide understand that the primary audience for his film is the evangelical Protestants and Catholics who saw the film repeatedly (Biema 2004, 66; L. Smith 2004, 47). Leslie E. Smith has noted this trend in her article on evangelical support for the film, and reviewers such as Richard Corliss and David Gates have also noted the narrow audience for the film. As Corliss writes, this audience consists of "true believers with cast-iron stomachs; people who can stand to be grossed out as they are edified" (Corliss 2004, 65).[8] Neal Smith goes further, arguing that evangelicals understood seeing and lauding the movie as both a stance against morally bankrupt values and a way to shore up "communal solidarity" and identity (2004, 159, 161). As such, the target of the film was evangelical believers, and Gibson's goal was to increase the piety of these viewers with his brutal depiction of the last hours of Jesus' life.

---

focalize Jesus through the eyes of a young girl whom he heals of blindness. See Stern, Jefford, and De Bona 1999, 45 and 53. For the popularity of *The King of Kings*, see Tatum 1997, 45.

8. See also Gates 2004, 50–52.

Inculcation of piety is also seen in the multimillion-dollar business of modern Christian fiction. However, a glance at the most popular titles, as of this writing, indicates that modern Christian authors of historical fiction generally shy away from retelling the story of Jesus. Instead, like films such as *Ben-Hur* and *The Robe*, Bodie and Brock Thoene's A.D. Chronicles series, as well as Hank Hanegraaf and Sigmund Brouwer's *The Last Disciple* and *The Last Sacrifice*, are composed of narratives that focus on how Jesus' life affects others during "Bible times." In so doing, they serve up role models for Christians today to emulate but only deal with Jesus in a very indirect way.

There are, of course, some authors of fiction who retell the stories of Jesus. One of the most popular recent treatments is *The Book of God: The Bible as a Novel*, by Walter Wangerin Jr. (1996). A less-known modern graphic rendering can be found in Robert James Luedke's *Eye Witness: A Fictional Tale of Absolute Truth*, published in 2004. Therein, Luedke interweaves two stories, one focusing on a modern archaeological discovery of an ancient account of Jesus' career and death, written by Joseph of Arimathea, and the other representing a retelling of the contents of Joseph's account. The translator of the text is a die-hard religious skeptic who, through the course of translating the text, realizes the error of his ways and becomes a Christian moments before a car bomb kills him. Luedke uses not only this plot but also the story of Jesus as told by Joseph to bring "the Passion story of Jesus to the youth of the world, in a format that they are both familiar and comfortable with" (Luedke 2004, n.p.). Even though I think Luedke's work ultimately subverts his goal, his efforts reflect the trend under discussion here, viz., the retelling of stories about Jesus in the hopes of engendering religious devotion in believers (Clanton 2007a).

This emphasis on creating or reinforcing faith in believers via a narrative retelling of Jesus' life and death is also found in material culture. As Timothy K. Beal argues, the nostalgia people feel for sacred space sometimes leads to the recreation of biblical scenes or events, a form of production stemming from "geopiety" (2005, 26–28). Included in this category of "biblical recreations" are spectacles such as Passion plays, the roadside displays that Beal examines in his book, and even theme parks like the Holy Land Experience in Orlando, Florida. Recently lampooned by Bill Maher in his 2008 film *Religulous*, the Holy Land Experience features a handsome Jesus who recites parables to the throngs of attendees prior to being crucified in an elaborate stage show. Beal calls it "Christian edutainment" but also notes that its goal seems more attuned to informing park-goers about, and thus preparing them for, the second coming (63–67).

Finally, one of the most important areas in which we find our biblical or devotional Christ is in music, specifically country and bluegrass music. It has long been noticed by scholars that music can serve as a repository of theological thinking,[9] and it should not surprise anyone with ears to hear that Jesus looms large in both country and bluegrass music. There seems to be a discrepancy, though, in the way that Jesus is portrayed in these two fundamentally interrelated genres. Some songs emphasize the human aspect of Jesus, as Maxine L. Grossman has noted:

> If God is the stern but deeply loving father, the Jesus of country music appears as an even more intimate and immanent divinity. The tendency in country music is to emphasize the human aspects of Jesus, focusing on his role as a man, whose actions might be emulated and whose sufferings might be familiar to an average person. (2005, 273–74)

This presentation of a human Jesus is certainly evident in songs like the title track from Joe Diffie's 2004 album *Tougher Than Nails*, in which a father uses the story of Jesus "turning the other cheek" to advise his bullied son not to retaliate. Remember, the father urges, in the end Jesus showed everyone he was "tougher than nails." Similarly, a son who has a tenuous and perhaps abusive relationship with his father ruminates on reconciliation while staring at a crucifix in Jimmy Wayne's song "I Love You This Much" (2003). In 1996, Gillian Welch sang on her album *Revival* that she will know her savior "By the Mark" where nails were driven into his hands and as such will rejoice when she sees him. Welch also tapped into a common theme—popularized by songs like the Stanley Brothers' "He Said If I Be Lifted Up"—when in her song "Orphan Girl" she connected being in heaven with reuniting with her lost family. On her 2004 album *Lifeline*, in the song "He Reached Down," Iris DeMent retells the stories of the Good Samaritan (Luke 10:29–37) and the woman accused of adultery (John 7:53–8:11) to highlight Jesus' compassion on those in need. And who can forget Johnny Cash's classic "I Talk To Jesus Every Day," in which the Man in Black assures us that he never has to wait for Jesus' secretary to have a word with him?

While Grossman is correct in noting the emphasis in much country music on the humanness of Jesus, it is equally obvious that many country songs, and especially bluegrass songs, focus more on the divine, even miraculous, aspects of Jesus' life. Returning to Johnny Cash, we find songs about Jesus' feeding the five thousand as well as his healings ("It Was Jesus"), along with tunes about the apocalyptic return of Jesus ("When He Comes" and "The Man Comes Around"), not to mention one of the most heartfelt pleas for forgiveness and atonement on record ("Spiritual"). The protagonist in Carrie Underwood's megahit "Jesus Take the Wheel" is not interested in a human Jesus and his suffering; she needs divine

---

9. See, e.g., Cone 1991 and Fillingim 2003.

intervention and spiritual guidance, and fast. This emphasis on a more divine Jesus is even more obvious in bluegrass, with its long tradition of gospel influences. In 2001, Patty Loveless retold the story of the raising of Lazarus in her song "Rise Up Lazarus" and assured her listeners that if they believed, they would be raised as well. On his 2005 album *Shine On*, Dr. Ralph Stanley sings about Jesus' divine return in "King of All Kings" and asks his hearers to "Sing Songs About Jesus" dealing with miracles and healings. Similarly, Ricky Skaggs, on his classic 1999 album *Soldier of the Cross*, covers several Bill Monroe songs, including "A Voice From On High" and "Remember the Cross," that deal with Jesus' death and resurrection and the ethical demands they should make on the listener.

In sum, what all these songs demonstrate is a focus on Jesus—be it an emphasis on his human or on his divine aspects—for the purposes of nurturing faith. They therefore cohere nicely with the other genres I consider above. All of these examples taken together show a remarkable interest in re-presenting Jesus in various genres of aesthetic and material expressions as both a model to be emulated as well as a redeemer to worship and petition. The ways in which this interest is manifest is an example of what Conrad Ostwalt refers to as "the secularization of the sacred," that is, when religious institutions and groups use modern media and other forms of secular cultural expression to disseminate their sacred message (2003, 7). As we shall see, not all aesthetic or cultural renderings of Jesus stem from religious organizations, nor are they intended to carry a specifically religious message.

JESUS IN ELSEWORLDS

Around 1950, Lowell Blanchard and the Valley Trio recorded Lee V. McCullom's song "Jesus Hits Like the Atom Bomb." Therein, Blanchard warns his listeners that they should be more worried about Jesus' return than about getting vaporized by an atomic bomb. While this connection may sound odd, it is demonstrative of the manifold ways in which modern comics, television shows, and films resituate Jesus into strange and often surreal settings. Not specifically concerned with encouraging faith, these examples of Jesus in Elseworlds illustrate, rather, a cultural preoccupation with Jesus and a playful willingness to engage in ahistoric aesthetic experiments in order to ask "What Would Jesus Do?" if he were dropped into weird environments.

One of the most common places to find Jesus transported into "What if?" situations is in comics and graphic novels. As early as 1964, Frank Stack was creating underground comics about Jesus, that is, he was a creator-publisher-distributor working outside the mainstream of comics, and his subject was Jesus.

But Stack's Jesus is not the pious, long-suffering, or helpful Jesus we find in the interpretations I discuss above. Rather, as I have noted, Stack's purpose is to satirize popular devotional understandings of Jesus, and, as such, his Jesus is sarcastic, humorous, and even critical of society and his followers (Clanton 2007b). For example, Jesus confesses that he is confused about how to be a messiah and decides to join academia as a guest lecturer at a large state school. Wearing his trademark linen shirt and halo, Jesus proceeds to spout sound bites from the Gospels to his students. Their responses are, as one might imagine, mixed. One asks how long it has been since Jesus has bathed, another inquires as to the number of "cuts" the students have, while a buff frat boy notes, "All that mystical shit went out with the Middle Ages!" In this, as in all his work, Stack intends to provoke his audience into a reconsideration of their views of Jesus by highlighting the difference between platitudinous proclamation and considered confession.

In 2000, Robert Kirkman and Tony Moore began advertising a comic they called "Christ-a-licious!" and noted "He's Back! Maybe he'll last a little longer this time." These ads heralded the arrival of *Battle Pope*, which Image Comics began reissuing in graphic novel form in 2005. The premise behind the four-volume collection is simple enough. God inaugurates the eschaton and finds humanity wanting. In fact, so few are righteous that the vast majority of humans remain on Earth where the doorway to hell is breached, and demons run amok. Eventually, a truce is signed that permits the escaped demons to remain on Earth but bars any more demonic immigration. In order to control the escaped demons and protect the sinful humans "left behind," God turns to Pope Oswald Leopold II, a hard-drinking, philandering pontiff. God transforms Oswald into a superhero, assigns his son Jesus H. Christ to be Oswald's sidekick, and the adventure begins. This Jesus, or "J" as he likes to be called, always appears in cutoff jean shorts and flip-flops, wearing Hawaiian shirts over novelty T-shirts with catchy phrases like "Finger Licking God" or "In God We Thrust." Even though he is drawn with a halo, "J" seems more like an underexperienced college nerd; even God has little faith in him. And Pope surely has little tolerance for "J," as he constantly interrupts Pope's womanizing. Despite the requisite slugfests, the standard portrayal of "J" bears all the hallmarks of classic comic relief. Only once does he get angry, and this divine wrath is directed at Santa Claus, in volume 3 of the series, *Pillow Talk*. The two soon reconcile, and we even see Santa—sporting a wicked-looking eye patch—and "J" partnering to fight demons in volume 4, *The Wrath of God*. In that volume, the last image we see of "J" is as a flower girl of sorts at the wedding of God and Mary. Upon seeing "J" walking down the aisle in cutoffs and a tuxedo T-shirt, God leans over to Pope and wryly notes, "Damn. I'll never be able to retire."

Both Stack's Jesus and "J" from *Battle Pope* fit nicely into the "Hippie" Jesus rubric delineated by Stephen Prothero. In his *American Jesus*, Prothero surveys different manifestations of Jesus in American culture, and one of the most influential is the Jesus that emerges in the 1960s. The "Hippie" Jesus was a product of the Jesus People, or "Jesus Freaks," who had their origins in the Haight-Ashbury district in San Francisco. Prothero notes,

> A long-haired rebel who somehow tuned into God long before the Summer of Love of 1967, their Jesus made love, not war.... More politicized Jesus People depicted Jesus as a Social Gospel hero, a "professional agitator" trying "to overthrow the established government." Less politicized Jesus Freaks accented their hero's fight against the religious establishment.... This hippie Jesus was not to be domesticated. He gloried in the road and in intimate comradeship with his male companions. (2003, 130–31)

Stack's Jesus obviously fits with the "Hippie" Jesus' struggles against the government and religious establishment, whereas the characterization of "J" embraces a pacifistic demeanor as well as the quality of male camaraderie. As such, while both Jesuses represent a new trend of displacing Jesus, they tap into an established topos.

Prothero also discusses a trend in interpreting Jesus that occurred in the late nineteenth century as a response to the seeming predominance of women in American Christianity. The importance of masculinity and its accompanying character traits—strength, confidence, and self-assertion among them—began to be touted by organizations like the Freemasons and the Boy Scouts. As a result, understandings of Jesus began to emphasize these traits, and the "Manly" Jesus was born (Prothero 2003, 87–94). In contrast to the slender, naïve, almost childlike Jesus we see in Stack's work and *Battle Pope*, this "Manly" Jesus is found most obviously in Tim Seeley's series *Loaded Bible: The "Jesus vs. Vampires" Gospels*, the first issue of which was published in 2008. In an interview with Dave Richards for the Web site Comic Book Resources that same year, Seeley described the setting of the story:

> After 9/11, Americans become more insular, more routed [*sic*] in Christian faith, to the point where church and state become inseparable. Then, one day, we find out that vampires exist. And from there, everything goes to hell. *Bible* takes place in the aftermath of a nuclear war with the Vampire Nation. The last outpost of humanity is a giant theocratic church-state called New Vatican City. Vampires are everywhere, most of them starving due to a lack of human prey. They're getting desperate. And then, our boy Jesus comes along. (Richards 2008)

"Our boy Jesus" is a spandex-wearing, sword-wielding, vampire-killing machine. He is so skilled at killing vampires—he can even take them down with his "holy spit"—that flying "cambots" record his exploits, which serve as the basis for a new type of televised, spectator-oriented Mass. Trouble ensues when the head vampire, Lilith (yes, *that* Lilith), sends her best assassin, Sistine Centuria, to New Vatican City (NVC) to deal with Jesus. Instead of killing him, Sistine reveals to him that he is not actually the son of God. She tells him, "The leaders of the city saw that the world had ended. But they had no Christ to lead them to Heaven. So, they found some relics ... a foreskin, some blood.... They **jump started** the Second Coming. They **cloned** you" (Seeley 2008, n.p.). Sistine then tells Jesus that the leaders who cloned him continually hope that he will be martyred, as that will increase the faith of their flock and make it easier to declare war on the remaining vampires. She even shows him a vast room filled with more Jesus clones waiting to be activated in case of such a war. Following this revelation, Jesus escapes NVC and forges an unlikely bond with Sistine. The third issue ends with Jesus and Sistine invading NVC to rescue Lilith, who has been captured and sentenced to die. Only Jesus makes it out alive, and while he vows to use his powers to help everyone, the leaders of NVC begin their war with the vampires, using their clone army.

And speaking of Jesus and vampires, we find a modification of Prothero's "Manly" Jesus in the 2001 film *Jesus Christ Vampire Hunter*. Directed by Lee Gordon Demarbre—and screened at the 2002 AAR/SBL annual meeting in Toronto—this low-budget endeavor defies easy summary. Its Web site describes it as follows:

> The second coming is upon us, and Jesus has returned to earth. But before he can get down to the serious business of judging the living and the dead, he has to contend with an army of vampires that can walk in the daylight. Combining kung-fu action with biblical prophecy and a liberal dose of humour, the film teams the Savior with Mexican wrestling hero El Santos [*sic*] against mythological horrors and science gone mad, and also manages to address contemporary sexual politics. And did we mention that it's a musical? This sure ain't Sunday school. (Jesus Christ Vampire Hunter)

We first meet Jesus (Phil Caracas) dressed in flowing robes with long hair. After being attacked by lesbian vampires and angry atheists, Jesus decides that he needs to update his image in order to combat this threat to his church. He gets a haircut, pierces both ears, and dons cool vintage clothing. Even this makeover proves to be no help, as he is attacked and beaten by the two head vampires, Maxine Schreck[10]

---

10. Her name is a nod to the actor Max Schreck who starred in the classic 1922 vampire film, Nosferatu.

and Johnny Golgotha. Jesus wanders out into the street, and the film retells the Lukan parable of the Good Samaritan after he collapses. A priest and a cop ignore his pleas, but finally a transvestite picks him up and cares for him. The following day, God speaks to Jesus through a bowl of cherry ice cream and instructs him to "seek out the saint of the wrestling ring." So, Jesus enlists the help of a Mexican wrestler named Santos in order to fight the growing horde of vampires.

Obviously this sounds like a silly premise, and in many ways it is. However, the film has a surprisingly interesting emphasis on Jesus' attitude toward sexuality as well as the religion that has grown up around his teachings. After surrendering to the vampires in the hopes of saving a captive Santos, Jesus asks why the vampires enslave so many lesbians. A vampire priest named Father Eustace replies, "They're deviants; no one will miss them." Jesus responds, "There's nothing deviant about love," and Santos wholeheartedly agrees with him. In the ensuing fight, Eustace stabs Jesus in the heart with a wooden stake, and Jesus seems to die. The screen goes red, and we see Jesus pull the stake out. A white light emanates from the wound, and when Jesus shines this light on the vampires, they turn to dust. So, Jesus is only able to defeat evil with his death. The final scene of the film is modeled on the Sermon on the Plain, except that it takes place in a public park. Jesus addresses a crowd with Santos at his side and tells them that they should not follow him just because he tells them to; rather, they should decide for themselves what to do. They should pay attention not to him, he says, but to his message. By downplaying the importance of Jesus' life and actions, the film seems to undercut its focus on Jesus, especially when it spends so much time showcasing his fighting skills. However, the inclusion of a more open sexual ethic successfully places Jesus' message in a specific twenty-first-century context; by showing Jesus being aided by a transsexual and condoning same-sex relations as an example of acceptable love, Demarbre presents us with a decidedly liberal Jesus, unbound by denominational squabbles, working to foster community at the same time that he preaches an antiestablishment message. As such, the film seems to unite Prothero's "Hippie" Jesus and "Manly" Jesus into a sort of hybrid "Skater" Jesus, a Jesus who is antiestablishment and pro-love, who embodies pacifism up to a point but who is also manly enough to take down any vampires in his way.

Sexual ethics and the issue of cultural relevancy lie at the heart of the 2003 film *Ultrachrist!* Like *Vampire Hunter*, its Jesus is an amalgam of Prothero's "Hippie" and "Manly" Jesuses, but the emphasis here is much more on the former. The plot is easy enough to follow, at least at first. Jesus (Jonathan C. Green) returns to earth in a scene that references the *Terminator* films and begins his mission to try to stomp out sin. Finding that he is unable to connect with young people today, and having watched copious amounts of Japanese anime and visited a comic book store, Jesus decides to dress himself up in a spandex suit—complete with a cape and a shining cross on his chest—and reinvent himself as Ultrachrist, so that he can "fight sin in all its forms," because, after all, "that's what Christs do." After Ultrachrist starts his ministry, though, the film's plots and characters get more convoluted and confusing, including an archangel named Ira, who is the patron saint of erotic massage, and even a plot by the Antichrist (in the guise of the New York parks commissioner) to defeat Ultrachrist through the employment of the Sin Monsters (Hitler, Dracula, Nixon, and Jim Morrison). Along the way, Ultrachrist comes to the realization that Christianity's trouble with sex was the result of a misunderstanding: when he was young, he saw the archangel Ira give his mother Mary a back rub but mistook this for adultery. As a result, he became sexually repressed and thus so did Christianity. After this epiphany and his first sexual experience, Ultrachrist decides to endorse sexual activity and become a "new, pro-sex kind of savior." Ultimately, Ultrachrist fulfills his mission of reaching today's youth with a musical show designed to preach this new pro-sex message, and Ultrachrist foresees it causing a massive wave of conversions to Christianity.[11]

As I said, the film seems a bit schizophrenic in its portrayal of Jesus/Ultra-christ. One minute he is a superhero fighting sin with his fists, and the next he is a naïve, anxious man struggling with his own sexuality. Like Demarbre's film, then, director Kerry Douglas Dye portrays Ultrachrist as both manly and sensitive, both strong and weak, and most definitely interested in sex and sexual ethics. For example, after learning that he has no place to live, Jesus rents a room from two self-described "lipstick lesbian lovers." Asked whether he has a problem with that, Jesus replies cautiously, "All love is holy in the eyes of God." At the same time, Jesus is so anxious about his own sexuality that whenever he gets aroused, he begins bleeding from his stigmata. As such, Dye's Jesus comes off as less cool and "in" than Demarbre's vampire-hunting Jesus, but this Jesus seems to be more focused on ministry and evangelization.

When we move from film to television, we have a more difficult time finding Jesus, especially in prime-time network shows. To be sure, Jesus has appeared as a regular character in the short-lived 2006 series *The Book of Daniel*, in which he dispensed advice to a pill-popping priest who has to deal not only with the mob but also with his dysfunctional family. Jesus has fared better in animated shows, even though he has appeared only once in *The Simpsons*.[12] Seth McFarlane's series *Family Guy* regularly uses Jesus in their trademark flashback scenes—

---

11. Luckily, the lyrics from the song that Ultrachrist sings at this show are available from the film's Web site; see Sing Along with the Ultrachrist! Songs.

12. Jesus had a cameo in the episode "Thank God It's Doomsday" (season 16; originally aired May 8, 2005).

including a particularly hilarious film trailer advertising a sequel to *The Passion of the Christ*—and recently devoted an entire episode to the story of what happens when Peter discovers Jesus working at a used record store and convinces him to make his second coming a public event.[13] However, the show that has demonstrated the most sustained engagement with Jesus has been *South Park*.

Beginning with their 1995 short film "Jesus vs. Santa," creators Trey Parker and Matt Stone and their Peabody Award–winning series regularly feature Jesus. For example, in season 1, not only do we see Jesus hosting a public access talk show called "Jesus and Pals" but he also appears in an episode titled "Damien," in which he must fight Satan in a boxing match.[14] We learn that the title character, Damien, is Satan's son, whose presence heralds the arrival of Satan. Satan challenges Jesus, who accepts, but instead of running in fear, the residents of South Park run to their bookies to place bets on Jesus to win. This attitude should surprise no one who has seen the show, as it routinely satirizes beliefs and institutions, especially religious ones. Once Satan shows up, looking large and muscular, all of the residents decide to change their bets in favor of Satan. The fight does not go well for Jesus, as he notes that everyone has forsaken him by changing their bets. This seems an obvious reference to the disciples' abandonment of Jesus in the Passion Narrative, as well as an allusion to Mark 6:1–6, in which Jesus could not work any powerful deeds due to the unbelief he encountered in Nazareth. After some inspiring words from the boys, which they curiously misattribute to Jesus, Jesus finally throws a weak punch and Satan falls. Of course, we learn soon enough that Satan was the only one in South Park who bet that Jesus would win. So, Satan takes a dive, collects all his winnings, and returns to hell, while Jesus forgives everyone for turning against him. By reframing the apocalyptic battle depicted in Revelation as a pay-per-view boxing match with a weak Jesus, Parker and Stone not only force the audience to reconsider their understanding of these texts, they also present us with a Jesus who seems incapable of defeating evil.

This characterization of Jesus, then, marks a major departure from those I have mentioned above, in that this Jesus rejects the "Manly" aspect discussed by Prothero and instead seems to adopt another interpretive rubric that Prothero calls the "Sweet Savior" (2003, 56–86). That is, owing to the increasing involvement of women in American Christianity in the eighteenth and nineteenth centuries, interpretations of Jesus naturally changed to fit the times. Jesus was often presented during this period as "pious and pure, loving and merciful, meek

---

13   Peter and Lois find the film trailer when they sneak into Mel Gibson's hotel room in the episode "North by North Quahog" (season 4; originally aired May 1, 2005). The recent episode with Jesus is titled "I Dream of Jesus" (season 7; originally aired October 5, 2008).

14.   Season 1; originally aired February 4, 1998.

and humble" (Prothero 2003, 59). In my opinion, the early presentation of Jesus in *South Park* accords nicely with this understanding of Jesus, which also appears in other early episodes that focus on Jesus, including "Are You There, God? It's Me, Jesus," an episode about Jesus' renewed popularity at the turn of the millennium.[15]

This portrayal of Jesus changes in the middle of the series, when Jesus begins to take on more of the "Manly" characteristics Prothero delineates. Specifically, in the episode "Super Best Friends," Jesus emerges as the leader of an organization of historical religious figures banded together to fight magician David Blaine and his followers, called Blainetologists.[16] Because of Blaine's magical abilities and Jesus' unimpressive, weak attempts at performing miracles, more and more people begin to follow Blaine. Only with the help of Buddha, Muhammad, Krishna, Joseph Smith, Moses, and Lao-tzu can Jesus succeed in keeping Blainetology from gaining tax-exempt status as a governmentally recognized religion.[17] Jesus returns in "Red Sleigh Down," in which Cartman—angling to be placed on the "nice" list—convinces Santa to bring Christmas to Iraq.[18] While delivering presents, Santa's sleigh is shot down and Jesus must lead the rescue party with guns blazing. During the rescue, Jesus is killed, prompting the newly freed Santa to announce that, from now on, Christmas should be a day on which we all remember Jesus for his sacrifice. Finally, in a 2007 episode based on Dan Brown's *The Da Vinci Code*, titled "Fantastic Easter Special," Jesus returns from the dead to prevent Bill Donohue (president of the Catholic League) from covering up the true connection between Jesus' resurrection and the Easter Bunny.[19] The secret connection is that Peter was originally a rabbit: Peter Rabbit. Therefore, the popes should have been rabbits, not men, because rabbits are innocent and pure and as such are not corruptible. In the penultimate scene, Jesus and Kyle are imprisoned and helpless to stop Donohue from destroying the heir of Peter Rabbit. To stop Donohue, Jesus asks Kyle to kill him so that he can resurrect himself outside their cell. Kyle, who is Jewish, expresses some hesitation at killing Jesus on Easter but fulfills Jesus' wish. Jesus is then raised in the midst of the throng of people outside the Vatican, where he publicly denounces Donohue

15. Season 3; originally aired December 29, 1999.

16. Season 5; originally aired July 4, 2001. This episode is obviously based on the Hanna-Barbera animated series *Superfriends*.

17. For an examination of this episode and its implications for interreligious dialogue, see Dueck 2007.

18. Season 6; originally aired December 11, 2002. This episode is adapted from the 2001 film *Black Hawk Down*.

19. Season 11; originally aired April 4, 2007.

before killing him with a ninja throwing star. It seems obvious from these examples that the more recent presentation of Jesus in *South Park* accords more closely with the amalgam of the "Hippie" and "Manly" Jesus we saw in *Jesus Christ Vampire Hunter* than with the "Sweet Savior" paradigm found in earlier episodes.

What do these examples of Jesus in Elseworlds have in common? They all exhibit a cultural, historical, and religious willingness to place, remold, and reinterpret Jesus within various aesthetic genres of popular culture, and in so doing, they force us, as consumers of pop culture and perhaps even religious believers, to develop our own understandings of Jesus, either against them or in dialogue with them. Unless you are a vampire, in which case you are out of luck.

CONCLUSION

When I was in college, one of the texts I was assigned to read made the following claim:

> We believe that purely personal interpretation of the Bible from the viewpoint of our modern culture will inevitably miss the mark when it comes to capturing the full richness of God's revelation through these ancient writers. What modern people *think* the Bible says is secondary to *what its writers thought they were saying*. (Ord and Coote 1994, viii)

These authors were obviously discussing the old exegesis-vs.-eisegesis debate, and their preference for exegesis is clear. However, it should be clear by this point in the development of the field of biblical studies that this dichotomy is a false one, as all interpretation involves one's own various contextual "locations." It has long been noted that no one can approach the text, let alone interpret it, with no presuppositions.[20] As such, we cannot simply ignore the above renderings as being the result of inadequate scholarly engagement, sophomoric humor, or poor judgment. Rather, we must ask why so many people are still so interested in doing things with Jesus.

The obvious answer is that America is a highly Christian nation, and Christians are interested in Jesus. As Prothero notes, though, that answer is only partly adequate, since non-Christians are also interested in Jesus (2003, 300–303). More basically, I think Jesus functions as an empty shell into which various meanings or significations can be poured. That is, the figure of Jesus functions mythically in our culture. Historians of religion have long noted that one of the key functions

---

20. The classic statement of this position is Bultmann 1984.

of myth is to provide a paradigm for action and identity (Livingston 1998, 82). Given Jesus' historical, cultural, and religious importance, it makes perfect sense that various interpreters would see in him and his life and teachings a rationale for their current identities and practices. And for those who have less of a religious interest in Jesus, he can also serve as a useful target of satire and humor. Again, though, the focus in the best of these renderings is on a critical reevaluation of Jesus' foundational status in our culture, so that identity and practice are once again highlighted.[21]

All of this is to say that in order to understand what people think of Jesus today, we must engage the reception history of Jesus and stories about him. It is imperative that we understand the myriad interpretations of Jesus in their own context(s) so as to free ourselves from the false claim that only scholars, theologians, and religious leaders have valid and meaningful insights into and about Jesus. Popular and lay understandings of Jesus in various aesthetic genres within popular culture have arguably done more to shape how people understand Jesus today than all the councils in church history. Given this—which can be good or bad, depending on your viewpoint—attention must be paid to renderings of Jesus in popular culture. As the Beatles sing in the song from which I take the title to this article, "Nobody can deny that there's something there." As long as people care about Christianity or the New Testament or Jesus himself, he will continue to be "here, there, and everywhere."

Works Cited

Alter, Robert. 1992. Scripture and Culture. Pages 191–210 in *The World of Biblical Literature*. New York: Basic Books.

Beal, Timothy K. 2005. *Roadside Religion: In Search of the Sacred, the Strange, and the Substance of Faith*. Boston: Beacon.

Biema, David Van. 2004. Why It's So Bloody. *Time*, March 1, 66.

Birchard, Robert S. 2004. The King of Kings. Pages 216–26 in *Cecil B. DeMille's Hollywood*. By Robert S. Birchard. Lexington: University Press of Kentucky.

Bultmann, Rudolf. 1984. Is Exegesis without Presuppositions Possible? Pages 145–53 in *New Testament and Mythology, and Other Basic Writings*. Edited and translated by Schubert M. Ogden. Philadelphia: Fortress.

Clanton, Dan W., Jr. 2007a. Scriptural Education and Entertainment: Evangelism, Didacticism, and Satire in Graphic Novels (Part 1). *SBL Forum* 5, no. 5. Online: http://www.sbl-site.org/Article.aspx?ArticleId=676.

———. 2007b. Scriptural Education and Entertainment: Evangelism, Didacticism, and

---

21. For an examination of this function of satire, see Griffin 1994, 35–94.

Satire in Graphic Novels (Part 3). *SBL Forum* 5, no. 7. Online: http://www.sbl-site. org/Article.aspx?ArticleId=704.

Cone, James H. 1991. *The Spiritual and the Blues: An Interpretation*. Maryknoll, N.Y.: Orbis.

Corliss, Richard. 2004. The Goriest Story Ever Told. *Time*, March 1, 64–65.

DeMille, Cecil B. 1927. The Screen as a Religious Teacher. Pages 31–33 in *The King of Kings*, booklet included with DVD. New York: Criterion Collection, 2004.

Dueck, Jeffrey. 2007. Religious Pluralism and "The Super Best Friends." Pages 224–35 in *South Park and Philosophy: You Know, I Learned Something Today*. Edited by Robert Arp. Blackwell Philosophy and PopCulture. Malden, Mass.: Blackwell.

Fillingim, David. 2003. *Redneck Liberation: Country Music as Theology*. Macon, Ga.: Mercer University Press.

Gates, David. 2004. Jesus Christ Movie Star. *Newsweek*, March 8, 50–52.

Griffin, Dustin. 1994. *Satire: A Critical Reintroduction*. Lexington: University Press of Kentucky.

Grossman, Maxine L. 2005. Jesus, Mama, and the Constraints on Salvific Love in Contemporary Country Music. Pages 267–98 in *Call Me the Seeker: Listening to Religion in Popular Music*. Edited by Michael J. Gilmour. New York: Continuum.

Guidelines for Authors. *Blackwell Bible Commentaries*. Online: http://www. bbibcomm. net/reference/guidelines.html.

Hanegraaf, Hank, and Sigmund Brouwer. 2004. *The Last Disciple*. Wheaton, Ill.: Tyndale.

———. 2005. *The Last Sacrifice*. Wheaton, Ill.: Tyndale.

Hollingsworth, Heather. 2008. 400 Dress as Jesus to Put Christ Back in Christmas. *World-Wide Religious News*, December 24. Cited 30 March 2009. Online: http://wwrn.org/ sparse.php?idd=29898.

Holub, Robert C. 1984. *Reception Theory: A Critical Introduction*. New York: Routledge.

Jesus Christ Vampire Hunter. Official Web site. Online: http://www. odessafilmworks. com/jcvh/.

Kirkman, Robert, et al. 2007a. *Battle Pope, Volume Three: Pillow Talk*. Berkeley, Calif.: Image Comics.

———. 2007b. *Battle Pope, Volume Four: Wrath of God*. Berkeley, Calif.: Image Comics.

Kugel, James L. 1994. *In Potiphar's House: The Interpretive Life of Biblical Texts*. 2nd ed. Cambridge, Mass.: Harvard University Press.

———. 1999. *The Bible as It Was*. Cambridge, Mass.: Harvard University Press.

———. 2006. *The Ladder of Jacob: Ancient Interpretations of the Biblical Story of Jacob and His Children*. Princeton: Princeton University Press.

Livingston, James C. 1998. *Anatomy of the Sacred: An Introduction to Religion*. 3rd ed. Upper Saddle River, N.J.: Prentice Hall.

Luedke, Robert James. 2004. *Eye Witness: A Fictional Tale of Absolute Truth*. Flower Mound, Tex.: Head.

Luz, Ulrich. 2006. The Contribution of Reception History to a Theology of the New Testament. Pages 123–34 in *The Nature of New Testament Theology: Essays in Honour of Robert Morgan*. Edited by Christopher Rowland and Christopher Tuckett. Oxford: Blackwell.

Ord, David Robert, and Robert B. Coote. 1994. *Is the Bible True? Understanding the Bible Today*. Maryknoll, N.Y.: Orbis.

Ostwalt, Conrad. 2003. *Secular Steeples: Popular Culture and the Religious Imagination.* Harrisburg, Pa.: Trinity.

Parris, David Paul. 2009. *Reception Theory and Biblical Hermeneutics.* Eugene, Ore.: Pickwick.

Prothero, Stephen. 2003. *American Jesus: How the Son of God Became a National Icon.* New York: Farrar, Straus & Giroux.

Richards, Dave. 2008. Jesus Saves: Seeley Talks *Loaded Bible. Comic Book Resources.* Online: http://comicbookresources.com/? page=article& id=6313.

Riches, John. 2000. *The Bible: A Very Short Introduction.* Oxford: Oxford University Press.

Sawyer, John. 2004. The Role of Reception Theory, Reader-Response Criticism and/or Impact History in the Study of the Bible: Definition and Evaluation. Paper presented at the biennial meeting of the authors of the series Evangelisch-Katholischer Kommentar. Germany. March 21–23.

Schniedewind, William M. 1999. *Society and the Promise to David: The Reception History of 2 Samuel 7:1-17.* Oxford: Oxford University Press.

Seeley, Tim. 2008. Loaded Bible, Book 1: The "Jesus vs. Vampires" Gospels. Berkeley, Calif.: Image Comics.

Sing Along with the Ultrachrist! Songs. Online: http://www.leisuresuit.net/content/ultrachrist_songs.shtml.

Smith, Leslie E. 2004. Living *in* the World, but Not *of* the World: Understanding Evangelical Support for *The Passion of the Christ.* Pages 47–58 in *After "The Passion" Is Gone: American Religious Consequences.* Edited by J. Shawn Landres and Michael Berenbaum. Walnut Creek, Calif.: AltaMira.

Smith, Neal. 2004. Truth at Last: Evangelical Communities Embrace *The Passion of the Christ.* Pages 151–62 in *Re-viewing The Passion: Mel Gibson's Film and Its Critics.* Edited by S. Brent Plate. New York: Palgrave Macmillan.

Stack, Frank. 2006. *The New Adventures of Jesus: The Second Coming.* Seattle, Wash.: Fantagraphics Books.

Stern, Richard C., Clayton N. Jefford, and Guerric DeBona. 1999. *Savior on the Silver Screen.* Mahwah, N.J.: Paulist.

Tatum, W. Barnes. 1997. *Jesus at the Movies: A Guide to the First Hundred Years.* Santa Rosa, Calif.: Polebridge.

Thoene, Bodie, and Brock Thoene. 2003. *First Light.* A.D. Chronicles, Book 1. Wheaton, Ill.: Tyndale.

'Tis a Pity She's (Still) a Whore: Popular Music's Ambivalent Resistance to the Reclamation of Mary Magdalene

Philip Culbertson

In 2006 and 2007, Elaine Wainwright and I co-taught a semester-long undergraduate course at the University of Auckland called The Bible in Popular Culture. Because the course was offered as part of a policy change at the university requiring undergraduates to take two courses outside the field of their declared major, we weren't sure what to expect. We had struggled over what to name the course— The Bible *in* Popular Culture, or The Bible *and* Popular Culture—but settled on the former because we wanted to examine the many ways in which the Bible was interpreted *in* film, art, popular music, and, indeed, in popular culture as a whole.

Both of us were experienced teachers of academic theology, and we were also active members of religious communities that struggled with the hermeneutics of biblical interpretation. But neither of us had taught a course on popular culture before, and, more importantly, neither of us had vast experience in teaching undergraduate students who were not majoring in theology or religious studies. Course enrollment in 2006 was 132 students and in 2007, 221. Both years we finished the course exhausted, stretched, challenged, and delighted with the integrity of the students who had completed it, many of whom came from the non-religiously affiliated background typical of so many New Zealanders.

For the first assignment, we gave students a choice of essay topics, one of which was: "Choose one song and/or image of Mary Magdalene in contemporary or historical culture; discuss how that cultural portrayal relates to the biblical images of Mary Magdalene." Approximately one-quarter of the students chose to write on that topic in each year we offered the course. The majority of those students were women, interestingly, but what surprised us most was the number of students (male and female) who rejected the deconstruction of the traditional image of Mary Magdalene as a prostitute. As one female student remarked, "Well,

I know that the Bible doesn't say she was a prostitute, but I still believe she was, and my opinion is confirmed by church history."

We carefully taught a two-hour unit, in week three of the course, entitled "Popular Culture Questioning the Bible: Mary Magdalene as a Case Study." All of the gospel texts pertaining to Mary Magdalene were examined by setting them side by side on a huge data-projector screen. Our arguments were supported by assigned readings from Esther deBoer's *Mary Magdalene: Beyond the Myth* (1997), Karen King's *The Gospel of Mary of Magdala* (2003), Jane Schaberg's *Mary Magdalene Understood* (2006), and, because *The Da Vinci Code* was the hot movie of the moment in Auckland theatres, we also assigned Lynn Picknett's essay "Sacred Sex and Divine Love" (2004). Following an examination of the biblical texts, Elaine carefully explained to the students the history of the sexualization of Mary Magdalene by tracing sermons, commentaries, and papal decisions, mostly from the third to the sixth centuries C.E., that conflated the Magdalene stories with Mary of Bethany (John 12:1–8) and the unnamed woman who was a sinner in the city (Luke 7:36–50). We also presented students with other images of Mary as they were shaped to fit subsequent historical periods—for example, as the penitent during the period of the Black Death or the evocative reclining nude in the period of nineteenth-century sexual repression. Having journeyed with the students through all this evidence from reception history, right up to the twenty-first century, we were sure that the problem was "done and dusted" and students would be well-equipped in the future to correctly defend Mary Magdalene as "the apostle of apostles," "the disciple that Jesus loved," the *prima inter pares*. Imagine our surprise, then, when a number of students rejected our careful reconstruction of the Magdalene, opting instead to revert back to a different hermeneutic altogether, of Mary as a common harlot before meeting Christ and a "healed" and "redeemed" woman afterwards, yet voluntarily submissive to the greater authority of the males in her life.

This raised the question of what the students had to gain by hanging on to an image of Mary Magdalene that had no clear support in the New Testament text. I have puzzled through this for a year and a half, ever since I last taught the course. Contributing to this volume has given me an opportunity to explore a possible explanation, though through a hermeneutical lens as complex as the archaeology of New Testament Migdal. I began my thinking with Sigmund Freud's theory of primary and secondary gains, which I continue to believe is a hermeneutic sadly neglected by biblical scholars, who may get frustrated when the general public finds academic exegesis too complicated to stomach. But the Freudian hermeneutic alone was not enough to answer all the questions, so I will augment Freud's theory of gains with an insight from Jung, a comment on the particularist logic of the human unconscious, a bit of social constructionism, a Ricoeurdian horizon, and a brief exploration of reverse hermeneutics. To say it in a simpler manner, no matter how well we teach the exegesis of Scripture and the hermeneutics of culture, there will still be people who actively resist what we are trying to teach because they have uniquely individual reasons for hanging on to some alternative meaning that better serves their personal needs, values, and life experience. These people have something to gain by not changing their minds.

Loss, Gain, and the Defense against Change

Sigmund Freud (1856–1939) first used the term "gain" in relation to the human psychological construct in a letter to Wilhelm Fleiss (Freud 1950). The term "secondary gain" appears for the first time in his "Fragment of an Analysis of a Case of Hysteria" (1905; the case of Dora) and "Some General Remarks on Hysterical Attacks" (1909). But he most clearly drew the distinction between primary gain and secondary gain in his *Introductory Lectures on Psycho-Analysis* (1917), lecture 24: "The Common Neurotic State," and again in his *New Introductory Lectures on Psycho-Analysis* (1933), lecture 34.

Freud never quite got around to developing fully his theory of primary and secondary gains, though his brief comments on the topic were suggestive enough that the theory went on to become one of the more important assumptions underpinning psychotherapeutic treatment. Basically, the theory attempts to identify what we gain by becoming sick, though subsequently the idea of gains has been broadened. Now, it is true that Freud's writings about women are both confused and confusing. Yet recent feminist reclamations of Freud (Chasseguet-Smirgel 1976; Roith 1987, 14–15) have argued that Freud understood the late-Victorian "femininity" that he encountered as a neurotic reaction to the oppressive power of patriarchalism—and in that sense *alone*, an "illness." Accommodation to the demands of that hegemonic form of masculinity, then, could be understood as a primary (paranosic) gain, an *internal and unconscious* adaptation to whom Victorian men expected women to be. Chasseguet-Smirgel further argues that males vigorously maintain patriarchalism in order to defend against their castration anxiety (their loss of power), thereby automatically generating the female primary gain of subservience and inferiority. Secondary (epinosic) gain, an involuntary form of attention-seeking behavior, is socially co-constructed between the woman and the society in which she lives and is structured both to reinforce the primary gain and to generate a reaction of sympathy or attention from society at large. In this sense, the hackneyed understanding of female hysteria, often attributed to Freud, would be a secondary gain, in that it positioned a woman in a particular way in relation to society but defended her primary gain of choosing to abdicate her own power in the face of an oppressive patriarchalism that felt life-threatening. In this sense, the protectionist superiority of men, which is their secondary gain in response to their fear of losing power (being castrated), and women's acquiescence to oppressive patriarchalism are mutually complementary and mutually constructed gains. Both are, in Freudian terms, considered reactions unconsciously generated in order to control a neurotic anxiety, however perverse they might appear to us today.

Of interest here is the way that this intergender dynamic is so heavily entrenched in most of pop culture's lyrics about Mary Magdalene. The dynamic is there because it appeals to listeners, including, I would argue, some of the students in our course, who project their own struggles with gender roles and gender identity onto the texts. But before exploring what the primary and secondary gains for our students might have been, we must first examine the ways that Mary Magdalene is imaged in contemporary pop lyrics.

IMAGES OF MARY MAGDALENE IN POPULAR SONGS

The question that I am struggling to address is what some students had to gain by rejecting the best recent New Testament scholarship about Mary Magdalene in favor of their own information about the character and life of Mary Magdalene, since their position clearly was not based on our careful close readings of the gospels but on information sourced from popular culture. Some of our students were involved in local congregations, but many weren't. This apparently made no difference, for those involved in congregations were just as likely to reject the biblical image as were those not involved in congregations. As we discovered, the students were much more familiar with pop lyrics than with the biblical texts and, apparently, often more willing to grant greater credence to those lyrics. In the clash between the biblical portrayal and the popular-cultural appropriation, the latter clearly had the upper hand!

A number of recent studies have highlighted how ignorant most Americans are of the biblical text, in spite of professing a public Christianity and having a Bible available in the home (see, for example, Popa 2009, reporting a study in which half of all high school seniors in the US believed that Sodom and Gomorrah were married to each other). Suspecting that the students were privileging the "canonicity" of popular culture's interpretation (and why would they not?), I began to explore how Mary Magdalene is constructed in the music that was so much a part of our students' lives. Through a combination of internet searches, taking note of the songs that students wrote about, and asking my own friends if they knew any songs about Mary Magdalene, I was easily able to locate the lyrics for ninety-two topical songs in the pop repertoire. The songs crossed virtually all the musical genres, including hip-hop and rap (for example, Immortal Technique, Tricky), rock (Jethro Tull, Franz Ferdinand, Jefferson Airplane), country and western (Kris Kristofferson, Linda Davis), heavy metal (Sethian), jazz and blues (Patty Larkin, Kate Cerebrano), Broadway (*Jesus Christ Superstar*), reggae (the UPpressors), easy listening (Neil Diamond, Roy Orbison), and pop (Tori Amos, David Gray, Elvis Costello). An analysis of the lyrics of the ninety-two songs suggested that they fell into four relatively clear-cut categories: lyrics that make no overt mention of Mary Magdalene but that are understood by some listeners to echo her story; lyrics that make no overt mention of Mary Magdalene but that are claimed by the author/lyricist to tell her story; lyrics that mention Mary or Magdalen/e in ways that refer ambiguously, if at all, to Mary Magdalene; and lyrics that overtly refer to the biblical Mary Magdalene.

LYRICS THAT MAKE NO OVERT MENTION OF MARY MAGDALENE BUT THAT ARE
UNDERSTOOD BY SOME TO ECHO HER STORY

One student in our Auckland course wrote an essay comparing the lyrics of "Maxine," by New Zealand artist Sharon O'Neill, with the plot of the movie *Pretty Woman* and the gospel texts that mention Mary Magdalene by name. The O'Neill song speaks of a woman with "creases in your white dress / bruises on your bare skin" who "takes on the whole world" and ultimately loses everything. The connection was tenuous to course presenters; to the student, it was powerful. The lyrics are archetypal—a "hard" woman with her "smacked-up face," attracted to "bad boys," seeking "cold comfort." She is, to quote a song that another Auckland student used for the same assignment—"I Cried for You," by New Zealand's Katie Melua—"a hopeless drifter," who cries when the man she loves leaves her because he wanted a life so different from what she had to offer him. A similarly archetypal song was pointed out to me by a friend, who insisted that "it's really all about Mary Magdalene." The song was "Fancy," originally sung in 1970 by Bobbye Gentry and recently revived (brilliantly) by Reba McEntire. As Fancy's momma is turned out of the house because they are so poor, she is told, "Just be nice to the gentlemen, Fancy, and they'll be nice to you." Fancy leaves home with only two possessions: a "red velvet dress, split on the side clean up to my hip" and a heart-shaped locket that said "To thine own self be true." Of course, "in this world there's a lot of self-righteous hypocrites" who would condemn a young woman who "had no way out," but because this is an American dream, Fancy makes good and only a week later is pouring tea for "a benevolent man ... in a five-room hotel suite." None of the songs in this category are actually about Mary

Magdalene, but because of the power of the inherited assumption that she was a prostitute, people are quick to connect them.

This is the first example of many that we will see in this article of deeply rooted, traditional archetypes about women that are *read back into* the stories of Scripture—the good-hearted whore, the homeless drifter who can only support herself "on her back," the abused woman who is so angry that she becomes self-destructive. None of these are the Mary Magdalene of the gospels, but, as we shall see, they are often the Mary Magdalene of popular culture.

LYRICS THAT MAKE NO OVERT MENTION OF MARY MAGDALENE BUT THAT ARE UNDERSTOOD BY THE AUTHOR/LYRICIST TO TELL HER STORY

Pop star Tori Amos has described Mary Magdalene as a "blueprint for women which was never carried over and passed down" (Rogers 1996, 33). Elsewhere, Amos explains:

> Mary Magdalene is really someone who has made the church very uncomfortable. That is why you have two Marys in the Bible: one that is very sexual, and one that is virtuous and spiritual, cut off from her sexuality. In doing so, they take away all her wisdom. So instead of people having to align with one or the other, the Marys need to become married—joined together. (Particle by Particle)

While Amos's quotation captures the classically misogynist tradition of "the virgin and the whore" that has shaped so much of Christianity's historical attitudes toward women, Amos does not write of her muse with an accuracy faithful to the biblical tradition but writes of her from a more gnostic tradition. Though Mary Magdalene is not mentioned by name in Amos's famous song "Marys of the Sea," the referent is obvious in the third verse: "You must go, must flee / For they will hunt you down / You and your unborn seed / In all of Gaul is there safety?" (2005). In her lyrics, then, Amos seems to grant as much credence to the early medieval legends about Mary Magdalene's flight to France as she does to the gospel texts. At the same time, other of Amos's claims echo the assertions of contemporary biblical scholarship about Mary: "She wasn't this 'anything for a fiver, honey.' She was a peer to Jesus" (Particle by Particle). Ultimately, Mary Magdalene is she who gives inspiration to so many of Amos's songs—I could count at least eleven such songs, only two of which mentioned the Magdalene overtly—though it is the archetypal Mary that Amos writes about. In her own words: "I don't fall in love much. I mean, I fall in love every five seconds with something but I don't go from boy to boy. I go from archetype to archetype" (Particle by Particle).

If Tori Amos falls in love with archetypes, she is in the company of Carl Jung. To Jung, all gender performance is driven by archetype, with the masculine and feminine archetypes, as filtered through culture, being particularly powerful. Furthermore, in Jungian thought, the gender archetypes are particularly influential in adolescence, as one struggles with them in preparation for assuming the responsibilities of mature roles in the social arena. However, to address an archetype as though it were universal ignores the fact that the contents of an archetype are constructed particularly, that is to say, particular human individuals socially construct the "applied" contents of every universal archetype. Your Wild Man and my Wild Man, your Damsel in Distress and mine, may be very different one from another. There is a level of psychological sophistication that has yet to be fully realized in analyzing the field of the Bible in popular culture.

I have no wish to denigrate the importance of the archetypal feminine in the lives of the kind of young women who enrolled in our course, but there is much more to Mary Magdalene than just the archetypal feminine, at the same time that there is nothing about the character of Magdalene in the gospels that suggests, however scant the material, that as a historical figure she was anything other than a flesh-and-blood woman whose sense of discipleship alongside Jesus qualified her for a leadership role in the subsequent apostolic formulation of the faith. Nor is there any indication that she fled to Gaul with Jesus and/or their biological children.

LYRICS THAT MENTION MARY OR MAGDALEN/E IN WAYS THAT REFER ONLY AMBIGUOUSLY, IF AT ALL, TO MARY MAGDALENE

In various blogs where the public discusses song lyrics, disagreements often break out about whether the name Mary is an intentional reference to Mary Magdalene. This happens, for example, in blogs that discuss the lyrics of Tori Amos, given how oblique some of Amos's references can be. Bloggers will argue that Mary is such a common name—indeed, a synonym for "everywoman"—that no connection to the Magdalene is justifiable. The same confusion surrounds the word Magdalen/e, which, according to the *Oxford English Dictionary*, had by the late 1600s become a synonym for "prostitute" or "a reformatory for prostitutes" (see also Hannay 1992 [488], who attributes the re-entry of Magdalene the prostitute into English literature to William Blake). To illustrate: Lenny Kravitz has a song called "Magdalene." The lyrics tell of a seventeen-year-old young woman, "in the prime of her life," from North Baltimore, though "her mama says she'd end up a whore." She packs her suitcase and runs away to Hollywood, where she becomes a stripper. In the penultimate line, Kravitz says, "She's magdalene." But she's not Magdalene of the New Testament, however much Kravitz plays on the traditional archetype of the loose woman who dreams of taking on "this town; I'm gonna be queen." Internet research made it obvious that lyrics which at first glance seemed to indicate Mary Magdalene as the subject needed to be examined carefully. Fully one-third of the songs I located based on the titles Mary and Magdalene turned out not to be about the biblical Magdalene nor any of the biblical Marys.

LYRICS THAT DIRECTLY REFER TO MARY MAGDALENE

But another third of the pop songs I located did turn out to be about Mary Magdalene, at least in part, sometimes relatively faithful to the gospel image and other times with "additions" from the later development of her image within church history. Several of these songs were wonderful, and teachable, though the majority of them also spoke of a sexual relationship, and even marriage, between Jesus and Mary Magdalene. Of note are the Rainmakers' "The Wages of Sin"; Tom Flannery's "If Jesus Had a Wife"; Johnny Cash's "If Jesus Ever Loved a Woman"; Jefferson Airplane's "The Son of Jesus"; Boston's "Magdalene"; Patty Larkin's "Mary Magdalene"; Redgum's "Working Girls"; Richard Shindell's "The Ballad of Mary Magdalene" (also covered beautifully by Dar Williams); Grinch's "Mother Magdalene"; and Meshell Ndegeocello's "Mary Magdalene" (of which I will write more).

     Some lyrics shock but still drive the point home, such as the Rainmakers' claim that Mary Magdalene was still a hooker after the crucifixion. Redgum (1982) makes the same claim, commenting that if Mary Magdalene were still working the streets of Kings Cross, Sydney (Australia), "wives would clutch their husbands" because of Mary's beauty. Tom Flannery suggests that Jesus and Mary had at least two children together: "Can his daughter become a priest?" and "a jr. Jesus would have big shoes to fill" (2003). Jefferson Airplane offers the "runaway" hypothesis, adding that Mary Magdalene rescued the two children that Jesus sired with her by hiding them "from the slaughter in the deep Black Sea" (1972). Sometimes the lyrics conflate biblical verses (a practice common in the early church, too), such as Johnny Cash's "From seven dirty devils did He free the soul of Mary Magdalene" (2006; see Mark 16:9; Luke 8:2) or Redgum's confusion of Mary with the woman caught in adultery (John 8:1–11). The lyrics of both Patty Larkin and Richard Shindell speak of Mary's enormous sacrifice in giving up her own future to become the lover of Jesus, while Boston's lyrics speak of the loneliness of Jesus that inevitably drove him into Mary's arms. Grinch presents the striking image of an angel lying in the gutter in the local housing project, soaked in her own fluids. With a glass eye and a toothless grin, she announces that her name is Mary and asks if the young man singing would like to take her home. And then, "She took my hand and led me to salvation" (1992).

In every one of these songs, Mary Magdalene is highly sexualized. In fact, I was not able to find a popular song about Mary Magdalene in which she was *not* sexualized or at least made to conform to the heteronormative metanarrative, except for one (below). She is not always portrayed as the seductress, but she is always a willing participant, because she loves Jesus passionately, just as he loved her.

Perhaps the most iconoclastic lyrics portraying Mary Magdalene are found in the eponymous song composed and sung by Meshell Ndegeocello (the spelling of her names has changed from time to time over the course of her singing career). Born in 1968, Ndegeocello identifies herself as bisexual, and one of her former partners was Rebecca Walker, daughter of feminist author Alice Walker. She has sung on recordings by John Cougar Mellencamp, the Indigo Girls, and the Blind Boys of Alabama; has been heard in the soundtracks of a number of movies, including *How Stella Got Her Groove Back*, *Batman and Robin*, and *Higher Learning*; and has played instrumentals on recordings by the Rolling Stones and Alanis Morissette, among others. Her 1996 CD, *Peace beyond Passion*, includes a number of songs based on biblical characters. Her deep, husky voice is almost unmistakable for anyone else's, yet it reminds me somewhat of a young Billie Holiday singing "Strange Fruit" or Nina Simone singing "Lilac Wine."

The opening verse of the song "Mary Magdalene" sounds at first as though it is Jesus speaking: "I often watch you the way you whore yourself. You're so beautiful.... I wish you'd flirt with me" (Ndegeocello 1996). But then listeners are surprised by the singer's invitation to "Mary Magdalene" to "jump the broom," an antebellum marriage ritual customary among African American slaves, who were often prevented from marrying legally (see *Jumping the Broom* 2005, and Tori Amos's claim, above, that "the two Marys need to become married to each other"). The singer describes "Mary Magdalene" as one who "lives alone in a crowded bed, never remembering faces" but pleads with her, "Tell me I'm the only one; I want to marry you." In the second verse, she describes the woman she desires: "In a harlot's dress you wear the smile of a child with the faith of Mary Magdalene, yet you wash the feet of unworthy men" (cf. Luke 7:36–50). Dreaming of a sexually charged marriage between the two, the singer woos "Mary" with verses of Scripture: "Blessed are the pure at heart, for they shall see God. So close your eyes and dream, for the world will bind you, and I'll judge not so that I may not be judged" (referencing, in order, Matt 5:8; a love song by Ten; Bhagavad Gita 3:9; Matt 7:1). These words could have been recited by any religious Jew in the late Second Temple period, including Jesus. The ambiguity of whether these are words of male-female ardor or female-female ardor is overcome by the powerful passion that provokes them.

These four categories into which songs about Mary Magdalene can be divided suggest that in popular culture, Mary Magdalene is more often purported to be present than she actually is. But where she purports to be, but is no longer, a hole is left, into which Jungian archetypes of the feminine can be inserted. This in turn raises the question of what happens when the Bible is imported into popular culture. Does the importing actually cause the Bible to disappear?

A Smorgasbord of Hermeneutics

When we were teaching our course on the Bible in popular culture, we employed a variety of schemata, borrowed from other scholars in the field, that we hoped would ground the students' thinking by providing them analytical categories. One such schema was the analysis by Bruce David Forbes and Jeffrey Mahan (2005). We charted it as follows:

Religion into Popular Culture	Explicit and implicit references to religious themes and characters in various media.
Popular Culture in Religion	Conscious and unconscious borrowing from religious traditions and texts in order to serve the purposes of popular culture.
Popular Culture as Religion	Overlaying popular culture with quasi-religious symbols, language, and devotion, such as in the case of sports.
Religion and Popular Culture in Dialogue	The forms by which religion and culture enter into dialogue, both positive and negative, and values and tradition.

Of these categories, the most pertinent to understanding the role of popular lyrics about Mary Magdalene is the second category, Popular Culture in Religion, particularly if we change the category's phraseology slightly: "Popular Culture in the Bible" nails the issue I am struggling with in this essay, namely that, in fact, some of our students seemed unable to read the gospel texts about Mary Magdalene and accept them for what (little) they said about her, wanting instead to read the stereotypical magdalenic images, or the imagined emotional lives of Jesus and Mary, into the text—*when they are not there*. When imported into popular culture, the facts of the biblical text seemed to disappear all of a sudden; the needs and values of popular culture seemed to make the biblical text invisible. In that sense, what we were dealing with was a "reverse hermeneutical flow." In his essay "Merleau-Ponty and the 'Backward Flow' of Time" (1992), Glen Mavis explores Merleau-Ponty's concept that time flows two-directionally, both forward and backward, from the past to the future as well as from the future to the past. Both Larry Kreitzer (2007) and Robert Johnston (2004) have found applications for Merleau-Ponty's theory in investigating the relationships among the Bible, film, and the audience for film. The same can be said here: the needs of the lyricists and singers who produce contemporary images of Mary Magdalene, as well as the needs of some of the students in our class, seem unable to resist the flow from the "pop culture present" back into the biblical text, unable to tolerate both the simple directness of the gospel texts about Mary Magdalene and the insufficiency of the received texts' description of her relationship with Jesus. This irresistibility—the Bible being recruited into the service of, and then read by, popular culture—makes it much more difficult for biblical scholars to reclaim ground for Mary Magdalene and reverse the damage done by centuries of institutional and ecclesiastical sexism. In a sense, the classical hermeneutical theories of Bultmann, Gadamer, Ricoeur, and others seem to have been displaced by the "lenses" of Andrew Lloyd Weber, Jerry and the Outlaws, Tricky, Frank Zappa, Tori Amos, Jethro Tull, Franz Ferdinand, and White Zombie.

These and similar lyricists adopt a late twentieth- and early twenty-first-century hermeneutic that leaves the habitués of popular culture dissatisfied. They want to know more—whether it is how degraded women like the Magdalene really are or how like the listeners they are, to the point of affirming their human desires for emotional understanding and deep relationship. Perhaps the majority cultures to which these lyrics appeal want Jesus and Mary Magdalene to be relationally intimate and mutually influenced, and the normative model they have for cross-gender relationships is sexual. In this way, popular culture not only influences biblical interpretation but also opens up new perspectives and challenges and confronts the conventional, stylized hermeneutical frameworks of the "industry" of the academic study of biblical texts. When Paul Ricoeur and Tori Amos go head-to-head, it is Amos who will win, because she expresses the world that young people live in, or wish they did.

But why? How can we understand the desire of some students to preserve the worst of Mary Magdalene's ill-deserved reputation? What can we hypothesize about their drive for the sort of primary and secondary gains that Freud theorized? Unless we understand these questions, we will not be able to understand why the scriptural interpretations of contemporary scholars of Mary Magdalene, such as Jane Schaberg and others, are not as influential in shaping students' hermeneutics as are the lyrics of Meshell Ndegeocello, for example.

UNDERSTANDING SOME OF THE RESISTANCE

Four recent studies have some relevance in understanding the resistance of some college-age students to the inroads of feminist and pro-feminist readings of the gospel texts.

A study by Janet Parks and Mary Ann Roberton, published in 2008, revealed that among the 370 American college students aged between eighteen and twenty-two surveyed, the merits of inclusive language were less supported than they were among any other age group, including participants in their eighties. The issues fought so hard for by first- and second-wave feminists are either taken for granted among Generation Y, or the Dot-Net Generation, or are of little interest to students at this stage of their development. These results suggest a possible lack of motivation among the current generation of college students to challenge, deconstruct, and reconstruct the image of Mary Magdalene that has been so long held in the church, a nearly exclusively patriarchal institution. Perhaps some students haven't found a way to engage the feminist critique, or perhaps they don't see the point.

A 2006 study published by New York University identifies the issues that Gen-Y students bring to university counseling centers as including low self-esteem, separation difficulties, eating disorders, sexual abuse, substance abuse, family dysfunction, stress, depression, anxiety, and career indecision (Hernandez 2006). The results of these and related issues are "high levels of distress and dysfunction." Among other things, this suggests a trend among American college-age students of wanting to return to a world in which they are safe and secure, where heterosexual desire between men and women is predictable, and in which change is not happening too quickly or their parents' values and attitudes are respected.

A study in 2005 by the Kaiser Family Foundation, sampling more than two thousand participants in the third through twelfth grades in the Uunited States, reported that teens are spending over sixty hours per week on average accessing new media like computers, the Internet, and video games without cutting back on old media such as television, print, and music. The amount of time that young people spend listening to music lyrics, for example, is a measure both of the level to which they are influenced by those lyrics and of how little reading of the biblical text they are doing. Many of our students in Auckland didn't know whether the gospels were in the New Testament or the Old Testament, but given a computer, they would immediately have been able to find the lyrics to Dave Alvin's "Sinful Daughter," which lumps together Delilah, Jezebel, and Mary Magdalene. For Gen-Y students, why should the biblical claims be more authoritative than the claims of popular lyrics?

In a 2007 survey of more than one thousand adults aged between eighteen and thirty conducted by LifeWay, a research organization within the Southern Baptist Convention, findings suggest 70 percent of young adults aged eighteen to twenty-two drop out of church for at least a year. The most frequent reason given was, "I simply wanted a break from the Church." The ages of eighteen to twenty-two describe the majority of university students who were taking our courses, and, ironically, this is also the age at which those who are churched are mostly likely to be looking for a break.

Of course, emotional and identity issues vary widely among eighteen- to twenty-two-year-olds in university settings, and these are also affected by nationality, regional and ethnic culture, and family background. However, this combination of seeming disinterest in the pro-feminist reclamation of biblical characters, the yearning for a safer and more secure world, the exaggerated imbalance between hours spent absorbing the popular media versus almost no exposure to the Bible at all, and the Gen-Y attraction to "a break from the church" can all be read as discouraging; or as explaining the students' enrolling in The Bible in Popular Culture as being the result of an attraction to popular culture rather than Scripture; or as a roadblock to engaging the challenging task of explaining the value of biblical hermeneutics to the students. Yet our students were very enthusiastic about the course—even the parts where their interpretations baffled us. How, then, might we think about what students gained?

Thinking about Primary and Secondary Gains

Students were not interviewed for this essay. I needed to pull back from the course to gain the perspective explored here, so what I write in this section is, admittedly, conjecture. But the topic of student resistance to seeing Mary Magdalene as the apostle of apostles seems to me, nonetheless, to be worthy of musing upon. The following are, therefore, my own ruminations.

We all get primary and secondary gains from reading biblical passages and stories. We read the Bible to feel good about ourselves, to feel superior to others, to be reassured about God's love for us and about our fate after death, to remind ourselves of our social responsibilities, to find our way through life's problems, and so forth. From these, we receive primary gains, which then allow us to co-construct, within our social environment, secondary gains such as being seen as faithful, having good values, being socially responsible, etc. We think "they're not like us," "we wouldn't do that," "we do do that so we're included among the elect of God," "this is how I need to change," and in general try to lead an examined life.

Perhaps that's the "fun" of hermeneutics: articulating the gains we get from read-ing the biblical text, each from our own unique social location.

But for students who are not biblically literate, what might they achieve through learning about the historically and biblically accurate portrayal of Mary Magdalene, beyond the fact that the poor woman has been dreadfully misrepre-sented throughout most of the course of church history? And why might some of them have rejected the very information that we were trying to impart?

Students may have gained a sense of social affirmation and of belonging. They worked hard in the course and its tutorials, we gave them lots of supportive feedback, and a sense of community was formed in the class—a community of people with new skills in the analysis of popular media and a new fascination with exploring what the Bible actually said. I believe they felt good about this.

Students may have moved beyond an assumed "splitting"—that the Bible is one world, and popular culture is another, and the two have little to say to each other. By putting the popular lyrics about Mary Magdalene in dialogue with the New Testament text, I believe we opened up some new avenues of communica-tion and interest between two worlds that are often assumed to have little to say to each other. This as well should have reduced students' cognitive dissonance, that seeming clash between the lives of people two thousand years ago in the Middle East and the lives of young people today in the vibrant city of Auckland, New Zealand—about as far away from Jerusalem as one can get.

I am not convinced of how successful we were in making the world of Second Temple Judaism accessible to them. I'm sure, from the students' point of view, the world of popular culture was still a lot easier to understand than the world in which Mary Magdalene lived. Most of our students were in the first year of their degree program and had not yet acquired the sorts of critical skills that we could build on. Very few, if any, had experience in applying critical skills to products of popular culture. So we were trying to create two different, but related, skill sets at the same time: how to do a close reading of, say, Luke, and how to do a close reading of, say, the lyrics of Franz Ferdinand. I suspect that this is a problem in all interdisciplinary courses that are taught at beginning stages of a university education.

This still leaves the question of why some students reaffirmed Mary Magda-lene's identity as a prostitute, in spite of the lack of gospel evidence. What would they have had to gain through their rejection? I suspect that what we did was to accidentally make Mary Magdalene into a two-dimensional character. We pre-sented her as "the apostle of apostles"—a faithful follower of Jesus and the first witness to the resurrection, who had subsequently been falsely maligned by a misogynistic church. In a sense, we set up a false dichotomy between the good woman and the bad male church. Judith Butler could have helped us rethink this. In *Gender Trouble*, she writes:

> Feminist critique ought to explore the totalizing claims of a masculinist sig-
> nifying economy, but also remain self-critical with respect to the totalizing
> gestures of feminism. The effort to identify the enemy as singular in form
> is a reverse-discourse that uncritically mimics the strategy of the oppressor
> instead of offering a different set of terms. (1990, 18–19)

Out of our concern to teach students to be sensitive to the feminist biblical hermeneutic, and by de-linking the very texts used by the patristic church to paint
Mary Magdalene as the epitome of the fallen woman and sexual temptress, we
must have removed from our students some possible levels of identification.
As Catherine Keller argues, "The dismissive approach to such phenomena of
popular culture betrays our own failure as academics to reach a wide enough
public—and to read its fickle, collective eros as inextricable from our own" (2006,
237). Our students, for the most part, were robust, active young men and women
in their late teens and early twenties. Based on present New Zealand statistics, at
least half of the students in the class would have been sexually active (Crisp and
Taylor 2008, 218–19). Comments such as "Well, I know that the Bible doesn't say
she was sexually active, but I still believe she was" reclaim Mary Magdalene from
being two-dimensional and make her into a three-dimensional character that the
students could identify with more closely. In so doing, those students made an
admirable effort to reclaim their own primary and secondary gains, not simply
the ones we desired to impart. Perhaps:

- in spite of the gains of second- and third-wave feminism, the traditions of patriarchal heteronormativity are too "comforting" to overturn,
  making the traditional primary and secondary gains of being powerful and defended men and subservient and overemotive women more
  preferable than a life in which egalitarian gender roles still need to be
  hammered out;
- a sexually active Mary is more attractive to university students who are
  themselves coming into their own as young adults no longer living with
  their families;
- the biblical stories, in an increasingly secular world, are simply such
  strange fruit for some students that they cannot always grant equal
  authority to the biblical world in conversation with their own, setting up
  a competition between Ricoeurdian horizons in which the need for the
  safety of the familiar predetermines that the reader's horizon will always
  win;

⤳   or perhaps we can never know. The human unconscious, perhaps the
ultimate determiner of which hermeneutic interpretations appeal and
which do not, is that six-sevenths of the human psyche that can never be
directly accessed. Perhaps the truest answer to the question of why, for
some, Mary Magdalene will forever be the repentant sinner and healed
submissive is that some people will always need her to be, for their security in a scary world.

In short, the reverse hermeneutical flow must have provided a more comforting
and attractive Mary Magdalene to some students than our lectures did.

And why shouldn't students make her into a three-dimensional character
that they could identify with more closely? Why *can't* she be a sexually active
woman who was apostle to the apostles? Martin Hugo Cordova Quero argues
that we have been simply too defensive of the Magdalene in our attempt to
reclaim her from Origen, Tertullian, and Gregory the Great:

> Theology has historically invested huge amounts of energy into fitting the
> *decent* patterns of societies (supported by the so-called *orthodoxy*) and
> condemning those that are considered *indecent* (related to those classified
> as *heterodox*). But the result is almost always fractured discourses that re-
> main unresolved. Mary of Magdala is one of those *unresolved fractures* in
> the decent discourse of Christianity. As with many human beings around
> the world, in past or present times, she has been historically trapped in bi-
> nary thinking. She is *either* sinner *or* saint; *either* decent *or* indecent. Binary
> thinking does not allow for further alternatives. (Quero 2006, 81)

CONCLUSION

If we are going to challenge students to engage the Bible in its endless hermeneutical glories, we should be very careful of binaries, or dichotomies, and should
therefore teach Mary Magdalene as being as complex a character as, for example,
Jesus:

> In a society where men were not even expected to talk to women in public
> (John 4), Mary of Magdala felt free to grasp Jesus' feet (Matt. 28:9), and she
> even had to be rebuked for clinging to him (the famous *Noli me tangere* of
> John 20:17). Evidently she was a woman who felt comfortable (not "sexually
> harassed") with socially disapproved physical contact with males. In both
> Matthew and John, therefore, it is not the male Jesus who takes the initiative
> in physical contact but Mary of Magdala. (Hanks 2000, 189–90)

This will be a fraught task, for once the conflations are removed, the textual witness to Mary Magdalene is slim indeed. Yet perhaps this is where the reverse hermeneutical flow can most help us as biblical scholars, by creating the middle ground where our careful academic readings of the text can meet the day-to-day lives of our students.

Works Cited

Amos, Tori. 2005. Marys of the Sea. *The Beekeeper*. Sony Records B00076EPQM.

———. Particle by Particle: A Page of Tori Amos Inspired Thoughts, Pictures, Quotes, and Downloads. Online: http://www.phrizbie-design.com/TORI_AMOS/quotes.html.

Butler, Judith. 1990. *Gender Trouble: Feminism and the Subversion of Identity*. New York: Routledge.

Cash, Johnny. 2006. If Jesus Ever Loved a Woman. *Personal File*. Sony Records B000F6YW08.

Chasseguet-Smirgel, Janine. 1976. Freud and Female Sexuality: The Consideration of Some Blind Spots in the Exploration of the Dark Continent. *International Journal of Psycho-Analysis* 57: 275–87.

Crisp, Jackie, and Catherine Taylor, eds. 2008. *Potter and Perry's Fundamentals of Nursing*. 2nd ed. Chatswood: Elsevier Australia.

deBoer, Esther. 1997. *Mary Magdalene: Beyond the Myth*. London: SCM.

Flannery, Tom. 2003. If Jesus Had a Wife. Online: http://www.songaweek.com/lyrics/11042003_ifjesushadawife.html.

Forbes, Bruce David, and Jeffrey Mahan. 2005. Introduction: Finding Religion in Unexpected Places. Pages 1–20 in *Religion and Popular Culture in America*. Edited by Bruce David Forbes and Jeffrey Mahan. Rev. ed. Berkeley and Los Angeles: University of California Press.

Freud, Sigmund. 1917. *Introductory Lectures on Psycho-Analysis*. Vol. 15 of *The Standard Edition of the Complete Psychological Works of Sigmund Freud*. Edited and translated by J. Strachey. London: Hogarth.

———. 1933. *New Introductory Lectures on Psycho-Analysis*. Vol. 22 of *The Standard Edition of the Complete Psychological Works of Sigmund Freud*. Edited and translated by J. Strachey. London: Hogarth.

———. 1950. Letter 76, to Wilhelm Fleiss. Pages 76–77 in *The Freud/Jung Letters: The Correspondence between Sigmund Freud and C. G. Jung*. Edited by William McGuire; translated by R. F. C. Hull and Ralph Manheim. Princeton: Princeton University Press, 1994.

Grinch. 1992. Mother Magdalene. *The Blackening Factory*. Online: http://www.elyrics.net/read/g/grinch-lyrics/mother-magdalene-lyrics.html.

Hanks, Tom. 2000. Matthew and Mary of Magdala: Good News for Sex Workers. Pages 185–95 in *Take Back the Word: A Queer Reading of the Bible*. Edited by Robert E. Goss and Mona West. Cleveland, Ohio: Pilgrim.

Hannay, Margaret. 1992. Mary Magdalene. Pages 486–89 in *A Dictionary of Biblical*

Tradition in English Literature. Edited by David Lyle Jeffery. Grand Rapids, Mich.: Eerdmans.

Hernandez, Nilda E. 2006. The Mental Health of College Students: Challenges, Obstacles, and Solutions. New York University Faculty Resource Network, November 17–18. Online: http://www.nyu.edu/frn/publications/millennial.student/Mental-Health-Hernandez.html.

Jefferson Airplane. 1972. The Son of Jesus. *Long John Silver*. RCA Fs Imports B000059L9A.

Johnston, Robert K. 2004. *Useless Beauty: Ecclesiastes through the Lens of Contemporary Film*. Grand Rapids, Mich.: Baker.

Jumping the Broom: A Black Perspective on Same-Gender Marriage. 2005. Published jointly by Equality Maryland Foundation, Silver Spring, Md., and National Black Justice Coalition, Washington, D.C. Online: http://www.nbjcoalition.org/jump_broom1.pdf.

Kaiser Family Foundation. 2005. *Generation M: Media in the Lives of 8–18 Year Olds*. Online: http://www.kff.org/entmedia/upload/Executive-Summary-Generation-M-Media-in-the-Lives-of-8-18-Year-olds.pdf.

Keller, Catherine. 2006. "She Talks Too Much": Magdalene Meditations. Pages 234–54 in *Toward a Theology of Eros: Transfiguring Passion at the Limits of Discipline*. Edited by Virginia Burrus and Catherine Keller. New York: Fordham University Press.

King, Karen L. 2003. *The Gospel of Mary of Magdala: Jesus and the First Woman Apostle*. Santa Rosa, Calif.: Polebridge.

Kravitz, Lenny. 1995. Magdalene. *Circus*. Virgin Records B000000W9V.

Kreitzer, Larry. 2007. The New Testament in Fiction and Film: On Reversing the Hermeneutical Flow (1993). Pages 370–73 in *The Religion and Film Reader*. Edited by Jolyon Mitchell and S. Brent Plate. London: Routledge.

LifeWay. 2007. *LifeWay Research Uncovers Reasons 18- to 22-Year-Olds Drop Out Of Church*. August 7. Online: http://www.lifeway.com/lwc/article_main_page/0%2C170 3%2CA%25253D165951%252526M%25253D201117%2C00.html.

Mavis, Glen A. 1992. Merleau-Ponty and the "Backward Flow" of Time: The Reversibility of Temporality and the Temporality of Reversibility. Pages 53–68 in *Merleau-Ponty, Hermeneutics, and Postmodernism*. Edited by Thomas Busch and Shaun Gallagher. Albany: SUNY Press.

McEntire, Reba. 1990. Fancy. *Rumor Has It*. MCA Nashville B0000020CW.

Melua, Katie. 2005. I Cried For You. *Piece by Piece*. UMVD Labels B000FBHCQ4.

Ndegeocello, Meshell. 1996. Mary Magdalene. *Peace beyond Passion*. Maverick B000002N2B.

O'Neill, Sharon. 1995. Maxine. *Foreign Affairs*. Columbia 469359-2.

Parks, Janet, and Mary Ann Roberton. 2008. Generation Gaps in Attitudes toward Sexist/Nonsexist Language. *Journal of Language and Social Psychology* 27: 276–83.

Picknett, Lynn. 2004. Sacred Sex and Divine Love: A Radical Reconceptualization of Mary Magdalene. Pages 19–28 in *Secrets of the Code: The Unauthorized Guide to the Mysteries behind the Da Vinci Code*. Edited by Dan Burstein. London: Orion.

Popa, Christian. 2009. Are Americans Faking Religiosity? *Reason Weekly*, October 17. Online: http://reasonweekly.com/christopher-hitchens/are-americans-faking-religiosity.

Quero, Martin Hugo Cordova. 2006. The Prostitutes Also Go into the Kingdom of God: A Queer Reading of Mary of Magdala. Pages 81–110 in *Liberation Theology and Sexuality*. Edited by Marcella Althaus-Reid. Aldershot, Eng.: Ashgate.

Redgum. 1982. Working Girls. *Cut to the Quick*. Epic 462552-2.

Rogers, Kalen. 1996. *Tori Amos: Images and Insights*. New York: Omnibus.

Roith, Estelle. 1987. *The Riddle of Freud: Jewish Influences on His Theory of Sexuality*. London: Routledge.

Schaberg, Jane, with Melanie Johnson-Debaufre. 2006. *Mary Magdalene Understood*. New York: Continuum.

Spittin', Cursin', and Outin': Hip-Hop Apocalypse in the Imperial Necropolis

Jim Perkinson

This essay constitutes a thought experiment attempting neither a scriptural reading of hip-hop nor a hip-hop reading of Scripture, but rather a "mini-sample"[1] in between the two traditions, rebounding onto both in unforeseen ways. The "phat note"[2] played here is one of giving hip-hop a place of power *inside as well as alongside* the Bible in a way that seeks to rock the sacred page with the rage of postindustrial street sages reincarnate in the peasant phrases of Holy Writ. The beat in such a backspin[3] is one that breaks open the biblical code to a question of rhythm—salvation as not just meaning but audition, a mobilization of syncopation, hitting *off* the beat of empire. Such a reading divines for possibility in the sonic underground of the text, imaginatively plumbing its *terra infirma,* its black humus of possibility, its base frequency. What happens if the Bible narrative is approached as encoding not straightforward witness but a "scratch-riff"[4] of Spirit interrupting the coherence of ideology?

---

1. The reference here is to hip-hop's "sampling" of past music, cutting particular beats from older songs into the new track of music being produced.

2. "Phat" as in "thick," "rich," "attractive."

3. A deejaying technique that flips the record backwards to once again pick up a particular "break" where the beat is most pronounced.

4. "Scratching" is another deejaying technique that involves moving the record back and forth rapidly under the needle, producing a novel set of sounds that in skilled hands becomes almost an alternative vocabulary.

A Hip-Hop Hermeneutic of Holy Writ

There is need today for a hip-hop aesthetic in urban activism and Bible study alike. Revelation is frozen on the mere page; the word is living and dangerous, dancing unrecognized on grimaced lips, spinning on its head in dark bodies, groaning inchoate in the bellies of homeless mothers and dying refugees—whether or not they can confess the right name! (Exod 2:23; Matt 25:31–46). Even inside the privileged page, the "word up"[5] is often a "throw down."[6] The psalmist exalts in ears excavated like an underground garage (Ps 40:6); the prophet in a tongue like a drill bit (Isa 49:2). Jesus learned his message from peasant diggers, telling stories of seed and weeds and rain clouds … and young bodies nailed to the imperial stake! (Mark 4:1–9; Matt 13:31–32; Luke 12:54–56; 13:2–3). Salvation in the code of the folk is about ground work and spilled blood! All of our love-theology to the good—the gospel is a matter of eating and being eaten, hard sayings, driving away wannabes, but music to the trapped (John 6:56–69). Today, Tupac's rap[7] is right, even when it's wrong. "They" (the powers) do have the darkened body locked down in a gun-sight and headed to an early grave. An urban ministry worthy of the age must stage its displays in the heavy gage of the ground-down.

My effort here does not offer either careful exegesis or scholarly paraphrase. It presumes a globalized planet organized in urban enclaves of ostentation pirating the fat of the forsaken gathered from elsewhere, living large in Disney-world dreams of trivial pursuits, protected by Defense Department lies and spies and eye-in-the-sky-guided smart bombs, while consuming a biosphere.

Hip-hop is not the gospel, but it is the percussive pound of an instinctual defiance (Perkinson 2005, 95–97). It is the code of a body refusing the electric chair, in spite of being destined there by the code of empire. It is the mode of the Jesus-word screaming against the quiet of torture, before it is tamed in the commercial … or the Bible verse.

Hip-hop is here offered as breakdown of the ghetto-bound—precisely in the breakout of the African pound of Middle Passage–drowned drum beats—breaking back up onto the surface of Western culture.[8] The issue is not the

---

5. "Word up" is a hip-hop expression generally meaning "agreement" or "truly."

6. A challenge that demands response.

7. Tupac Shakur's video release, "They Got Me Trapped," describes the dilemma of young black men who are so readily "trapped" by circumstance and policing tactics into contact with and control by the criminal justice system.

8. Yale art historian Robert Farris Thompson (1983) would say that one of the unforeseen consequences of the slave trade was that now the entire Western world "rocks to an African beat."

lyrical frown on the face of the CD cover.[9] It is rather the code of the unheard—
Afro-diaspora street funk striking against the memory and reality of European
colonial hegemony in the mode of syncopated heat,[10] tinged with Latino repeats
of mambo and rumba feats of mobility,[11] Filipino streaks of scratch-dream
sagacity,[12] and all manner of techno-digitalized Third World threats and bets and
meetings and greetings, promising concrete comeuppance![13]

Reading the writ of salvation in the grip of such a phat titillation means,
somehow, sounding out the delirium below the doctrine, representing the tic-toc
rip-rock inside the teaching. Since the text can't sing by itself, the demand is for
detonation inside the reading body—a use of words to infuse the surge of percussive memories of refusing the grave. Resurrection—not as tame reflection, but
sonic apocalypse! What follows are a series of improvisations in the key of flow
on certain "passages" that tease the possibility of such an aesthetic.

SPITTIN' RHYME: REVELATION

EXODUS 17:1–7 AND THE OG BEDOUIN

The tale begins with an outlaw witness. After escaping—compliments of his
momma—an imperial Egyptian policy of Hebrew infanticide, Moses grew up
privileged and posh in Pharaoh's court, until in midlife, troubled by his "pass-
ing" as an Egyptian, hearing the blood sing, he steps beyond the suburb and tries
to intervene back in the "ghetto" of hard labor. An Egyptian soon lies curled in
a white chalk outline (Exod 2:11–15, 22). The Hebrew crew beefs[14] when he
intervenes like a chief. The heat will fall hard now on both slave and would-
be deliverer. The chosen boy bolts. As Big Syke, Tupac-teacher-of-the-street,
reminds, Moses has here joined the killaz (Dyson 2001, 212). But without a posse.

---

9. Such as you might find staring back from a CD by, say, the Wu Tang Clan or N.W.A.

10. Syncopation is a well-known African and Afro-diaspora style of embroidering on
rhythm to make it yield multiple time signatures and meanings (Thompson 1983, xiii; Lattany
1994, 166).

11. Afro-Cuban dance forms that reference the contributions of the fusion of Spanish
and African cultural mixes to Western aesthetics in general and to hip-hop style in particular
(Perkins 1995, 6; Roberts 1999, 76–77, 127–28, 264; Spencer 1995, xi; Thompson 1983, 215).

12. One of the most innovative DJs to have emerged in the second phase of hip-hop DJ
history is the Filipino wizard of the turntables, DJ Qbert of the Invisible Skratch Picklz.

13. See, e.g., Olaniyan 2004 on the resistive creativity of West African genius Fela Kuti.

14. Complains; has an issue.

Becomes a refugee. The original gangsta Bedouin, wandering the sand wastes of Sinai with a warrant waiting back home.[15] But Moses went AWOL without a homeboy hope to call in. Had to become another kind of n … r. Neither street-wise nor poverty-propped,[16] he was taken in by an African clan, hooked up with a homegirl woman and taught the survival code of a Desert-Genie with a thuggish game (burning bushes and cracking mountains in demanding respect).[17] For the years to come, on the run from the Five-O,[18] Moses went old, old school, in the bosom of a rhythm learned at the hip of Mother Guinea. On a tip, after forty years of roaming the rock and herding the local product, Basket Boy could survive with only a flock at his side. It would soon enough become vocation.

In chapter 17—after the Hebrew groan has galvanized a god-in-the-dock—Moses has been cold-clocked by a hot leaf speaking the lyric of collision (Exod 3:1–7), returned against all counsel to the scene to free the whole block, been fronted[19] by Pharaoh, gone fabulous in motto and battle-rhyme against Pharaoh's best crew, mobilized the mob, conjured up drive-by plagues, looted the chunk,[20] parted the street, and found sweet refuge under open skies back in his Sinai 'hood—the beef begins. No Mackey D's or Pepsi here, not even Gatorade. The people rumor revolt. But we are given then a strange omen. The man has learned the rock. Bedouin lore today has the same tale. Harsh circumstance came be made to yield life sustenance. Infrequent rains and flash floods in certain places crust up crevices with pools locked in behind mineral deposits. Knowing the locale under the need to survive teaches where to strike and make stone yield water. Even present-day nomads can repeat the trick. Recognition of such a "local knowledge" does not lessen the idea of providential provision—but in this case it is a product of human familiarity with an ecology and intimacy with its seasons and cycles. Moses had been "schooled" by his sands. And learned how to drum a living flow out of a no-go land. And thereby offers us a "joint"[21]

---

15. In hip-hop culture, OGs or "original gangstas" are those who have participated in serious crime as opposed to those "studio gangstas" who only boast about such in rhyme.

16. "Props" are kudos or credit or respect, given to support an artist or performer. Here, the meaning is that Moses could not command respect from those whose lot he now shared as disenfranchised; he had no personal history of having survived a hard circumstance.

17. Yahweh's first appearance to Moses is in terms of a "plant revelation"—a bush that burns but doesn't burn up. Yahweh's next major appearance is as storm over Mount Sinai or even earthquake at the base of the mountain.

18. Police.

19. To be deceived by pretense.

20. Reference to "chunk" gold worn by hip-hoppers, beginning especially with the second wave.

21. Something positive, such as referring to a Spike Lee movie as "Spike's new joint."

not different from what rap represents. Hip-hop, too, encodes a savvy born of a harsh ecology—cold concrete forced to yield a clairvoyant beat. Hard places teach deep rhythms and can be made to yield profound revelation. For those who pay attention to the pace, who face the dread possibility of death and refuse to go down before downtime is up, the result is a mentality of steel and indigo, a consciousness of night and fire, a capacity for vision at the edge of nonbeing. Skills incubated in such a cauldron flash with apparition. The god who appears is indistinct from Ferocity writ large as a mode of Spirit and will not tolerate the substitution of "nice manners" for "exodus movement." Knowing how to find and free living vitality inside gritty reality is the honored ability. Hip-hop syncopation is not itself liberation, but can be its burning bush and does grant cold drink.

GENESIS 11 AND THE BREAK-BEAT OF BABEL

The setting, obviously—today and for ten-times-ten centuries now—is the city. The task—lighting a fuse in a toe to incite flight from the terror-dome (Abram will leave Ur in chapter 12 as the first moment of faith)! Urban enclaves since Cain[22] have always posed architectural claims on heaven. Like the archetypal Babel, they seek to organize labor and nature into a re-engineered version of the Great Garden, bloodied limbs and severed roots buried deep below the feet of well-fed self-congratulation.[23] In the tradition here, it is Abel who stands as emblem of the primordial murder victim—ghost figure for the graced lifestyle (nomadic relationship to the earth as "garden" is originally propped as "good" in Gen 1) sacrificed at the altar of settled agriculture … and the beginning of the ziggurat-cum-World Trade Center lifestyle of aggrandizing elites that has defined history ever since.[24] Every city is a theological monstrosity—the divine comeback to which is babble.[25] A solicitation of tongues in a tricked-up tandem of confu-

---

22. In Genesis, Cain is a name that signifies a particular kind of lifestyle choice—the turn to settled agriculture at the expense of pastoral nomad and hunter-gatherer ways that has as its inevitable consequence the killing off and "disappearing" of the latter by the former to gain control of land to cultivate. Cain is also—in that lifestyle logic—the first city-builder, as cities emerge as the ruling centers of settled agricultural societies and model themselves as earthly realizations of the heavenly patterns they claim as the divinely legitimizing sanction for their policies.

23. A city historically is a structure of injustice, concentrating resources gathered from elsewhere through the violence of conquest and slave (or at least exploitatively coerced) labor.

24. Again, cities ancient and new are notorious for developing vaunted opinions of themselves and creating architecture that "towers" over the rest of mundane life and reaches toward a "heavenly" achievement.

25. "Babble" in the biblical text is actually clarified as gift in the Pentecost outbreak of

sion! A riot of bodies obeying beats unlicensed—and indeed unrepeatable—at the seat of control! Hip-hop today is not itself the spell of divine deconstruction of urban self-deification. And indeed, it is quickly co-opted and bent to serve. But for the moment in our moment, it is the code of the clamor, the mode in which the city challenges its own meaning, the expression of contradiction that belies the homogenization and salvation claimed by the rulers. And thus—for now it defines the groundswell of groan that revelation must learn to moan as it loans Spirit an articulate Word. Ironically, for ears well-versed in the tinkle-chimes of middle class porches, it is "gospel" as liberating "curse."[26]

Cold[27] Cursin': Enculturation

Psalm 137 and the Criminal Code

Despite Samuel's griot-rage against betrayal of an originally anti-imperial vision (1 Sam 8:1–22), Exodus-delivered-Israel eventually goes monarchical under Saul, urban under David, and melts down within two generations. As prophecy glows hot, exploitation waxes fat, and for four hundred years a tragic tale of kings and catastrophe, farmers and poverty, is woven (the "history" of Israel from Solomon to Jehoiakim). Doglike and hungry, Assyria springs forth from the north in 721 and leaves only bones and "Samaritans" in place of ten of the tribes; Babylon swoops in with bared fangs in 587, and the remaining elites are reduced to a refugee state of exile by the River Chebar—there to sing as well as labor. And irony of ironies!—the fate is a date with comeuppance.[28] Not only is a homeboy beat now to be the treat of the Babble-on overlords,[29] but indeed the home-country-haughty-ness of the Israelite overclass is now schooled in singing "out of place." Would that they had learned.

The exile-lament of Ps 137 gives a peek at what anthropologists would call the "hidden transcript"—the meaning underneath the meaning, when oppressed

---

tongues in Acts.

26. "Cursing" is actually one of the weapons of the weak in the biblical tradition—one taken up and used by Jesus with great potency as we shall see below (cf. Luke 6:20–26; Matt 23:13–39; Mark 11:14). It too (along with parable, proverb, sermon, song, etc.) is a form of "gospel."

27. "Good," "nice," "mean."

28. It is primarily the Israelite overclass that is taken off into Babylonian exile—a group that had become oppressive within Israel itself now given a taste of its own medicine.

29. The Israelite elites being forced to treat their Babylonian captors to some local Jerusalem melodies as depicted in Ps 137.

peoples must publicly serenade or otherwise "obsequiate" their oppressors (Scott 1990, xii–xiii, 8–9, 14, 191–92). Forced to palliate the powers, the clever often conceal curse under cover of the requisite "sorrow song" or the slave's carefully donned "be happy." To dominant ears, it all sounds nicely plaintive ("such sweet darkies singing for the chariot to swing low") or else like a party ("sho' enuff got rhythm!"). But the code is likely a verbal spear in the belly. Like the Auschwitz prisoner commanded to make a Torah-scroll suit for his German captor in World War II, who carefully selected only curse-sections of the Holy Writ and wove a textile of warbling maledictions for his guard to wear! The Hebrew guttural in a Babylon court undoubtedly groaned the coming fate of Babylon ahead of time— "May you be blessed … into an early grave and your children's splattered brains decorate your golden gates!" Singing fate! Singing late comeuppance in an early refrain! Mixing mirth and tears in a compound palaver of sheer rage. But carefully couched in foreign babble.

The psalm as we have it is clear shorthand for the agony/ecstasy of producing entertainment from ravagement. (And there *is* a certain bliss inside such bombast, managing to "get over," in spite of the surveillance and control.) But how quickly forgotten when the younger offspring of such exiles are released to return home and, not too far down the road, set up a new version of the old show, priestly pretenders and scribal pontificators and other cooperators with whichever empire currently reigned (first Persia, then Greece, then Rome)—living large off the produce of the ground-down "land people" who remained, as before, regularly pushed "out of place," Jubilee proscriptions to the contrary (Mal 2:1–3:5). Peasants, on the other hand, already knew the tune. They had long had to sing the songs of torment *inside* of Israel! Simply to survive.

But here then is the very epitome of hip-hop's origins! A criminalized population of Bronx streets, boomboxing the beating of their dominant-culture demonization, figuring a party line over a percussive lynching served up in return to the white-mindset. Grandmaster Flash's DJ-fingers flying "F… you" sounds up suburban ears so irresistible under the lyrical lament of Bronx concrete that parents still can't control the teenage fallout twenty years later. Apocalyptic curse-crunk in a party beat. The next thing after Bob Marley's singing down Babylon through white tongues at reggae clubs. And indeed the actuality of a certain kind of "end" for the country at large may not be far behind (especially given the coming peaking of oil and its relationship to contemporary global exploitation). Should we lament? Or sing? Is there a difference inside empire?

LUKE 6 AND INSURGENT FUNK

There are whole sections of the biblical witness that are off-limits today, in cultures dedicated to a polite rape of the planet. For most of us on the upside of the great global grab, our mask of etiquette disallows the habit of public cursing, even as, in an earlier moment, we'd pinch our white-pink noses closed if we got anywhere near the thick funk[30] of knowing god as a mode of sweat. Afro-diaspora religious sensibility has historically trusted rousing rhythm above limp text as the vocabulary of incarnation. "God" shows through flesh only when the body gets down into the beat, funks up with heat and posturing, speaks in tongues and struts the subtext of the community in a healing reveling—and revealing—of its unsolved conflicts. In the late '60s, that communal working of spirit went public. In Black Power's courage to put a closed fist and a thundercloud 'Fro in the public eye, the African-revelation-of-America shifted from off-timed[31] savvy to sharply defined stridency. The Word on whiteness went boldly straight up. Whether speaking obscenity or marching politically, black bodies signified the public saliency of a curse-form. And in the shot-up flesh of Black Panther fighters like Fred Hampton, paid the price.[32] Successor-griots like Baraka[33] or the Last Poets[34] translated the bullets into verbs and shot up the ensuing conspiracies of silence. Hip-hop percussivity traces its immediate root to that reverberation, even when its recitation is merely "party time." Theo-musicologist Jon Michael Spencer discerns razor blades on throats in the scratch-line, striking back on the base-beat memories of batons thumping nappy heads (1995, 143–46). The music is code for war. And its word-underneath-the-word is a clairvoyance of curse.

Jesus here is model for a mode lost to our time. In Luke's Sermon on the Plain—a leveling riff on Matthew's Mountain version—the messianic mouth inverts the social signs of his day (Luke 6:17–26). It is the poor, hungered, grieving, demonized peasant crowd that is "blessed"—and in the same breath, the rich, roast-duck-stuffed, refined-ly laughing reputables who find a curse-code falling on their heads. This is not mere woe-speaking, but rather an ironic "return serve" of patriarchal court oaths[35]—sworn on Bibles in all-male ensembles of

---

30. "Funk" refers historically to "stink," getting sweat-soaked and body-worked in dance or sex and just living.

31. "Off-timing" is an ironic technique of "signifying," offering public commentary that is humorous, critical, and multi-referential, leveling the playing field of encounter through indirection and innuendo.

32. Chicago Black Panther leaders Fred Hampton and Mark Clark were murdered as they slept in 1969 in a raid initiated under J. Edgar Hoover's COINTELPRO program.

33. Imiri Baraka (formerly Leroi Jones), leader in the Black Arts movement of the 1970s and internationally renowned poet.

34. The Last Poets of the Black Arts movement are propped today as proto-rappers, gathering Black Power passion into sharp-edged chants and hard-hitting refrains.

35. Cf. Ps 109 for a psalmic version of the use of curses by the powerful in the court system to "underwrite" their legal machinations, effecting property transfers out of the hands of the

elites to "transfer" (i.e., steal) the estates of widows and waifs—back at the feet of their originators, as the "holy" word of the Human One. More simply said: Jesus returns the legal grenade like a hot potato and names the game. Living off of the surplus product of the hard-labored and calling it "blessing" while family members bury such "worn-out ones"[36] early is indeed an omen. The emperor may not have clothes on, but his local collaborators do, and the clothes are not their own, and the "provision" is not a gift! It is plunder. And its significance is ominous. Jesus is not inventing a form of recompense here as much as naming a reality. The curse is the devilry of complicity in the silent pleasantries of profit-taking while the peasantry that supplies the surplus dies early. Speaking it is not so much wishing it, as naming the obvious to the face of the oblivious. The apocalypse-coded-as-curse that he tenders as public pillory does eventually come home in the form of the Roman endgame on revolutionary Zealotry (in 70 C.E., some forty years after his death). But his frame was third-world and peripheral. The equivalent in our day from inside the belly of the new ("Roman") beast (rather than its maquiladora margins) would mean calling America today Thug No.1, clarifying the primary "gangbanging" as the latest oil-war, and Coolio's "Paradise"[37] as the average boardroom. Hip-hop's sublime hook-line[38] could be geared down to a simple unrhyme: Will the real criminal please stand up (and by the way, pay back what is owed before the rage-in-return goes nuclear)?

OUTIN' ILLIN'[39]: EXORCISM

JOHN 8 AND THE REAL KILLAZ

The Gangsta joint points to the profound issue. How discern the day? What is the real deal and who's who in the mix? Will the real Crips[40] please stand up and disclose their Blood(s)letting? Jesus' debate with the gate-keeping scribes and

---

poor and less powerful and into their own control.

36. Cf. Matt 11:28 for a classic Jesus-word addressing this circumstance, calling those so labored into a new community of Jubilee release and Sabbath rest that his movement initiated.

37. Coolio's release called "Gangsta's Paradise," sketching out (and sending up) the gangster lifestyle and consequences.

38. The "hook" in hip-hop refers to the refrain in rap lyrics that hooks the audience.

39. "Ill/illin'" is an AC/DC word that can mean something like "weird," "strange," "crazy-good," "awesome."

40. The Crips and the Bloods are Los Angeles gangs whose ongoing struggle for control of the streets became legendary in the 1980s and 1990s.

evangelical tribe of his day in John 8 illumines the stakes. John is the gospel with a difference. At least one scholar (Stephan Davies) suggests that the unique tone may reflect a zone of ecstasy-offering—folk-healer Jesus, speaking-by-the-Spirit when tranced-out and hyped-up in the shaman-struggle to make affliction yield its opposite (Davies 1995, 66–77, 151–69). According to Davies, the great "I am" statements characteristic of this gospel may actually reference a tongue-torrent under the influence of another world, Spirit-speech rich with the edge of vision, uttered by a messiah under the duress of possession. But in any case, the spate of creative signifyin'[41] in John 8 is a virtual clinic in "tropic[42] contestation"—a form of "dozens-playing"[43] drumming hard on the father-line. The state of things in the narrative design (John 7) is that Jesus is on the authorities' hit list to become supine before his time. He dare not go up to the great Festival Barbeque except incognito (John 7:1–10) and engage in guerilla rhyming on the run. As long as the sun and the people are out in full shine, no problem (John 7:14, 30–37). But when the dark falls, the crow calls. He better be out of Dodge (John 8:1). So he pops up like a tart in a toaster, roasts the rulers like a West Coaster,[44] on the last day of the feast throws up the Big Daddy of all boasts, and then goes subterranean again like a river. The Pharisees are furious. No arrest made, the guards red-faced with confusion, Nicodemus muttering something about justice.

The next day, the freestyle battle is on again, and the holds have no bars (John 8:1–59). The conversation is theological; the stakes are the people.[45] As the hands

---

41. A reference to longstanding African American practices of using language creatively and ironically, to play with the hidden possibilities of language and displace, or at least relativize, dominating power.

42. "Tropes" refer to the shifts of reference involved in signifying, in which words are deployed "tropically" as modes of metaphor, metonymy, synecdoche, or irony, thereby simultaneously masking and multiplying meaning underneath the misleading "plain" sense of the words.

43. "Playing the dozens" refers to an African American "ritual of insult" that invokes genealogy along the mother-line ("your Mama this" and "your Mama that") in seeking to put down an opponent who similarly is seeking to put you down. In net effect, the ritual is a bit of street pedagogy, training young people in verbal comebacks and ironic send-ups that are essential survival skills in a world of social abuse and ever-threatening physical coercion.

44. Referencing the emergence, in the late 1980s, of West Coast rap, seeking to establish itself over against East Coast (New York) hip-hop by offering its own distinctive "gangsta roast" of the country at large for creating, tolerating, and perpetuating the conditions of ghetto desperation.

45. Cf. a similar structure of interaction between Jesus and the leadership elites (priests, scribes, and elders) that is conducted in lofty theological terms about explicitly eternal concerns ("who gave you the authority to do these things"—that is to say, take over the Temple and shut it down for a day) whose real political stakes on the ground are the credence and allegiance of "the people" (Mark 12:27–33 RSV).

and hoots go up, the MCs throw down. The debate is cryptic until Jesus goes elliptic. The Focus on the Family crew goes ballistic. Abraham may be the name, but crime is the game and the scribes merely scholastic. The cap-down, buggaloo, bust-a-rhyme[46] grind is bombastic: party-line of the official crew is that Jesus is not really a Jew; Jesus' rejoinder in the stew is "neither are you" (John 8:38–47). The issue is the father; the charge is the devil; the real question on the level—who is trying to kill who? For today's Christian zoo, this is some deep doo! Spiritual discernment is finally not a matter of a particular linguistic ("Jesus is my personal Lord and savior"), but infer-ment of whose intention toward whom is actually terroristic. Any serious resister to the White House agenda of the "honorific" and self-ordained (John 5:44; 7:18; 8:15) is destined to become a mere statistic. Trying to name the spirit?—be realistic! Whose finger is on the trigger? The tricky few offer Jesus a trap: "You are just another N … r without a clear bloodline. Are we not right in saying your Mama was a hip-grind and you've done time in a straitjacket? Aren't you just a Samaritan with a demon?" (John 8:48). The return-rhyme is a bullet to the mind: "I have no demon—but your father was not even a twinkle in the eye of my own father's son when I first put a tooth through the gum. Better run! The 'I am' is come." Instructive for the doom of today: Jesus does not presume to deny a wandering genealogy. He is quite free to live inside a stigma, ally with the demonized (while denying the demon!), suffer with the racialized (without correcting the perception), die with the dammed. "Washed whiter than snow" in the old codes—in his own zone, he is black as night and feenin'[47] to blow up the lie.

MARK 7 AND THE DISSIN' SISTAH

As we move from the "insane" margins through the gangbanging center of the global banter (underwriting the decanting of world resources), it is also necessary to look within. As citizens of a planetary city now tentacle-d out in influence and dependence literally everywhere, we who live heavy on the backside of everyone else are without question "possessed." What we are possessed "by" is the sub-stance of stuff gathered from the farthest corners. Our "chronic" MJ high is the round of trinkets we buy and fry and fly and try not to let overwhelm the garage. The big lie is that we are entitled. So potent is the cry of the commercial that we usually die, in this country, pretending not to know. The sigh of global duress never enters our ears, even while it steals up as fears in our midnight dreams of

---

46. Rap with a "tight flow"—with power and finesse.
47. Craving; strongly desiring.

waking up. The quaking necessary to outing the Western world stake in the great global taking of stolen goods would be psychically seismic. The reversal involved in learning to make out the enemy in the mirror (as well as in the "other") is per-haps hinted in the aching alteration Jesus himself confronted in the shake-down, send-up he received while on leave from his vocation, in the Tyrean underworld.

Mark 7:24–31 recounts a strange encounter. On the run from the sum of misunderstandings and surveillance at home (Mark 1:37, 45; 2:24; 3:6, 21–22, 31; 4:11; 5:17; 6:1–6, 14, 35–36, 50; 7:1–13), a marked man counting his hours (John 2:4; 7:6; 12:23–27), the notorious Big Man-Teacher goes underground and silent—only to be found out and rounded up by a door-pounding out-rousting sistah of mixed blood and suspect repute (that she seeks him out in *his* quarters is presumptive evidence of another design than merely hoped-for healing). He is refugee at least, outlaw at worst, in a space of Jewish outcasts and exploitation. Tyre is historically a hard master of the north, pulling harvests from the hands and bread from the mouths of the displaced peasants around (Jewish and other-wise). He repels her hubris: "It is not right to take the little children's bread and throw it to the dogs!" (Perhaps much like Natives today would say to wannabe white sweat-lodgers: "No! Enough that you have taken our land and future, life and culture, you cannot have our spirituality as well!" Or maybe it was an origi-nally Tyrean proverb, used against the Jews as "dogs," that Jesus ironically puts back on her.)

But she goes under his word, comes up crafty and choppin',[48] specifyin' on his signifyin' (as Zora Neale would say):[49] "Yes, sir, yet even the little puppies under the table eat the little crumbs that fall from the little kids' plates!" (as it literally states in Greek). He has refused in the name of "littleness" as the street condition he most regularly champions; she repeats his prop back to him in a threefold "trump" of his rendition. This is dis' rap[50] without a mike or a mob to mediate! (Roxanne Shanté[51] to the fore, please! Show the man the door!) He instantly capitulates, notarizes her word as "up,"[52] "over," and "down" on his own

---

48. Talking.

49. "Specifying" (and "lying") is roughly equivalent to "signifying" (Willis 1987, 1–3).

50. In some accounts, a veritable genre of rap, but in any account, an integral part of the terrain of hip-hop, in which MCs compete in putting each other down and thus sharpening rhyme skills.

51. A reference to the first major dis' rap battle between a male and female rapper, in 1984, when Roxanne Shanté (14-year-old Lolita Shanté Gooden of Queensbridge) responded to the put-down lyric of the group UTFO by dissin' their dis' in a way that garnered national attention and respect.

52. See n. 5, above. This incident in Mark is the only time Jesus affirms someone for speaking "logos" back to him in any of the gospels.

round—a clown-faced "sounding out" of his frown that "throws down" without a crown to wear. This is bare truth, a tooth to the head, a spread of spoof like a rhyme was bread and the original hook uncouth! It is the only time in the gospel Jesus is recorded as losing a battle and affirming the hard-spit prattle of another as "Word." An unheard-of competition! Losing to a woman not of the tradition— pagan, single, without position! Vision! Call/response on a mission! Skill in the house! As they say at Café Nuba in Denver, "It's hot and it's black!" Whatever the skin color.

Yo Yo and the Real Flow

But we need to roll out the real dope here. This is soap in the mouth of the man-messiah. Wonder of wonders in a text hyping "Him," it is *her* word that pops open the possession; Jesus merely verifies what is already accomplished ("go your way, gone [past tense] is the demon from your daughter!"). Did that womanish word also clear a certain incipient patriarchy from outta his own psyche? Perhaps an early gangsta rap witnesses a similar show, a low female blow in a high rockin' "yo" directed to the brothas in a machine-gun flow, sampled by Ice Cube, throwing up "bitches" like "hoes" in a clockin'[53] mow-down, interrupted by Yo Yo.[54] Remarkable for a male-controlled rap (on *Amerikka's Most Wanted* album), in Cube's invocation of James Brown's "This is a Man's World," her word contests his own in a lyric of dissin' dozens that mocks the idea of brothers and sisters as merely kissin' cousins, once removed. Yo Yo interrupts the Richard Pryor, Eazy-E, Andrew Clay spray of sampled put-down, reinforced by Cube's macho throw down on what women are good for, by sending up Cube's lowdown as a failure of manhood, calling out his word-flood as inferior, and cutting down the rise of his size[55] as puny—literally. The echo-effect of her voice coming in over his is a heavy "thud" on the boast—a male-roasting of female function, toasted "black" in the comeback. But all kudos to this crunk[56] comeuppance to the good, the real key here is the opening of this male-dominated lyric-space—like the toast-place given the Syro-Phoenician *inside* the Messiah-boast—to more than one voice and agenda.

---

53. To hit; to see through pretense.

54. Yo Yo, a young female rapper concerned with building a progressive movement for black women, appears in the middle of an Ice Cube rap on *Amerikkka's Most Wanted*, engaging him in a version of the dozens (see n. 43, above).

55. That is to say, a clear sexual innuendo in her rap.

56. A word combining "crazy" and "drunk" (or "funk" as some would have it)—meaning hyper, hyped, excited, fun.

The model invites a serious rendering of the spirit-battle all of us face in the pace of globalization. Whose voice controls? How do we hear the thunder down-under? And in the males who regularly flail the word from the pulpit, what blend of gender soliloquizes the One? There is a Chronic within the church, a possessive addiction to the ten-millennia run of patriarchal constriction of the verb, as well as the resources. But the reverb is a vibe of mothers championing daughters—as indeed an ancient river of ancestral murmur[57] for more broadly shared bread—sounding in the silence under the male-dominated word. Whether such a black-robed masculinity can ever give place to this kind of up-welling multiplicity—a messianism of militant mamas and strident grand-papas up the spines and inside the rhymes and finally even in place of pontificating pastors—remains perhaps the gravest test of our citified mission. For us males—it is a question of who we are willing to ventriloquize and epitomize and ultimately legitimize. Can we really allow God an incarnation as both "woman" and "communion"—interior to our own flow? Can we channel more than just another vision of a world-dominating "bro"? Or do we insist on one gender alone under one Father's control as the only "real" show in our ever-changing flesh?

CONCLUSION

The above is a stable of biblical samples, flung skyward in a burst of examples trampling through a tradition anchored, exegetically, in inchoate expression, queried and quarried by percussion and groaning. Ancient Israel-as-yet-a-mere-twinkle-in-the-eye-of-an-exodus-God first commands attention as a mode of moan, memorialized in code and prophecy alike (Exod 2:23–24; 22:21–27; Isa 5:7, etc.). The insurrection of energy that the community first channels under the duress of slavery, not yet caressed with finesse, splitting lips of repression without infinitives, breaking silence like a spade in the soil, digging for Holy Ghost oil, feenin' for spoils, releasing coils of Jubilee jubilation in a boiled-over eruption of liberation, fairly demands elaboration under a beat. Hip-hop offers the concrete inundation of sound capable of pounding the text with its sonic equivalent. This is the real Bible-thumping aesthetic! A groan from a drum and a base-frequency quake, on the take for ears and wallets. The aural uptake of the ache of the poor, finished with obsequy and deference, echoing through the global somnambulance like apocalypse, in a Bomb Squad raid on the parade of gated community

---

57. Once again, think Abel's unrequited cry as cipher for the ongoing dying of indigenous folk the planet over .

(and country) propriety and nice manners, naming itself "Public Enemy." Bet! The sound of the blood of Abel, across the stage of civilized genocide, decried by the tenants of Babel's great tower as charade and mere babble, but in truth, an aural grenade of resurrection, still waiting its ethic and ecclesiology. The question it asks, in the pound of its swelling ground, is whether Christianity today has the ears to hear.

WORKS CITED

Davies, Stephan. 1995. *Jesus the Healer: Possession, Trance, and the Origins of Christianity.* New York: Continuum.

Dyson, Michael Eric. 2001. *Holler if You Hear Me: Searching for Tupac Shakur.* New York: Basic Civitas.

Lattany, Kristin Hunter. 1994. "Off-timing": Stepping to the Different Drummer. Pages 163–74 in *Lure and Loathing: Essays on Race, Identity, and the Ambivalence of Assimilation.* Edited by Gerald Early. New York: Penguin.

Murphy, Joseph M. 1994. *Working the Spirit: Ceremonies of the African Diaspora.* Boston: Beacon.

Olaniyan, Tejumola. 2004. *Arrest the Music! Fela and His Rebel Art and Politics.* Bloomington: Indiana University Press.

Perkins, William Eric. 1995. The Rap Attack: An Introduction. Pages 1–47 in *Droppin' Science: Critical Essays on Rap Music and Hip-Hop Culture.* Edited by William Eric Perkins. Philadelphia: Temple University Press.

Perkinson, James W. 2005. Constructing the Break. Pages 85–115 in *Shamanism, Racism, and Hip-Hop Culture: Essays on White Supremacy and Black Subversion.* New York: Palgrave Macmillan.

Roberts, John Storm. 1999. *The Latin Tinge: The Impact of Latin American Music on the United States.* New York: Oxford University Press.

Scott, James. 1990. *Domination and the Arts of Resistance: Hidden Transcripts.* New Haven: Yale University Press.

Spencer, Jon Michael. 1995. *The Rhythms of Black Folk: Race, Religion and Pan-Africanism.* Trenton, N.J.: Africa World Press.

Thompson, Robert Farris. 1983. Introduction: The Rise of the Black Atlantic Visual Tradition. Pages xiii–xvii in *Flash of the Spirit: African and Afro-American Art and Philosophy.* New York: Vintage.

Willis, Susan B. 1987. *Specifying: Black Women Writing the American Experience.* Madison: University of Wisconsin Press.

The Bible and Reggae: Liberation or Subjugation?

Noel Leo Erskine

It is not surprising that Bob Marley, the father of reggae, turned to the Bible for inspiration and social commentary on life in colonial Jamaica, where he was raised. He could not escape being religious because he was nurtured by his grandfather, Omeriah Malcolm, a Myalist (a form of African religion that survived in Jamaica) who believed in the mysterious powers of the Bible. Omeriah expressed regret that Bob was not given a biblical name, as was the tradition in the Malcolm family:

> And then into the world comes a creole pickney, named Robert after Marley's brother—not Omeriah's father—but, regardless, still a "slave name."
> (Robert Malcolm was believed by the family to have originally been a plantation owner's surname, which he then bestowed on Uncle Day.) And where is Captain Marley now that his son suffers? Gone-a Kingston in shame, under the mantle of disgrace from his own family.... At the very least the boy, the product of this regrettable union, could have been named from the Bible, bonding him to Africa and the folk culture of his people, like Omeriah and his brothers, Joseph, Nehemiah, Ramses and Isaac. (White 1991, 57)

Growing up in Jamaica at the same time as Bob Marley, it was instructive to me that as his music began to challenge poor and oppressed Jamaicans to leave Babylon (Jamaica) for Zion (Ethiopia), there was a sense among the populace that he was in fact another "brother Moses" and that his God, Jah, the God of Rastafari, had chosen him to lead Jamaica, through reggae music, on the journey from Babylon to Ethiopia. Perhaps it was the similarities that the Jamaican people saw between his movement and the biblical story of the Exodus from Egypt led by Moses that caused so many Jamaicans to make a connection between Marley and Moses. It is a connection he seems to allude to in his album, *Exodus* (1977), acknowledged by *Time* magazine as the best album of the century (December 31, 1999, 72). Marley's plea that Jah "would send us another brother Moses" (Hawke

2001, 48) was perhaps a wistful call for another Marcus Garvey to lead Jamaicans in a difficult time, when the political leadership had failed to implement promises made when Jamaica gained its independence. Even if Marley did not see himself as another Moses, the people of Jamaica did: "He saw himself as a singer, a psalmist, who would offer hope to those who were involved with the struggle, but he too was looking for another Moses. The cry is such a heartfelt and profound appeal that it would have resonated with struggling people all over the world who understood that the crisis of a society was marked by the crisis of leadership" (Dawes 2002, 207).

Marley's *Exodus* album was rendered with such conviction and passion that it was difficult for Jamaicans not to see him as another brother Moses, even if he himself was looking for Moses. "We know where we're going. We know where we're from. We are leaving Babylon. We are going to our Father's land. Exodus. Movement of Jah people. Movement of Jah people. Send us another brother Moses. Movement of Jah people. Gonna cross the Red Sea" (Hawke 2001, 48). Jamaicans were ready for Marley to lead us out of Babylon, to a new place of freedom, to a new and better life for all of Jah's children. If Martin Luther King Jr. represented a Moses figure for African Americans, Marley was our Moses. We knew that unlike Moses, whose journey was from Egypt to Canaan, Marley's was from Babylon to Zion, Ethiopia. We sang with him, "send us another brother Moses," while at the same time we believed he *was* our Moses:

> Exodus was a natural theme for Marley. Its issues of power, betrayal, hope, disillusionments, and the search for serenity were all uppermost in his mind as he created the *Exodus* album with the Wailers. The Book of Exodus deals with leaving familiar oppression behind, braving the unknown, and letting faith guide you to a brighter future. These ideas have increasing relevance as we are hit by a contemporary litany of troubles that can be read like the plagues at a Seder, the communal Passover meal at which, every spring for the last two thousand years, the escape from Egypt has been reenacted, sometimes at great peril, wherever there are Jews. (Goldman 2006, 14)

Marley was ahead of us. He knew all the time that the life of violence in Babylon was oppressive and that he could not provide the leadership needed. This leadership had to come from Jah (God) and through Jah. And so, in the *Exodus* album, he would remind us as he informed the world: "Jah come to break downpression [oppression], Rule equality, Wipe away transgression, Set captives free" (Hawke 2001, 49). As far as Marley was concerned, it was all right if he was not the brother Moses for whom we prayed because, as he joined faith and reggae, it was clear that help had to come not from human hands but from the divine.

BIBLE AS PRIMARY SOURCE

"Jah will rule equality, break downpression, wipe away transgression, and set the captives free." Kwame Dawes suggests that these lines in "Exodus" function as a benediction, and provide conclusive proof that Marley, drawing on the words of Isa 61:1–2 in a similar fashion to Jesus the Christ two thousand years before him, saw liberation and freedom from bondage in Babylon as a task for the divine. The goal was to transport victims from a place of desolation and despair to redemption and hope: "He makes it clear that salvation will come from Jah. Another 'brother Moses' will not bring the change, but the change will come from Jah whose authority is unassailable" (Dawes 2002, PP). It is Isaiah's prophecy that undergirds the language surrounding the work of Haile Selassie for the Rastafarians:

> The Spirit of God is upon me; because the Lord hath anointed me to preach good tidings unto the meek; he hath sent me to bind up the brokenhearted, to proclaim liberty to the captives, and the opening of the prison to them that are bound; To proclaim the acceptable year of the Lord, and the day of vengeance of our God; to comfort all that mourn. (Isa 61:1–2 KJV)

There are at least two other reasons that Marley could not avoid making the Bible central to his articulation of reggae. Earlier, I called attention to the home in which he was reared in Nine Miles, Saint Ann, Jamaica, where his grandfather Omeriah, a herbalist and Myalist, had a special affinity with the Bible. Here I should also mention the faith of his mother, Cedella, who was baptized in the local Pentecostal church and would see to it that Bob in his tender years was nurtured in the bosom of the church, learning its Scripture and singing its hymns. But the wider culture also had its impact, as the Bible was required reading in schools, whether public or private, in which there were always morning devotions replete with homilies, perhaps in part because most of our schools were administered and owned by churches.

For many of us in Jamaica, the first book we owned and learned to read was the Bible. The Bible had a central place in most homes and was often kept open at Ps 23 to keep away evil spirits. It provided a basis for our morality and gave us access to the mind and will of God. The Bible, being a resource of popular culture and a tool for the formation and enforcement of laws, was also a tool of colonialism and was used to keep things the way they were. One area in which the Bible was used against the populace was the insistence of many churches that its focus and emphasis is individualistic. Many churches taught that God would only relate to human beings individually and that according to the Bible, individuals were required to obey authority, including governmental authority, uncritically.

With the advent of Jamaica's independence in 1962, Jamaicans began to question institutions, including the church and the government, as a way of assessing the colonial bias, and they began to draw the conclusion that the church and the government had failed them and that the criticism of society should begin with the criticism of the church. Along these lines, there were hard questions concerning the understanding of the Bible and whether or not its authority was used in Jamaican society against the interests of poor people:

> In the surge of nationalism that accompanied Independence (in 1962) there was some suggestion that the English Bible, like the English language, should be spurned as the abandoned material of imperialism. But cultural commentators have since pursued the metaphor by declaring that these are the spoils of war, captured weapons that can be put to use in the continuing struggle for equal status among nations. This is essentially the Rastafarians' attitude toward the English Bible, though they conceive it more as recovered than as a captured weapon. The Rastas believe that the true Bible was originally written in Amharic by and about Ethiopians, the "Israelites." But as part of the punishment by which God led his people into exile, this Bible was allowed to fall into the hands of slave masters, who distorted it to serve their own oppressive purposes. (Breiner 1985–1986, 31–32)

This was the reasoning that informed Marley's embrace of Rastafari and provided a basis for joining faith and reggae together. The bottom line is that Marley's articulation of reggae is not understandable without reference to Rastafari. Reggae functions as a way of sharing the faith and allowing this faith to both critique and challenge the colonial agenda in Jamaica. Marley highlighted the issue for us: "When you say Rastafari, it's Jesus Christ with a new name, just like reggae use to be ska. So it really is the official thing for earth, and reggae is the music the Bible speak of" (Goldman 2006, 133). The Bible interlinks faith and music, Rastafari and reggae, and provides narratives and images as reggae exposes the tricks of Babylon:

> A chapter a day is the Rasta way, and Bob never went anywhere without his old King James Bible. Personalized with photos of Haile Selassie, it would lie beside him, a ribbon marking the place, as he played his guitar by candlelight in whichever city he found himself. He had a way of isolating himself with the book, withdrawing from the other laughing musicians on the tour bus to ponder a particular passage, then challenging the bed'ren to debate it as vigorously as if they were playing soccer. (Goldman 2006, 13–14)

Marley's music is sourced and inspired by the Bible. He sought in several of his songs to place the biblical text in tension with the contemporary context, allowing reggae to serve as a gadfly calling the oppressive ways of Babylon into question. It was a fitting tribute to Marley that at his death, his Bible, opened to Ps 23, was placed in his casket along with his guitar. One hand pointed to the Bible, the other to his guitar. As in life, so it was in death: the Bible and reggae were conjoined.

I would like at this time to identify some of the cardinal sources of Rasta-fari belief that shaped the worldview of Bob Marley. It is the linking of the Bible and reggae that is determinative. Perhaps it was the reality that Marley was abandoned by his father for most of his life, and at different points also by his mother, that made his turn to Rastafari all-embracing. Reggae is the music of Rastafari and Marley understood himself through his music as an apologist for Rastafari.

RASTAFARI BELIEFS AS CONTEXT

According to Rastas, there is both historical and biblical basis for believing that Haile Selassie I is the messiah. He is a descendant of King Solomon and the Queen of Sheba, and he is the one that Scripture speaks of in Rev 5:5: "And one of the elders saith unto me, weep not: behold, the Lion of the tribe of Judah the Root of David, hath prevailed to open the book, and loose the seven seals thereof." A cardinal tenet of Rastafari faith that was instructive for Marley is that King Solomon and the Queen of Sheba were the parents of Menelik I. This places in Ethiopia the Solomonic dynasty that ended with the disappearance of H.I.M. (His Imperial Majesty) Haile Selassie I in 1974. When Selassie became emperor of Ethiopia, he was given the title Lion of the Tribe of Judah. It must be kept in mind that discourse concerning the divinity of Haile Selassie I, and claims concerning biblical warrants that justify his messiahship, are made within the sociopolitical context in which the vast majority of Rastas, including Bob Marley for most of his life, were at the bottom of the socioeconomic ladder. Rastas, from this place at the bottom of the social stratum, saw themselves as prophets who lashed out through word, often with biblical allusions, against the evil system (which they called shitstem) that sought to sabotage the lives of poor Jamaicans. Reggae became the method and the art form through which the prophet would make his pronouncements against the exploitation of the poor and downpressed in Jamaica. The Rasta as prophet would, in speech or through reggae lyrics, guide all who would listen through the tricks of Babylon that were intended to thwart the lives of the people, rendering them second-class citizens or consigning them to a life of violence in Babylon. In language or in rhythms, Rasta speech would constitute a protest against the ways of Babylon. The point of their speech was "to resist against the shitstem," fomenting and bringing to the fore an alternative consciousness that would lead the way out of Babylon to Zion. It is in this sense that reference to the Bible becomes central, as it functions in a similar way as Africa, and especially Ethiopia, calling on the people to remember the divine activity in the past and thereby have confidence in the divine activity in the present. Historical memories, both biblical and African, became clues to liberation in the present.

If, on the one hand, a central question for Marley is, where do you stand in relation to Africa? then, on the other hand, an equally important question is, where do you stand in relation to the Bible? Africa and the Bible were the two poles within which Rastafari and its central art form, reggae, sought to articulate the teachings of H.I.M. Haile Selassie I. Africa and the Bible were united in the liberation of Jah's children:

> So no matter what stages, oh stages, Stages they put us through
> We'll be forever loving Jah. Cause there's no end.
> 'Cause only a fool lean upon, lean upon
> His own misunderstanding. Oh yeah. (Hawke 2001, 51)

It is clear that Babylon is doing its worst to Jah's people. A typical day in the life of victims in Babylon meant dealing with police brutality, the injustice of the courts, unemployment, racism, and violence against the poor. Marley chanted about the stages of suffering and the rages that excluded a person's experience. Yet he proffered an alternative consciousness, the antidote to life in Babylon: love for Jah. In spite of what transpires, "We'll be forever loving Jah." The temptation in Babylon is to lean on one's understanding, but this turns out to really be one's misunderstanding, because human beings are no match for the tricks of Babylon. The wise and prudent discover that love is the answer. Love for Jah is the way to deal with the different stages of violence that confront one in Babylon. Unfailingly, Marley's answer to the problems in Babylon is theological. The reality in Babylon is that people are confronted with "principalities and powers and wickedness in high and low places" (Eph 6:12). The only way out is for Jah to intervene and, through love, redeem Jah's people. We may "get up and stand up for our rights" (Hawke 2001, 55) but at the end of the day, hope resides in Jah. In gratitude, "We'll be forever loving Jah" (51).

Reggae and Rastafari

The theological and biblical emphases that suffuse Marley's reggae lyrics are largely the result of the conjoining of reggae and Rastafari. Their coming together was inevitable, as they emerged in similar social settings. Rastafari came on the Jamaican scene because of the impoverished conditions in which many working-class Jamaicans had to live. In addition to the harsh social and economic conditions that confronted Jamaicans, their lives were also determined by the policies of Great Britain, of which Jamaica was a colonial outpost for over three hundred years. Bob Marley was not insulated from the harsh conditions and grinding poverty that confronted most Jamaicans. Don Taylor, a close associate of Bob Marley, gives us a glimpse into the world that shaped our reggae superstar and made him turn to Rastafari for faith and inspiration:

> Trench town and the rest of West Kingston were beginning to show a flare-up of the ghetto problem which had started to become noticeable in the early fifties: there were large tracts of waste land crammed with makeshift houses of the iterant rural squatters who captured every square inch of living space, as they moved from country to town. The shacks were built cheek-by-jowl and somehow the politicians thought the way to solve the problem was to bulldoze them all down and build large and concrete structures.... This was where Bob ended up, in the area of the country later called Concrete Jungle. (1994, 23–24)

Reggae, like Rastafari, emerged in a context in which ghetto life is woven into a "black popular narrative." Through music, the poor and marginalized found their voice and were able to acknowledge and celebrate their identities. Reggae, born in a context in which the first artists were seen as social outcasts, turned to a religious faith that was itself outside the mainstream: Rastafari. The reggae artist became committed to the main themes in Rastafari: "Rastafarianism, whose roots are in Africa, in Jah, Haile Selassie, the emperor of Ethiopia. The themes of their message are rooted in the despair of dispossession, their hope is in Africa or diasporan solution. As a result, their messages emerge as ideology of social change" (Cooper 1993, 120–21).

As Bob Marley embraced Rastafari, he began to spend more time with Mortimo Planno, who is regarded by Jamaicans as the foremost authority on Rastafari. Planno took Marley under his tutelage and became the primary inspiration for Marley's journey into Rastafari:

> Planno took Bob through the stages of Rastafarianism, taking him to the settlements deep in the interior of the country where he learned about the groundation ceremonies, and the all night convocations which meant feasting on coconut meat, rice and peas (ital, or "natural living" cooking). It was here that he listened to the chants of the traditional Bongo Man and humba and Nyabinghi chants, while hundreds of Rastas sat on their haunches passing the chillum pipe. (Taylor 1994, 26–27)

The relationship between Marley and Planno was so all-embracing that on his public declaration as a Rasta, Marley chose to sing a song whose title Planno had given him. "Over a molasses-slow Nyabinghi drum track, Bob chanted: 'Haile Selassie is the Chapel, power of the trinity, conquering lion of the tribe of Judah, He is the only King of Kings'" (Steffens 1998, 257). It seems that Bob may have also acquired his love for the Bible from Planno, as his Bible was adorned with pictures, similar to Planno's Bible: "So I started to read from Planno's well-thumbed black King James Bible that his grandmother gave him 'back in the old village,' noting that it's been adorned with pictures of Rasta lions and H.I.M., just like Bob's" (Goldman 2006, 136).

Another significant influence on Marley's turn to the Bible is the foremost prophet of Black liberation in Jamaica and the African diaspora, Marcus Garvey. He envisioned the return of Jamaicans to their homeland, Africa, claiming that Black Jamaicans, like the children of Israel, were captives in the white man's land, and it was God's will that they experience exodus. "As children of captivity we look forward to a new, yet ever old, land of our fathers, the land of God's crowning glory. We shall gather together our children, our treasures and our loved ones, and as the children of Israel, by the command of God, face the promise land" (Garvey 1974, 121). A key text for Garvey, and one that is foundational for Rastafari, is Ps 68:31: "Princes shall come out of Egypt; Ethiopia shall soon stretch out her hands unto God." For Garvey, as for Rastafari, the exodus was not from Egypt but from Babylon to the homeland, Ethiopia.

Both reggae and Rastafari owe their existence to Garvey's call that, in the spirit of Ps 68, they should look to Ethiopia for liberation and identification. Prophesying in the spirit of Marcus Garvey, replete with biblical allusions, Marley wails:

> All and all you see a gwaan, is to fight against the Rastaman
> So they build their world on great confusion, to force on us the devil's illusion
> But the stone that the builder refuse, shall become the head corner stone.
> (Hawke 2001, 123)

Presented in the style of an Old Testament prophet, Marley bore witness, through reggae, to the apocalyptic end that will come to all who are invested in life in Babylon. Two stones that were rejected by Jamaican society are Marcus Garvey and Bob Marley, but they have become head cornerstones. Garvey was made a national hero in Jamaica and Marley received one of the highest titles, the Order of Merit, from the government of Jamaica, which allows us to refer to him as the Honorable Robert Nesta Marley.

Reggae as Songs of Freedom

Through reggae, Marley awakened Jamaica's poor, who were urged to "Get up and stand up for your rights." Through music, the consciousness of the masses was raised as no other medium, including Christianity, had ever done. Marley had the rare ability to make the poor keenly aware, through reggae, of their situation, as he prodded them to organize. This call to consciousness that exploded on the airwaves was presented as a right belonging to all Jamaicans. The poor were no longer nobodies but were armed with these "songs of freedom" (Hawke 2001, 119) as they become agents of their own liberation. "Build your penitentiary, we build our schools," Bob Marley wails in "Crazy Baldhead."

Reggae music points to a clear option for the poor and powerless. Jamaicans began to learn and to take seriously that all people, including the dispossessed, have inalienable rights and a responsibility to change their world and affirm their dignity. They have a moral responsibility to stand up for their rights. Marley captured this in his song "No Woman No Cry." The bottom line is that Jah is on the side of those who weep and are victimized. Jah is the one who stands up for the weak and all who are disabled. In Kingston, where Marley lived, each day he would see hundreds of women who could find no employment and thousands who were landless and homeless. As far as Babylon was concerned, these people did not exist. The reggae artist cried out on their behalf, and Marley explained:

> no one gives Jamaican people a chance, that's why we say the earth is corrupted and everyone has to die and leave we.... How long will they pressure we? We are the people who realize the place where they thieved us from, so we say, *Ah,* you took us from there, *ah,* this is where we are. But they still tell us, No, no, this is what you are! This is what you must be.... The greatest thing that could happen would never happen, so you could say God has we for a purpose and reason. (Goldman 1997, 46)

It was important for Marley that reggae did not neglect the history of the people and that their history was joined with biblical history. Through reggae, Marley was able to help oppressed Jamaicans fashion their identity as they placed their oppressive history within the larger context of the narrative history of the biblical story. This meant, among other things, that the oppressive history of Babylon was no longer decisive in shaping the image and the identity of oppressed Jamaicans: "That is, it is by the conscious 'indwelling' of a larger story of meaning, a story larger than the individual self, and beyond the confines of the dehumanizing present, that we find meaning for our lives and come to a sense of identity, in a manner that enables us to resist the dehumanization of a world system undergirded by its own large story of meta-narrative. So memory shapes identity" (Middleton 2000, 190).

The appeal to biblical stories, and the history of freedom fighters such as Marcus Garvey and Paul Bogle, helps the Rastafari community and the audience in Babylon to whom reggae is addressed to begin to shape an alternative identity founded on the songs of redemption and stories of protest and resistance. Through songs such as "Exodus, Movement of Jah's People," Rastafari and all who are willing can participate in ancient and contemporary stories as a basis for fashioning their identities. As the people discover their story conjoined with the biblical story, they begin to leave Babylon; they begin to recognize that their sojourn in Babylon is temporary as they discover they are meant for Zion. This is certainly another illustration of history in the service of liberation.

Another strategy of liberation in Babylon is the appeal made in reggae lyrics to the biblical doctrine of creation: "The other strategy is by appeal to creation, specifically to God's creational intent from the beginning which can call into question the status quo, that is, the present unjust order of things. Thus we have Marley's famous song, 'One love.' … The power of creation theology to sustain hope is evident in these lines found in the very center of the song: As it was in the beginning (One love!) So shall it be in the end (One heart!)" (Middleton 2000, 191). The key here is that in the lyric "as it was in the beginning (One love!) So shall it be in the end (One heart!)," the purpose of creation is revisited. The purpose is one love and one heart. The point here is that the love of God, which constitutes the meaning and purpose of creation, calls the present order of injustice into question. God's love, that is the cause and reason for creation, calls into question the present order of society and presses for reconciliation, the uniting of hearts. The human choice is one love and one heart, "because there ain't no hiding place from the father of creation." Marley's creation theology serves as the basis for a theology of hope. There is hope for all creation because God's purpose and plan is one love and one heart and certainly one song. The song is one of exodus, of people leaving oppressive traditions and histories and moving to their father's land. The basis of this hope is love, One Love rooted and grounded in God because this love provides hope for the "hopeless sinner." Love's call is identical with reconciliation:

In January 1978, Bob was approached by rival gunmen from the two main political factions in Jamaica, who came to his temporary headquarters in England with a special request. A spontaneous peace truce had broken out in the ghettoes of West Kingston, and to cement this momentous occurrence, a giant musical event, called the "One Love Peace Concert," was to be held in Kingston on April 21, the twelfth anniversary of Selassie's visit. The gunmen begged Marley to return to headline the event. He did, and on that evening, under a full moon in a jammed National Stadium, he implored "the two leading people in this land to come on stage and shake hands, to show the people that you love them right, show the people that you're gonna unite!" Leaping in a frenzy, Bob forced right-wing leader Edward Seaga to shake hands in public with the socialist prime minister Michael Manley, a moment that has been immortalized in Jamaican mythology. (Steffens 1998, 260)

Bob Marley was instrumental in making the call to "One Love" the basis for a peace movement in Jamaica. With the coming together of the rival factions in the political parties, new reggae songs such as "The Peace Treaty Special" and "War is Over" became immediate favorites in Jamaica. However, Marley was also aware that a peace concert was not enough and that years of colonial rule and oppression of poor people would not disappear overnight. What in fact the peace concert brought to the fore was the importance of continuing the struggle and the value of using a method and a means—namely reggae—to expose the atrocities meted out to the poor and to articulate a vision of what things could look like in an independent Jamaica.

The year following the peace concert, Bob Marley dedicated an album to children, entitled *Children Playing in the Street*. He sang about the plight of Jamaican children born in poverty and diminished by existence in darkness but who continued to search for the light of a new day. Marley wailed, "Woman hold her head and cry, Cause her son, Had been shot down in the street, And died, From a stray bullet; 'Can a woman tender care', She cried, "Cease toward the child she bear?" (Cooper 1993, 130).

THE WAY FORWARD

Several women performed with Bob Marley during his singing career. Among them were Rita Marley, Judy Mowatt, and Marcia Griffiths, all gifted singers in their own right. Obiagele Lake, in her important text *Rastafari Women* (1998), points out that while several of Bob Marley's songs may be regarded as revolutionary, there are others that portray the misogynist ideas that objectify women as sexual beings and regard women in a subordinate role to men. According to Lake, there is a profound sense in which reggae becomes a part of the Babylon that it seeks to critique and remains enmeshed in a system that it counsels its audience to flee for Zion.

In *Noises in the Blood*, Carolyn Cooper indicates that the ambivalence we sense in Marley's lyrics indicates his wrestling with Rastafari beliefs on the one hand and the Bible on the other. Several of Marley's songs about women call attention to "the Adamic Rastaman, susceptible to the wiles of Babylonian Eve,

[who] becomes the passive victim of female cunning. The biblical image of Babylon as whore, the fallen woman of *Revelation*, defines contemporary gender relations, founded on the essential frailty of (fe)male flesh. The female is perceived as both deceiving and vulnerable to deception" (Cooper 1993, 130–31).

The way forward should come from Rasta women, claims Obiagele Lake. While the reggae lyrics of Rita Marley (Bob's wife) are promising, they do not go far enough, because, like Bob's and Judy Mowatt's reggae lyrics, these too reflect endemic social values that reify life in Babylon. "Lillian Allen is one of the few Rasta sisters who deals directly with the subject of violence against women in contemporary Jamaican society. [Her music] is exceptional since most female Rasta artists sing all praises to Jah (God), the Black man, and Ethiopia" (Lake 1998, 126–27).

Marley understood his music as a "sermon" for freedom. Freedom was not merely the removal of physical chains, as Marley indicated that in many instances the chains were removed from people's feet only to be placed on their minds. Because of this, he would wail, "Emancipate yourself from mental slavery. None but ourselves can free our minds" (Cooper 1993, 124). There are different kinds of chains. If mental slavery was one chain that Marley addressed, it is clear that misogyny is one that he failed to chant down in Babylon. Perhaps, as women such as Lillian Allen and Rita Marley lead, we will be able to truly sing this time, "We are leaving Babylon" (where it is the practice for women to be subjugated), "we are going to Zion" (a new place of liberation where the ways of Babylon have no currency). This is possible because Jah has come to break the back of "downpression," to wipe away transgression and to set captives free. The power of the song resides in Jah's decision to make the song transformative in Babylon.

WORKS CITED

Breiner, Laurence A. 1985–1986. The English Bible in Jamaican Rastafarianism. *Journal of Religious Thought* 42, no. 2: 30–43.

Cooper, Carolyn. 1993. *Noises in the Blood*. London: Macmillan.

Dawes, Kwame. 2002. *Bob Marley: Lyrical Genius*. London: Sanctuary.

Garvey, Amy Jacques, ed. 1974. *Philosophy and Opinions of Marcus Garvey*. Vol. 1. New York: Atheneum.

Goldman, Vivien. 1997. *Uptown Ghetto Living: Bob Marley in His Own Backyard*. Pages 39–47 in Reggae, Rasta, Revolution. Edited by Chris Potash. London: Schumer.

———. 2006. *The Book of Exodus*. New York: Three Rivers.

Gossai, Hemchand, and Nathaniel Samuel Murrell, eds. 2000. *Religion, Culture, and Tradition in the Caribbean*. New York: St. Martin's.

Hawke, Harry, ed. 2001. *Complete Lyrics of Bob Marley*. London: Omnibus.

Lake, Obiagele. 1998. *Rastafari Women: Subordination in the Midst of Liberation Theology.* Durham, N.C.: Carolina Academic Press.

Middleton, Richard J. 2000. Identity and Subversion in Babylon. Pages 181–98 in *Religion, Culture, and Tradition in the Caribbean.* Edited by Gossai Hemchand and Nathaniel Samuel Murrell. New York: St. Martin's.

Murrell, Nathaniel Samuel, William David Spencer, and Adrian McFarlane, eds. 1998. *Chanting Down Babylon: The Rastafari Reader.* Philadelphia: Temple University Press.

Potash, Chris, ed. 1997. *Reggae, Rasta, Revolution.* London: Schumer.

Steffens, Roger. 1998. Bob Marley: Rasta Warrior. Pages 253–64 in *Chanting Down Babylon: The Rastafari Reader.* Edited by Nathaniel Samuel Murrell, William David Spencer, and Adrian McFarlane. Philadelphia: Temple University Press.

Taylor, Don. 1994. *Marley and Me.* Kingston, Jamaica: Kingston Publishers.

White, Timothy. 1991. *Catch a Fire: The Life of Bob Marley.* London: Omnibus.

"Help Me Make It through the Night": Narrating Class and Country Music in the Theology of Paul

Tex Sample

Kris Kristofferson's songs "Help Me Make It through the Night" and "Me and Bobby McGee," along with "For the Good Times," were three of the five nominees for the Grammy Award for Best Country Song in 1971, which "Help Me" won. All of these songs have become classics in country music as well as attaining popularity as crossover hits. In this paper I focus on "Help Me" and "Bobby."

The sustained popularity of these two songs for nearly forty years as country music classics, and the role of country music in working-class life in the United States, raise the question of why these songs speak in such a sustained and powerful way to working Americans (Malone 1993, 114; Bufwack and Oermann 1993, ix; Sample 1996, 13–15). The twofold purpose of this paper is to hear (working people do more hearing than reading) these songs in the context of American working-class life and then to narrate this account into the theology of Paul, especially, but not exclusively, in Galatians. To begin, I turn first to an "exegesis" of these two songs.

"Help Me Make It through the Night"

"Help Me Make It through the Night" begins as a very sexy and sensual song. The singer asks his partner to remove the ribbon holding her hair and allow it to fall upon his skin, where it can lie lightly like "shadows on the wall." Then asking her to join him at his side on the bed and stay till morning, he clarifies that all he is asking is for her time in order to get him through the night.

A lyric that troubles some, including at least one theologian, is Kristofferson's stated lack of concern for the morality of what he is asking. Neither does he have any interest in understanding what he and his partner are about to do. He states clearly that as far as tomorrow is concerned, the Devil can have it all for himself.

His reason is simply that, on this night, he needs a friend. It was this expression of a lack of moral concern and Kristofferson's willingness to leave the future to the Devil that led theologian Albert Outler to describe the song as "defiant hedonism" with a "self-conscious a-moralism" (1971, 98).

I read the song differently. These lines can be seen as a prayer. In the line that consigns the future to the Devil, there is a calling on the "Lord" and then the claim of the need for a friend. Furthermore, a world without a past or a future is not defiant hedonism but abject despair—not amoralism, but bankrupt desperation. The past is dead and the future is beyond consideration.

Two more things especially strike me about this song. First, nowhere in the song is there any suggestion that, after making it through the night, the coming tomorrows will be any different. There is no suggestion of an end to the futility. There is no promised revitalization of the dead yesterdays and there is no discernible future expectation. The only thing that seems to make the situation different is a friend, and that only to make it through the night.

This makes the second thing to be said even more striking. Nowhere in the song is the question raised of whether it is worth making it through the night. This song makes an unspoken assumption that one just does. Such an assumption does not even seem to have the status of an intention. It is certainly not a declared commitment. It is something you just do.

"Me and Bobby McGee"

"Busted flat" and with his feelings almost as "faded" as his jeans, the singer and Bobby are hitchhiking from Baton Rouge to New Orleans when Bobby hails down "a diesel" that takes them all the way. As they ride, the singer pulls his "harpoon" (harmonica) from his "red bandana" carrying case and accompanies Bobby as she sings the blues. Metronome-like windshield wipers and Bobby's percussive clapping beat out the rhythm while she sings all the songs the driver knows.

We know nothing about who they are, only, so far, that they are on the way to that great Crescent City at the end of the Mississippi River. It seems idyllic: a couple who clearly enjoy each other off on a lark, singing and playing together on the road to New Orleans.

Then comes the most famous line of the song, proclaiming that freedom is only one more word, but it stands for that time or place or situation of not having anything to lose. Anything one can lose is already gone. If such lacks worth, this "nothing'" nevertheless is free. And Bobby and the singer share this condition, or so it seems.

Yet, this kind of nothingness is accompanied by a powerful "feeling good" that comes from being with Bobby when she is singing the blues. The ease with which such feeling comes seems to be more than enough for this free-spirited couple. At this point the chorus is strange; indeed, how can the singer sing of nothing to lose? Hell, he's got Bobby! More than that, we learn in the next verse that they are crisscrossing the country. Their travels take them through Kentucky and California and, it seems, many places in between. In their travels, Bobby shares the deep unknowns of the singer's soul and stands close beside him through all he does, while keeping him warm from the cold. How can this be a state of having nothing to lose? It takes the second verse to make it clear.

In the second verse, he lets her "slip away" around Salinas. The only reason we are given for his losing her is that she was searching for a home, a home that the singer can only hope she will find. We are not told what kind of home Bobby wants. We are only told what she did for the singer of the song. Is there some suggestion here that the relationship they had was all about him? What did Bobby get from all of this? We don't know. Is it only now that the writer of the song hopes that she will find the home she seeks? His wish for Bobby seems to be a recognition that comes too late.

Then he confesses that he would forego the entirety of his future for just one bygone day when he could embrace her body right next to his own. That wonderful on-a-lark, "feeling good" of the first verse is gone, and he has now lost not only that feeling but, of course, Bobby as well and all that she means.

The chorus coming again at this point takes on a strange, even contradictory, character. If freedom were that state of not having anything to lose, it would seem that the singer is only now truly free. That seeming freedom of being on the move, that lyrical world of Bobby singing and clapping out the blues with his backup on harmonica while diesel truck, windshield wipers, and a rainstorm provide context, rhythmic power, and stage: all are gone. This is what seems like freedom, but the next chorus tells us otherwise.

In this chorus the lyrics change. She leaves him free, but it is freedom without her. Two more things are strange. First, the notion of freedom takes on the character of emptiness, and it seems now that the time with Bobby was better than the freedom of having nothing to lose. Or, are we looking at two different ways to use the notion of "nothing left to lose"? Was there with Bobby a different kind of freedom: the sense of being off together free and loose in the world?

Second, and even more strange, the singer states that feeling good was sufficient for him and for Bobby McGee. Yet, we already know that it was not sufficient for Bobby. Was it also a different kind of freedom that she sought, or perhaps something else and not only a home? There are no answers to these questions.

A Working-Class Reading

My contention is that "Help Me" and "Bobby" have remained popular, in part, because they name something fundamental about working-class life in the United States. My approach in this section is to connect these songs to key issues in the working-class world as a way to understand not only their initial popularity but also their ongoing use in the decades since their introduction.

Working-Class Americans, 1947–1973

The desperation and despair in "Help Me" and freedom as nothing to lose in "Bobby" may seem strange coming as they did in the late 1960s and early 1970s. Some working-class lives were never better. Following World War II, industry in the United States was well intact, highly productive, and not challenged by international competition, while that of Europe and Japan suffered the massive destruction of that global conflict.

In 1950, General Motors and the United Auto Workers signed the Treaty of Detroit, virtually guaranteeing autoworkers a 20 percent increase in living standards in the next five years, through annual upgrades in wages and benefits. By 1960, more than half the unions had similar agreements providing for yearly improvement upgrades and adjustments for cost of living. Labor unions represented one worker in three, and even nonunion businesses went along with these changes to keep workers satisfied and to prevent unionization (Greenhouse 2008, 75).

During these same years, a human-relations methodology was applied to employee relationships, sometimes called "the happy worker model." The perspective argued that the best way to high productivity was to keep workers satisfied and happy with their work (Greenhouse 2008). Along with this came a commitment by industry to worker-employment security. General Electric's Earl S. Willis wrote in 1962, "Maximizing employment security is a prime company goal." He maintained that the capacity of an employee to project his future job security "with reasonable certainty is an employer's most productive asset" (Greenhouse 2008, 78.)

From 1950 through 1973, average family income more than doubled in constant dollars, the greatest leap in affluence in the history of the United States (Yankelovich 1981, 21). Perhaps one of the most stunning statistics is that productivity in the United States rose 104 percent from 1947 to 1973, and median family income virtually equaled that rise, soaring up 103 percent (Greenhouse 2008, 75).

The years 1947 to 1973 were good years for the American working class, at least in these respects. Why, then, did Kristofferson's two songs reach so many working Americans? To what did the desperation and despair in "Help Me" speak? Why did freedom as nothing more to lose in "Bobby" resonate so powerfully?

Two fine qualitative studies on the working class in the United States came out at the end of this period. First, in a rich and nuanced description of issues of freedom and worth, Richard Sennett and Jonathan Cobb found that class took from working people "the feeling of secure dignity in the eyes of others and themselves." It happened in two ways. First, the images that determined the class to which one belonged were "presented as the ultimate outcome of personal ability." Second, the very social definitions of required actions to guarantee dignity "do not, cannot work and so reinforce the originating apprehension" (Sennett and Cobb 1972, 170–71).

The second study, by Lillian Rubin, found that even with the affluence of the 1950s and 1960s, the families she interviewed looked back not only on their parents' lives but on their own as being lives in which "the dominant theme is struggle and trouble. These realities not only reflect the past, but dominate the present" (1976, 48). In her conclusion, Rubin states that "the affluent and happy worker of whom we have heard so much in recent decades seems not to exist." Acknowledging the increase in median family income, she observes that this figure conceals the fact that a third of the families she studied made roughly half to three-quarters of that amount, "not much money on which to support a family of at least four" (204).

WORKING-CLASS AMERICANS, 1974–2008

If the conditions of working-class life were still tough during the 1950s, 1960s, and early 1970s, they have worsened considerably since. Increasing global competition, oil crises, foreign imports, loss of manufacturing, deregulation, recessions, layoffs, the corporate offensive against unions, the decline of union members, downsizing, off-shoring, and plant closings, to mention only a few, changed the circumstances of working people in the United States. In the 2000s, with the financial meltdown, the housing mortgage debacle, the loss of jobs, and more, the situation for working Americans is worse than it has been in the past fifty to sixty years (Greenhouse 2008; cf. Kuttner 2008). Ehrenreich reports that 30 percent of the labor force works for eight dollars or less an hour (2001, 3), that only 20 percent of the homeless are employed (26), and that while fourteen dollars an hour represents a living wage, 60 percent of American workers make less than that amount (213; cf. Newman and Chen 2007, 3).

One of the most stunning statistics of the period from 1973 to 2003 is that although productivity went up over 70 percent, the median income of families increased just over 20 percent. But if you take out of this figure the additional hours that wives worked, hardly any increase occurred at all, and the incomes of working-class people remained basically flat (Kuttner 2008, 21). The point, of course, is that the situation of a great many working-class people in the United States was difficult even following World War II but that it has deteriorated significantly since that time.

The Practices of Inequality and the Practices of Working People

We turn now to practices of inequality and those of class for further background in understanding class indignities and struggles and the way that Kristofferson's songs speak to these. The focus here on practices offers a concreteness to class and provides an alternative to a more abstract approach that uses primarily "values" or some broader concept of "culture." The practices we name in this paper, of course, can only be partial and illustrative.

Practices of Inequality

I draw on three basic forms of class domination, from the work of Randall Collins: giving and taking orders, giving and getting respect, and practices of deference and demeanor (1975, 49–66). Working-class people typically take orders from bosses and have to practice "sucking up" in giving respect. By practices of deference and demeanor, I mean to suggest the facial expressions, body postures, gestures, and forms of personal bearing that indicate and enact authority, esteem, honor, economic standing, and power by those higher in the class structure and indicate and enact obedience and submission by those who are lower. In the vernacular, working-class people have to "kiss ass." These microlevel practices populate the realities of class and ritualize inequality in everyday life.

Practices of Working People: Oral Culture

In terms of the practices of working-class people, most participate in oral cultures. By this I do not, of course, mean orality as in a primal culture without a written language but rather a range of practices that are not nearly so "printy" as that of the college-trained. These practices engage the world more through story and proverb than through the specialized discourses of business and the professions.

It is far more of a spoken culture than one of writing and reading. It is a culture where story is basic to grounding life and to understanding it and where sayings crystallize wisdom.

James Ault, in his ethnographic study of a Jerry Falwell–fundamentalist Baptist church outside Worcester, Massachusetts, found that congregation to be a decidedly oral culture. As a community of "the spoken word," it was also "a community of the Book" (Ault 2004, 154), and its communication was characterized by stories, sayings, aphorisms, or maxims (191). This congregation's use of the Bible was based in stories, proverbs, and verses from Scripture as well as in folk sayings. "Their artful, pithy, poetic cast makes them eminently repeatable and hence, memorable, and this is the sign of their unassailable character as traditional folk wisdom" (194; cf. 127, 211–12).

In my work, I find that oral culture characterizes a great majority of the people in working-class life, not only those in fundamentalist churches. The practices of storytelling and sayings are central in the everyday life of working people on the job, in the family, and in friendship networks (Sample 1994, 1996, 2006).

Furthermore, in keeping with an oral culture, family and kinship-like structures organize working-class life outside the job. Life is lived in terms of these kinds of relationships. It affects the way one thinks, the organization of one's life, the way things get done, and the morality of what is right and good (Ault 2004, 190–200). Working-class people look to these relationships for the formation of their judgments far more than to those of academic or national authorities.

PRACTICES OF RESISTANCE

Given their subordinate position in the practices of inequality, it is not surprising that working-class people develop resistance to practices of domination (Certeau 1984; Bakhtin 1984; Scott 1985, 1990). So practices of resistance will also be used here to interpret Kristofferson's music. This resistance takes a variety of forms, which we cannot cover in the space here, but includes such things as refusing correct grammar; the "proper"; established etiquette; upper-class taste; and more (Bourdieu 1991, 88; Sample 2006, 31–32).

I claim that working-class resistance takes the forms of a traditional politics and a populist anarchism. By the former I do not mean a political or laissez-faire conservatism but rather a sociomoral traditionalism. It is a form of life that attempts to protect the family against the corrosive effects of the dominant culture by commitments to basic institutions like the school and church and to a morality seen as supportive of these (Ault 2004, 204–17).

By the latter I mean a desire to be free from the dominant "institutional entrapments of the modern [established] world" (Bakhtin 1984, 275). Highly suspicious of control, populist anarchism does not trust experts and the dominant discourse, especially fine print. Love of country runs deep in this form of anarchism but is understood primarily as a way of life. Along with this love of country is an equally profound distrust of government. In the vernacular, it takes the form of wanting to be "left the hell alone" (Sample 2006, 40–46). Not all working people share these practices, but many do.

Narrating "Help Me" and "Bobby" into Paul

It is easy to do a moralistic reading of "Help Me" and "Bobby," but reading them against the horizon of the structure of inequality and the practices of the working class opens up an opportunity to narrate these songs into the theology of Paul.

Orality in Kristofferson

As a basic music of working people, it is not surprising that country is so pervasively a story music and one filled with pithy sayings and descriptions that take on the character of proverbs, aphorisms, and maxims, among others. In this regard, Kristofferson possesses an amazing ability to turn a short country song into a story with numerous inflections in a way that, with a light touch and by indirection, can convey powerful emotional responses. Furthermore, his one-liners lead one commentator to say that Kristofferson possesses "that particular, indefinable power that every straightforward and sentimental artist needs to elevate naïve clichés into native myths" (Miller 2008, 3). In "Help Me" and "Bobby," these characteristics are evident not only in the masterful narrative of the two songs but also in lines that characterize freedom, a dead past and an unforeseeable future, and the cry for help to make it through a dark night.

Story and the Apocalypse of God in Christ

In the working class, the stories of country music can be placed in the stories of Scripture and, for my purposes in this paper, in the story of Paul's theology (see Harink 2003, 67–70, 78–81, 148–49). In Paul's thought, history has a beginning, a center, and an end. Begun in creation, Jesus Christ is the center of history, the apocalypse of God's action (Gal 1:11–12; 2:16–21; 3:23–4:11; cf. Martyn 1997, 251–80). We live in the already of this action, in a creation that awaits "with eager longing for the revealing of the sons of God" (Rom 8:22 [transl.]).

Not only does Christ disclose God's plan for the ages, but this apocalypse is a history-making and cosmos-changing event. Entering the world, Christ empties himself, becomes a slave, and in suffering obedient love to God dies on the cross to the powers of sin, death, and oppression, both cosmic and human. God then exalts Christ in resurrection and defeats the powers of the world (Phil 2:5–11). By this action, a new creation is begun. The old opposition of Jew and Gentile has now been rectified, and other oppositions of the elemental spirits of the universe have been brought to nothing (Gal 4:3–7).

Further, Paul has his own pithy sayings (Gal 2:6b, 16; 2:20; 5:1, 13, 16a, 25; 6:10 and more). Romans 12:9–21 is an especially concentrated list of such one-liners that can take on the character of proverbs. These may certainly address the inequalities of class and its dominations—for example, Paul's call to associate with the lowly and never to be conceited (Rom 12:16).

"Help Me" and the Powers

The world of the working class is one where, in the best of times, the struggle for dignity is pervasive and, in the worst of times, surviving and coping are the order of the day. It is life without a living wage for most and of poverty and near-poverty for many. For most, it is a world where one faces, day after day, a dead-end job (or maybe its loss); where both spouses work for pay (provided there are two workers outside the home); where the bills never get completely paid; where free time at home, when shared, is exhaustion played out before the TV; when there never seem to be enough occasions for the kids; and where tomorrow means more of the same—indeed, the past seems "dead and gone" and the future is beyond one's vision. Not every minute of all of working-class life, of course, is filled with desperation and despair, but it is easy to see how profoundly, nevertheless, life is marked by struggle and futility.

With the working class, "Help Me" can be placed in Paul's understanding of the powers in a significantly interpretive and faithful way. In Gal 4:3–9, Paul addresses "the elemental spirits of the universe" to which we are enslaved. In the traditional view of the times, these elements were earth, air, fire, and water, with the addition of stars in some cases. Moreover, these elements existed as pairs of opposites and constituted the cosmos (Martyn 1997, 393–406). Martyn concludes, however, that Paul is not concerned with these traditional elements but rather with the elemental opposites he names in Gal 3:28: Jew and Greek, slave and free, and male and female (404).

More specifically, in Galatians, Paul is emphatically occupied with the opposite of Jew and Gentile and thereby the Law and the Not-Law (Gal 6:14–15; Martyn 1997, 404). But it is not a misuse of Paul to address the antinomies of our own time, such as those of race and class along with slavery and gender, in the light of his teaching. For Paul, the opposites of male and female and slave and free count for nothing because there is now a new creation, a new cosmos, as a result of the apocalypse of God in Christ and the outpouring of the Spirit. The cosmic powers and their opposites have been ultimately defeated, and the liberating work of the Spirit has now opened the world to a new community.

These are not naïve claims in Paul. In Rom 8, we find no little realism about the "not yet" character of Christ's victory over the powers (see Gal 5:5–6). The whole creation continues to groan in travail waiting for the sons of God to appear. While the Spirit calls out the community of the new creation in Christ, the community nevertheless continues to live in the midst of a creation not yet finally redeemed.

In this passage, however, we learn of the hope for those who are in Christ Jesus. No created power on earth or in heaven, visible or invisible, can prevail against the apocalypse of God's action: there is no desperation or despair, no isolation or dark night that can "separate us from the love of God in Christ Jesus our Lord" (Gal 8:35–39).

Freedom and Resistance

The theme of freedom is pervasive in Kristofferson's music. He says, "If you took freedom out of the songs [I have written] you'd have very few Kristofferson songs" (2009). When he wrote "Bobby," he says, he "was trying to show that freedom is a double-edged sword and that you may be free but it can be painful to be that free." He then suggests "at the very end," when you die, "you will be free, when you've nothing else to lose" (Denton 2009).

For Kristofferson, it is this double-edged character of freedom that the song crystallizes. That wonderful freedom of being on the road with Bobby does not last. Yet it speaks to a working-class dream of being free of bosses, released from sucking up, and no longer kissing ass. But in the working class world this is fantasy. That kind of freedom comes, as Kristofferson suggests, only in death.

Still, the song can be read in a way that represents resistance to the established order. There is no mention of work in the song except that of the driver of the diesel truck. Basic to the freedom of the first verse is the freedom from work, to be hitching around the country without bills and a mortgage or rent to pay. A certain resistance resides in the escape from that world.

Certeau works with a distinction between places and spaces. The powerful set up places in the world where they exercise strategies of control and hegemony, and the powerless set up spaces in the places of the powerful, where they engage in tactics of resistance (Certeau 1984, xix). These spaces are usually under the eye of the powerful and are typically covert or hidden. The riding of Bobby and Kris in the cab of the diesel can be understood as such a space, and they are there singing, playing, clapping, and colluding with the driver of the truck. In this connection, Bakhtin discusses the important role of "festival" in the resistance of working-class people during medieval times, just as the cab of the truck is the location of a festive time of singing and celebrating on the road to New Orleans. (1984, 196–276).

Paul's Vision of Freedom

When Kristofferson makes the claim that we are only free in death, he obviously has in mind a negative freedom. This claim can be juxtaposed with Gal 5:13, where Paul says, "For you were called to freedom, only do not use your freedom as an opportunity for the flesh." Martyn observes that in Paul there is no such thing as an autonomous free will, so that negative freedom—freedom from—is "nothing more than a transfer from one form of slavery to another" (1997, 485).

Further, Paul speaks of not using freedom as "an opportunity for the flesh" (Gal 5:16–17). Again, Martyn maintains that the word here translated "opportunity" is best understood as "a military base of operations," a place from which the flesh, with its impelling desires, can launch opposition against the Spirit, so that flesh is understood on a cosmic scale as one of the enslaving powers (485). Kristofferson's comment about freedom in death takes on a serious finality in Paul. Since death is one of the powers, a negative freedom understood as death is a full-scale submission to the slaveries of the powers. Yet for Paul, freedom is connected to death quite clearly in the cross: true freedom is to be crucified with Christ and to imitate him in obedient, suffering love. The death and resurrection of Christ introduces the new creation, the new age where we are liberated by the Spirit. Freedom is then obedience to God and the imitation of Christ by letting that mind be in us which was in him (Phil 2:5–11).

But too much of working-class church life has been subjected to an individualizing of what Christ did on the cross and to a substitutionary view of that atonement which blots out Christ's defeat of the powers. According to Martyn, Gal 3:13 involves more "than this standard formulation" of substitutionary atonement. Martyn acknowledges that Christ did take on the curse of the Law by dying on a cross "in our behalf." The point, however, is that Christ did this "not by simply taking onto himself a punishment due us but by embodying the curse, in such a way as to be, in his crucifixion, victorious over the enslaving powers" (Martyn 1997, 318n110).

Therefore, freedom is not finally nothing more to lose and certainly not the death offered by fallen powers, but rather the new creation where all is Christ's and all is ours (1 Cor 3:21b–23), a new world where we live as slaves of righteousness to God and to each other, and where we are called into the space of the church as an alternative to the dominations of class.

"BOBBY," POLITICS, AND THE CHURCH

Further, individualized, narrow, and wrongly focused substitutionary-atonement readings of Paul obscure the function of the church and its role in freedom and the possibility of a new and different politics. The word that Paul uses for the church is *ekklesia*, a word that derives from the ancient city-state of Greece. The ekklesia was an assembly of the town's citizens called to do the city's business. In Paul, it is the church coming together as an assembly in a given city where God's new creation and God's apocalyptic salvation are joined. It is the site of freedom in Christ, where the freedom of the Spirit is lived in vital enactment of the faith of Christ (Coenen 1975, 1:291). It is not the autonomous freedom, so-called, of American culture, but a communal freedom, a freedom in which to live out radical obedience to God in the day-to-day life of the church, "doing good to all, especially to those who are of the household of faith" (Gal 6:10).

This understanding of ekklesia is an alternative to the traditional politics and populist anarchism of working-class life, but, very importantly, it can take seriously the resistance embedded in these two important working-class commitments. The church as ekklesia can question the idolatries of the nation-state, promote a sagacious and faithful distrust of government and corporate America, and resist the "spiritualizing and privatizing" of faith in the secular order. These can be done without necessitating a withdrawal from the pursuit of the common good through citizenship. Still, traditional politics and populist anarchism require a different narration, one finding strength and focus in the support of an alternative ekklesia, a different politics.

Furthermore, great numbers of working-class people live in extended-family relations and tend to seek out family-like organizations in their live-a-day world (Ault 2004, 202; Sample 2006, 43–48). A kinship-like organization of the church can be a space of resistance and a radical alternative to establishment politics, in which working people see themselves as the family of God, as those who enact the body of Christ where the antinomies of contemporary powers of class are rejected as nothing, a community to help one make it through the night.

Here, the church carries out the tactics of a Christ-formed community in spaces within a class-dominated society, and as Christ's body, it can stand against the established powers of class—and race, gender, and others—and thereby be subversive of these powers (Hays 1997, 280). Here, too, the church can be a space of festival in worship, in eucharist, in church suppers, community outreach, and action.

Kinship-like community groups can, of course, be sinfully exclusive. Here again, Paul is instructive. Hays reports recent scholarship "that the Corinthians' differing views on 'knowledge' and spiritual gifts may have been related to class and status differences within the church" (1997, 12). Clearly, the conflict around the Lord's Supper had a class dimension. Those who had more than enough food humiliated those who had nothing (1 Cor 11:22). Passages like these stand as a corrective to churches that slide back into the antinomies of class, race, gender, and other fallen hierarchies of the powers.

Finally, the figure of Bobby in the song reflects another common feature of country music, in which women represent salvation (Sample 1996, 103–6). Ellison observes that secular country music "relies on the motif of salvation but replaces the love of Jesus with the love of women" (1995, 118–19). Certainly Bobby plays a temporary salvific role in this song. Yet the song displays a basic contradiction in which women are salvation but romantic relationships are vulnerable.

At this point, the song portrays a freedom that is finally negative with the only positive freedom—that of being with Bobby. In the working class world, a deep love relationship between a man and a woman may be the best that the world has to offer, at least for most, as vulnerable as that may be. The song "Bobby" names that hope, only to lose it.

An ekklesia that is a body of brothers and sisters (Gal 1:11; 3:12, 28; 4:12, 28; 6:1, 18) does not replace the love of couples for each other, but can surround them in supportive community where devotion to each other and to others can flourish, and where making it through the night is shared through even more extended "family" by means of the relational ligaments of a Christ-formed body (see Hays 1996, 55–56).

CONCLUSION

Country music is a music for working-class Americans. The country songs "Help Me" and "Bobby" have spoken to working-class people for forty years, in both the best and the worst of times. Their themes of desperation and despair, and of freedom as nothing left to lose, resonate with working-class life and take on a certain clarity through a class hearing of these songs. This paper narrates these songs and a working-class hearing of them into the theology of Paul. This theology provides a more compelling story in the apocalypse of God's action in Christ; names the role of the powers in rituals of structured social inequality; uses practices of orality, resistance, and politics from working-class life; and reads them into the politics of Paul, especially in the calling out of a concrete, living ekklesia of brothers and sisters. These moves suggest directions for the use of country music in biblical studies and offer avenues for the life of the church and for its mission and ministry with working-class people in the United States.

Works Cited

Ault, James M. 2004. *Spirit and Flesh: Life in a Fundamentalist Baptist Church.* New York: Knopf.

Bakhtin, Mikhail. 1984. *Rabelais and His World.* Translated by Helene Iswolsky. Bloomington: Indiana University Press.

Bernstein, Jared, and Lawrence Mishel. 2007. Economy's Gains Fail to Reach Most Workers' Paychecks. Economic Policy Institute. Briefing Paper no. 195, August 30. Online: http://www.epi.org/publications/entry/bp195/.

Bourdieu, Pierre. 1991. *Distinction: A Social Critique of Taste.* Trans. Richard Nice. Cambridge: Harvard University Press.

Bufwack, Mary A., and Robert K. Oermann. 1993. *Finding Her Voice: The Saga of Women in Country Music.* New York: Crown.

Certeau, Michel de. 1984. *The Practice of Everyday Life.* Translated by Steven Rendall. Berkeley and Los Angeles: University of California Press.

Coenen, Lothar. 1975. Church, Synagogue. Pages 291–307 in vol. 1 of *The New International Dictionary of New Testament Theology.* Edited by Colin Brown. 4 vols. Grand Rapids, Mich.: Zondervan.

Collins, Randall. 1975. *Conflict Sociology: Toward an Explanatory Science.* New York: Academic.

Denton, Andrew. 2009. "Enough Rope," ABC interview July 25, 2005. Online: http://www.abc.net.au/tv/enoughrope/transcripts/s1422317.htm.

Ehrenreich, Barbara. 2001. *Nickel and Dimed: On (Not) Getting By in America.* New York: Henry Holt.

Ellison, Curtis W. 1995. *Country Music Culture: From Hard Times to Heaven.* Jackson: University Press of Mississippi.

Greenhouse, Steven. 2008. *The Big Squeeze: Tough Times for the American Worker.* New York: Knopf.

Harink, Douglas. 2003. *Paul among the Postliberals: Pauline Theology beyond Christendom and Modernity.* Grand Rapids, Mich.: Brazos.

Hays, Richard B. 1996. *The Moral Vision of the New Testament: A Contemporary Introduction to New Testament Ethics.* San Francisco: HarperSanFrancisco.

———. 1997. *First Corinthians.* Interpretation series. Louisville: John Knox.

Kristofferson, Kris. 1970. Help Me Make It through the Night. Combine Music Corporation.

———. 2009. Official Web site. Online: www.kriskristofferson.com/.

———, and Fred Foster. 1969. Me and Bobby McGee. Combine Music Corporation.

Kuttner, Robert. 2008. *The Squandering of America: How the Failure of Our Politics Undermines Our Prosperity.* New York: Vintage.

Malone, Bill C. 1968. *Country Music U.S.A.: A Fifty-Year History*. Austin: University of Texas Press.

———. 1993. *Singing Cowboys and Musical Mountaineers: Southern Culture and the Roots of Country Music*. Athens: University of Georgia Press.

Martyn, J. Louis. 1997. *Galatians: A New Translation with Introduction and Commentary*. Anchor Bible 33A. New York: Doubleday.

Miller, Stephen. 2008. *Kristofferson: The Wild American*. New York: Omnibus.

Newman, Katherine S., and Victor Tan Chen. 2007. *The Missing Class: Portraits of the Near Poor in America*. Boston: Beacon.

Outler, Albert. 1971. *Evangelism in the Wesleyan Spirit*. Nashville: Tidings.

Rubin, Lillian. 1976. *Worlds of Pain: Life in the Working Class Family*. New York: Basic Books.

Ruhlman, William. 2004. Kris Kristofferson Biography. Online: http://new.music.yahoo.com/kris-kristofferson/.

Sample, Tex. 1994. *Ministry in an Oral Culture: Living with Will Rogers, Uncle Remus, and Minnie Pearl*. Louisville: Westminster John Knox.

———. 1996. *White Soul: Country Music, the Church, and Working Americans*. Nashville, Tenn.: Abingdon.

———. 2006. *Blue Collar Resistance and the Politics of Jesus: Doing Ministry with Working Class Whites*. Nashville, Tenn.: Abingdon.

Scott, James C. 1985. *The Weapons of the Weak: Everyday Forms of Peasant Resistance*. New Haven: Yale University Press.

———. 1990. *Domination and the Arts of Resistance: Hidden Transcripts*. New Haven: Yale University Press.

Sennett, Richard, and Jonathan B. Cobb. 1972. *The Hidden Injuries of Class*. New York: Vintage.

Yankelovich, Daniel. 1981. *New Rules: Searching for Self-Fulfillment in a World Turned Upside Down*. New York: Random House.

JESUS OF THE MOON: NICK CAVE'S CHRISTOLOGY

Roland Boer

In about the year 1990, a major event in music history happened: at the same time that Nicholas Edward Cave made his first serious attempt to give up heroin, he also became rather interested in Jesus. Although he would not finally kick the heroin habit until 1997 (leading to a four-year break in recording),[1] 1990 also marks a distinctive shift in his writing and music. As he put it, somewhat off-handedly, we can divide his work according to the Bible: while the 1970s and 1980s may be called his Old Testament period, from the 1990s onward it has been the New Testament: "After a while I started to feel a little kinder and warmer to the world, and at the same time started to read the New Testament" (Hattenstone 2008). Indeed, in his studio in Hove, near Brighton in England, there hangs a painting of Christ in all his suffering.

So why does Cave have such a fascination with the Bible, especially the figure of Christ? I have explored Cave's engagement with the Bible elsewhere (Boer 2005, 2006), so my attention here is drawn to Christology. He is an avid reader of the New Testament, has written an introduction to an edition of the Gospel of Mark (Cave 1998), depicts his relationship with his long-dead father in terms of Christ and the Father, and has written a string of songs with christological themes, such as "The Firstborn is Dead," "Brompton Oratory," "Messiah Ward," "Dig!!! Lazarus Dig!!!" and "Jesus of the Moon."

However, one of the difficulties in writing about music is that writing is a poor medium to deal with the expanse of music. As Elvis Costello once said, "Writing about music is like dancing about architecture" (Gracyk 1996, vii). One common response, especially for those of us accustomed to working with texts, is to focus on the lyrics. Another response is to analyze the music itself and leave

---

1. The last drug-fuelled album was *The Boatman's Call* (Cave 1997a); four years later he released *No More Shall We Part* (Cave 2001).

the lyrics aside. I wish to combine the two, inspired by the work of Theodore Gracyk and Jacques Attali and the music criticism of Theodor Adorno.[2] How does Cave's Christology emerge and what is its nature? I suggest we deal with this question in terms of three categories: volume and noise, sex and seduction, and heresy.

VOLUME AND NOISE

Anyone who takes time to listen to Nick Cave's pre-1990s music would character-ize it with one word—noise. Of course, many influences have helped to produce that noise, such as punk, psychedelic, krautrock, experimental, proto-industrial, and primitive rock, but the band always pushed the limits of music into noise. Cave's earlier bands, the Boys Next Door and the Birthday Party, were gothic and post-punk bands, exploring the capabilities of amplified music to see what new noises might come out of those electronic devices. And Cave himself was the wild, pouting, self-important, drug-taking, heavy-drinking, venue-destroying, prophetic figure who would stride out on stage and "let the curse of God" roar through him (Cave 1997b, 138). After the Birthday Party imploded in 1983, when the band moved to London, Cave settled in Berlin and gathered what would become the first Bad Seeds lineup. The new members came from the under-ground scene in Berlin; notably, Blixa Bargeld had played with the infamous Einstürzende Neubauten. Soon, the recording procedure went roughly as follows: inspired by a mix of drugs and alcohol, Cave would scribble down lyrics on rough pieces of paper, turn up at the studio and meet the other band members, and they would construct raw music around those lyrics. Other influences were to follow, such as the heavy sound of the Delta Blues and apocalyptic themes from the Bible.

However, around the year 1990, something changed in the music. Part of it was due to yet another change in lineup (Conway Savage and Martin Casey joined the group in the next year or two), part was due to Cave's move to São Paolo to follow a new love, and part was due to the influence of a long tradition of the saudade, love poetry that explored pain in the midst of love. But now we also start to find Jesus turning up in the lyrics and other writings of Cave. The title track of the new album from 1990, *The Good Son* (Cave 1990), draws directly

---

2. In writing this essay, I am caught in a curious situation, for there are as yet no academic assessments of the work of Nick Cave. There are interviews aplenty, as well as writings by Cave (1988; 1989; 1997b; 1998; 2000; 2004b) and that curious subgenre of the "rock musicians biog-raphy" (Brokenmouth 1996; Dax and Beck 1999; Johnston 1996).

upon the parable of the Prodigal. An increasing number of ballads also turned up, played slowly with lyrics clearly accentuated, speaking of love, pain, and Jesus. The quieter songs of this period enabled Cave to appeal to a wider audience: "Straight to You" (Cave 1992), "Foi Na Cruz" (Cave 1990), "The Ship Song" (Cave 1990), "Brother, My Cup is Empty" (Cave 1992), "Christina the Astonishing" (Cave 1992), "Where the Wild Roses Grow," with Kylie Minogue (Cave 1996), and "Henry Lee" (Cave 1996). Perhaps nothing sums up this period better than the opening lines of "Nobody's Baby Now" (Cave 1994b): "I've searched the holy books; I tried to unravel the mystery of Jesus Christ, the saviour." Up until the mid-1990s, these slower, quieter songs were interspersed with those that continued the older, raucous style. But by 1997, The Boatman's Call appeared (Cave 1997a). Pared back to the simplest of musical styles, it is a deeply introspective album that has song after song with Jesus present in some way or another: "Into My Arms," "Brompton Oratory," "There is a Kingdom," "Are You the One That I've Been Waiting For?" and "Idiot Prayer." And toward the end of the decade, Cave (1998) wrote an introduction to the Gospel of Mark for a popular release of the biblical book by Canongate Books. The theme continues throughout the next few albums and even up to the present (Cave 2001, 2003b, 2004a, 2008), although in the two most recent of these albums there has been something of a resolution of the two contrasting tendencies between noise and quiet, raw sound and ordered music, or, if you like, the Old Testament and the New.[3]

Clearly something is going on with this confluence of focus on the figure of Jesus and marked change in musical style. But let us stay with the music and the issue of noise, drawing upon the work of Jacques Attali and Theodore Gracyk. In his influential work, Noise (1977, 1985), Attali argues that music is nothing other than organized noise. Different cultures may order that noise in different ways, but the relation of noise to order is, he argues, structurally related to wider patterns in economics and society. For Attali, the emergence of noise, unstructured and cacophonous, is a signal of social unrest and economic mayhem. However, when that noise is once again channeled into recognizable patterns of music, it marks the return to ordered social patterns. Does this apply to Cave's music? Can we point to wider patterns of social unrest that show up in his music? Strange as it may seem, it is actually possible to do so, for Cave had lived from 1984 to 1989 in West Berlin, leaving just before the fall of the Berlin Wall to go and live in São Paolo. It is no stretch of the imagination to see that one of the most significant

---

3. These two tendencies are embodied dramatically in the creation of a second, pure rock band, called Grinderman, in 2007. Using exactly the same lineup as the Bad Seeds, Grinderman played as a support act for the Bad Seeds. Tellingly, the label under which the eponymous album (Grinderman 2007) was released is called "Anti-."

political events of the late twentieth century also makes its mark in his music. I must say I am surprised to see myself making such a direct connection, but it seems difficult to avoid.[4] The turmoil of a personal life notwithstanding (including the struggle with drugs and the traumatic memory of his father's death in a car accident when Cave was nineteen), Attali's theory has some currency at this point.

What about Jesus? Does the turn to the figure of Jesus in his thoughts, reading, and music also play a role? Yes it does, but not quite the way we might imagine. This is where Gracyk's unique proposal comes in. In a study that consciously avoids lyrics and focuses on all the other aspects of rock music—recording, the market, romanticization, rhythm, noise, and ideology—Gracyk argues that one of the defining features of rock is its volume (1996). Quite simply, pump up the volume, let the noise roar forth, and you have rock. It follows, then, that should we turn down the volume, pare back the music, and slow down the rhythm, we would have something else. It is certainly not rock—perhaps folk music, ballad, jazz, or classical. In other words, there is a decided shift in Cave's music beginning in about 1990. To be sure, there is still plenty of the older-style rock in Cave's music from the early years of the 1990s, but by the time we get to *The Boatman's Call*, the rock has well and truly gone (although it was not to disappear forever). Here we find hymns, somber ballads, and laments.

The subject matter of all these new songs is both painful love and Jesus. Does this mean that Cave's New Testament turn has brought about a change in his music? Indeed, has Cave "found" Jesus in some conversion? At a stretch, one could read some of his comments in this way. For example, Cave says that when he finally came to read the Gospels, beginning with Mark, "There, in those four wonderful prose poems of Mark, Matthew, Luke and John, I slowly reacquainted myself with the Jesus of my childhood ... and it was through him that I was given a chance to redefine my relationship with the world" (Cave 2003a). Further, in his introduction to Mark he points out: "The Christ that emerges from Mark, tramping through the haphazard events of His life, had a ringing intensity about him that I could not resist. Christ spoke to me through His isolation, through the burden of His death, through His rage at the mundane, through His sorrow" (Cave 1998, 7).[5]

---

4. I am usually wary of such "vulgar Marxist" connections between a moment in culture (superstructure) and socioeconomics (base), but it certainly has its place.

5. So also in an interview: "To me there are certain elements to the Christ story that are patently fiction: I don't believe in the Virgin Birth and I don't believe in the Resurrection.... The story of Christ interests me in that it concerns a human being's struggle with the concept of faith, which I, myself, feel very close to" (Cave 2003a).

However, rather than see this turn to Christ—from the spiteful God of the Old to the quiet, sad Christ of the New Testament—as the cause of Cave's evolution into the sad ballads of the 1990s, I would like to reverse the equation. Instead of taking an idealist line in which one's inner convictions, one's "attitudes" (as we hear so often) are the keys to change, I prefer to flip the whole equation over, stand them on their feet, so to speak, and connect them to the turn in Cave's music. Quite simply, the appearance of Christ acts as a signal of that shift.

Now, in case someone should object that I have engaged in a moment of vulgar Marxism (although there should always be "vulgar" Marxists), in which the economic base acts as the primary cause for anything that happens in the realms of ideology, culture, and above all religion, I should point out that Cave may think that Jesus and the New Testament are a major cause. He may even feel—and there is good evidence to suggest that this is the case—that Jesus has led his music down quieter paths. But this is more like an aftereffect, a reciprocal action that folds back on the reality of the music.

Sex and Seduction

There is one curious feature of these "Jesus songs" that has struck me for some time: more than one person has confided in me that they are extraordinarily seductive. At one level I can well understand the sentiment. For example, the haunting, longing music of "The Ship Song" (used more than once for weddings!) comes with the following words:

> Come sail your ships around me
> And burn your bridges down
> We make a little history, baby
> Every time you come around. (Cave 1990)

Although there is precious little of Jesus in such a song, we don't have to look too far to find him, for Cave has made a specialty of involving Jesus in a good number of love songs. Despite the fact that Cave claims he has written more than two hundred love songs (more than the total number released on all his albums),[6] some of these songs contain a specific feature that stands out—an erotic and seductive evocation of Jesus in a way that reminds one eerily of John Donne.

---

6. For a discussion of Cave's love songs, see Boer forthcoming.

Here I shift to a consideration of the lyrics. I would like to examine one song in particular, "Brompton Oratory." However, since I cannot quote the song in full due to copyright reasons, I refer the reader to http://www.metrolyrics.com/ brompton-oratory-lyrics-nick-cave.html (or http://www.allthelyrics.com/lyrics/ nick_cave/brompton_oratory-lyrics-12165.html) and paraphrase the song here. The songwriter begins by walking up the steps of the oratory, hailing the joyful day's return. It is Pentecost and the reading comes from Luke 24, especially the verses where Christ returns to his loved ones after the resurrection. But now the song turns and the singer looks at the "stone apostles," thinking to himself that such a joyful return is all right for some. But for him, he wishes he was made of stone so that he did not have to see a "beauty impossible to define," impossible to believe or to endure. The third stanza moves to the act of communion, in which the blood is "imparted in little sips" with the "smell of you still on my hands." And as he brings the cup to his lips, he reflects that no God in the skies or devil in the sea could "do the job that you did" of bringing him to his knees. We close with him sitting on the stone steps, feeling at a loss, forlorn and exhausted "by the absence of you."

The song opens with the lightest of percussion, a swish on the cymbals and a soft tap on a snare drum. The only other instrument is an organ that plays in an ecclesial fashion. One could be forgiven for thinking that it is an ever-so-slightly upbeat hymn, which might conceivably make its way into the repertoire of a church choir—except that the lyrics may not be as acceptable for such a context. However, that subversive element does not show up initially. The first four lines evoke hymnody, with images of the stone steps, the joyful day's return, the shadowed vault, and the hailing of the pentecostal morn.[7] Already there is a hint of the song's paradox of loss: the "joyful day's return" runs a contrary path to the painful disappearance of a lover.

Yet this tension in the lyrics is first established in a curious disjunction between the style of music and those first words of joy. The music may be hymn-like, but it is certainly not the hopeful tones of Pentecost; more appropriate to Good Friday, perhaps, or Jesus' temptation in the desert, or the murder of the innocents. When the words kick in, we hear of climbing up to a joyful pentecostal morn—an immediate jarring sets in. Add to this the way that Cave sings the words—mournfully slowly—and the song is full of tension.

One more tension completes the collection. The first stanza (the first four lines) evokes a collective scene of worship that the singer is about to join. We

---

7. It is not the only time Cave has entered a church at the beginning of a song; see "Darker With the Day" (Cave 2001).

follow him as he steps upward, entering the church to what we assume to be a Pentecost worship service. Yet as soon as the second stanza begins—"The reading is from Luke 24"—we undergo a shift from the collective to the personal or, rather, from participation to observation. Suddenly, the song shifts to the singer's reporting on what is going on. The feeling of being at the beginning of a hymn has been shattered, for this is very much an individual and personal song.

Now I can return to the tension I mentioned earlier, namely between the sense of return evoked by the Gospel passage and the singer's own palpable sense of loss. That loss is not stated until the last line: "By the absence of you." Yet it overshadows the whole song before that final line. So there is a gentle twist with the Gospel reading and the stone apostles. The words do not specify which verses from Luke 24 are read, but the various pericopes concern the women at the tomb on the Sunday morning, the appearance of Jesus to the two walking to Emmaus, his appearance among the gathered followers soon afterwards, and then the explanation of what had happened. It is quite clearly a story of return, although with Cave's own twist, "to his loved ones." This evocation of love stands in stark contrast with the stone apostles to whom he turns his gaze. Stone hearts, I wonder, or perhaps a reflection of the singer's own heart. Of course it is, for the stone apostles were once the lucky ones, but not the stone-dead heart of the singer. They found their lover coming back to them....

Up until this point, the song is interesting but not stunning: he goes into a church, hears a Bible reading, looks at some statues, and thinks about his own sad state. Many run-of-the-mill love songs have done better. But then something new enters the song, with the lines: "A beauty impossible to define / A beauty impossible to believe / A beauty impossible to endure."

This is the beauty he does not wish to see, a beauty that includes a hint of pain with the final word of the third line. A beauty impossible to endure is not necessarily a pleasurable one, or perhaps it is a pleasure found only through pain. But whose beauty? Is he referring to the apostles seeing the beauty of the risen Christ? Or is it Cave himself who does not wish to look upon that beauty? Or is it the beauty of the lover who has gone? We don't know quite yet, unless of course we have listened to the song countless times (as I have in writing this piece). What begins to happen is a merging of Christ and the loved one—the two begin to overlap, wash into one another, and the singer's passionate devotion applies to both.

Or perhaps they are one and the same—a trinity of Cave, Christ, and an unknown lover. But this is really only the beginning, for the abstract admiration and puzzlement over beauty passes over into physical, sensual contact, although not in the way we might expect. Blood is imparted in little sips: here we have the evocation of the cup of wine at the Eucharist, tipped gently by the priest or minister as the communicant kneels. Then he takes control and lifts the cup up to his own lips. Between these two acts is a line that shifts the whole register: "The smell of you still on my hands." Is this the smell of Christ? Or is it the smell of sex, of vaginal fluids, or perhaps of something else? If so, the sex must have been recent. Or is there a hint of something that pushes past the boundary into fetishized sex? The lines now evoke menstrual fluid, the blood in little sips slides toward pain and loss, and the cup is not necessarily a eucharistic cup but melds with the cup of suffering mentioned in Christ's prayer in Gethsemane—"My father, if it be possible, let this cup pass from me" (Matt 26:39). And if we recall the Song of Songs, then the cup of wine itself becomes a metaphor for the vagina and its fluids.

It is never clear whether Cave sings of his lost lover or of Christ, for the Eucharist becomes a moment of sensual and physical contact with both Christ and the lover. Or rather, it is a memory, a physical recovery, or even a transubstantiation of what was lost, for Christ, too, had gone and left his lovers behind. Does Cave hope that the act will bring back his lover? It does not seem to be the case. Instead, we have broached an area of sexual taboo, especially in light of history in which Christ has been desensualized and desexualized. It reminds me of the overt sexuality and passionate spirituality of the twelfth-century beguine, Hadewijch of Brabant, from the Netherlands (this is from her seventh vision):

On that day my mind was beset so fearfully and so painfully by desirous love that all my separate limbs threatened to break and all my veins were in travail. The longing in which I then was cannot be expressed by any language.... I desired to have full fruition of my beloved, and to understand and taste him to the full. I desired that his Humanity should to the fullest extent be one in fruition with my humanity, and that mine then should hold its stand and be strong enough to enter into perfection until I content him. (Hadewijch 1980, 280)

However, there is another feature of this taboo sensuality that may pass unnoticed: the sex of the lover is never specified. We assume the singer's lost lover is female, largely because of the biographical knowledge that Cave is heterosexual. But English does not specify gender with its second-person pronoun (the reference to "baby" is no giveaway). And so it is by no means clear whether the one who has gone is female or male. The boundaries between bodies, identities, and gender become quite blurred as they fold over and leak into one another—and that includes Christ. Cave's Christology has become decidedly queer, transgendered, and sensual.

So it is with the remaining words of the song: the lover, who does far more of a job on the singer than either God in heaven or the devil beneath the sea, is now both/and the sensual Christ and the lost lover. But as with so many of Cave's songs, that devotion and passion is not a source of joy. Exhausted pain washes over the end of the song and, as with Cave's best love songs, the pain is most exquisite when both God and pain are present—now in the figure of Christ.

Heresy

Nick Cave's Christology is becoming a little heretical. Not given to believing in the historical veracity of the virgin birth or the resurrection and then finding a sensual and sexual Christ who has a peccadillo for threesomes is not your run-of-the-mill orthodox Christology. I could add his observation that the Christ who draws Cave in is a creative and artistic Christ who is misunderstood and shunned. This Christ embodies the struggle of faith, trying to understand what it means to live in relation to God. Christ struggles and fails, only to be abandoned by those whom he felt were closest. Elsewhere, Cave presents a picture of a writer's God, saying that he most certainly believes in God but that he writes God into existence anew with each song or poem. Or he suggests that God is present only when "two or three are gathered" (see Cave 1994a, 1998, 2003; Hattenstone 2008). Then there is the existential effort to come to terms with the death of his father—who was an English teacher in a high school—in a car accident when Cave was nineteen (at the time, Cave was being bailed out of jail by his mother for burglary). He articulates this devastating and "palpable sense of loss" (Maume 2006) in terms of the relationship between Christ and the Father.

So how do we read this sensual, seductive, creative, uncertain, collective, and very personal lover Christ? What I do not propose to do is to take Cave's word on all this, for he is too well known for seeking to direct interpretation of his own work. Instead, I wish to play three theorists off against one another, particularly on the question of the romanticization of rock. For Alan Bloom (1987), the wild, barbaric, Dionysian jungle beat of rock is to be abhorred. Rock releases the primal urge; encourages people to wild, indiscriminate sex, drugs, and booze; and rolls back the achievements of order and culture as embodied in someone like Mozart. By contrast, for Camille Paglia (1992, 19–21) the primitive urge of rock is its great appeal. Rock releases the deeply repressed side of ourselves, offering an unmediated expression of our most individual and rebellious side. Paglia argues that rock has "sold out" by becoming commercialized, by pandering to the record companies and the market, and by seeking money over genuine and unique artistic expression.

There is nothing particularly new in either position. At heart, they share the same assumption, namely, that rock is fundamentally Dionysian. Bloom might want it banned and Paglia might want it released, but they are on the same ground. Musicians too will inevitably romanticize rock in similar ways. A young band bashing it out in someone's garage will swear never to sell out. There is endless speculation as to when Bob Dylan sold out—was it when he introduced electric sound in that fateful concert in 1966 when someone was heard to yell out "traitor" from the audience? Or did he do so when he made an advertisement for the new Cadillac Escalade in 2007? Or if a band moves from an underground recording label to one of the big multinationals, some will spit in disgust at the move.

However, as Gracyk (1996, 175–206) argues cogently, rock had been defined from the moment it began as a recording, commercial venture. Its aesthetic cannot be understood without such a reality. Even underground and alternative singers and groups find a place within a commercial network dominated by the market. So what are we to make of the claims to originality, to authenticity, and to individual expression? Cave is one who plays the line well, looking askance at critics, refusing the MTV Music Award for Best Male Artist, since his temperamental muse is not a racehorse, refusing to allow any of his music to be used for advertising, and pursuing the authenticity of the individual artist (see, for example, Goldman 1998). In response, it is all too easy to find examples where he has "sold out," such as seeking out interview after interview (they now run into the many hundreds over the last three decades), or becoming a commercial success with the "Jesus songs," or singing a duet with Kylie Minogue (Cave 1996), or being inducted into the ARIA Music Hall of Fame.

Let me bring all this back to the heretical Christology of Nick Cave. He has said time and again that he has no time for the insipid and colorless Christ of the churches, citing his experience as a choirboy in the Wangaratta Anglican Church. Instead, we are given a distinctive and individual picture of Christ, blending elements from here and there and offering his own original pieces to the mosaic. But this fits in perfectly well with the authentic, individual artist who seeks meaning by being true to himself. It is, I would suggest, nothing less than claiming to be an autonomous individual free to express his or her own position without constraint—in a word, heresy.

Although we can trace the lineage of such an individual back at least to Augustine, the private individual became a leitmotiv of the new ideology of liberalism that emerged with the Enlightenment. It was a very political move, for asserting the value of each individual threatened the vested interests of church, dogma, or God-given absolute power for a monarch. Following the French Revolution, in one European country after another, the claim to individual rights, to democracy, republicanism, and freedom of speech in the name of those rights, was regarded as a threat to the very foundations of society. Tom Paine's widely read *Rights of Man*, written in 1791 after he emigrated from England to North America, was proscribed and burned, and those who printed and distributed it were thrown in prison. The proponents of this new liberal ideology, centered in merchant groups in the towns, were watched by the police, their presses were censored or closed down, and their leaders often had to go into exile.

The ideology of the sacrosanct individual has of course gone into eclipse, although it shines out as brightly as ever after these periodic darknesses. Above all, it is alive and well in art and popular music, taking the form of the authentic artist who will not compromise her or his individual expression. It is this liberal tradition that lies at the heart of Cave's idiosyncratic Christology. I would also suggest that heresy is the best word for both this Christology and for the ideology of the authentic individual. After all, is not heresy the ability to make a choice, from the Greek *hairesis*, the ability of an individual to strike out on a path of his or her own? It is not for nothing that the churches have struggled to keep heresy on the list of damnable sins, for the ideology of liberalism is so much part of our landscape that the charge of heresy these days evokes the dark and dingy times of medieval power and usually brings forth a laugh or mere curiosity that it could still be invoked.

Conclusion

This heretical Christology, which I must admit has its appeal at certain points, is one that emerges out of a particular Enlightenment ideology of the sacrosanct and inviolable individual. The emergence of Nick Cave's heretical Christology may mark a profound shift in the nature of his music, from the crashing post-punk rock of the 1970s and 1980s to the slower, quieter love songs of the 1990s and beyond. It may collapse the boundaries of gender and sex in a uniquely sensual trinity; it may give expression to a bewildered Christ who is trying to sort out what faith means and who this "father" really is; and it may be an artist's Christology, one that brings God to life in writing, song, and the gathering of a few. But if we assume the right of the individual to "choose" his or her own heresy, then Cave's heresy is yet one more exercise of that choice. Nick Cave has "chosen" and constructed the heresy that means the most to him. I must admit that I am the last one to allow anyone else to tell me what to do or think, but I am troubled by the way Cave buys into the underlying ideology of the private individual in the very act of making his heretical choice. A more iconoclastic approach, as Adorno persistently argued (2006), would be to challenge that Enlightenment ideology of the individual rather than reinforce it.

Works Cited

Adorno, Theodor. 2006. *Philosophy of New Music*. Translated by R. Hullot-Kentor. Minneapolis: University of Minnesota Press.

Attali, Jacques. 1977. *Bruits: Essai sur l'économie politique de la musique*. Paris: Presses Universitaires de France.

———. 1985. *Noise: The Political Economy of Music*. Translated by Brian Massumi. Minneapolis: University of Minnesota Press.

Bloom, Alan. 1987. *The Closing of the American Mind*. New York: Simon and Schuster.

Boer, Roland. 2005. *Gates to the Garden: Nick Cave og bibelteksternes efterliv*. Fønix (Denmark) 29, nos. 3–4: 31–47.

———. 2006. Under the Influence? The Bible, Culture and Nick Cave. *Journal of Religion and Popular Culture* 12. Online: http://www.usask.ca/relst/jrpc/art12-nickcave.html.

———. Forthcoming. Nick Cave's Trinity: Love, Hate and Women. *Journal of Religion and Culture*.

Brokenmouth, Robert. 1996. *Nick Cave: The Birthday Party and Other Epic Adventures*. London: Omnibus.

Cave, Nick. 1988. *King Ink*. London: Black Spring.

———. 1989. *And the Ass Saw the Angel*. London: Black Spring.

———. 1990. *The Good Son*. Mute Records.

———. 1992. *Henry's Dream*. Mute Records.

———. 1994a. Interview in *Revue*, 13 August 2006. Online: http://www.nick-cave.com/index.php?option=com_content&task=view&id=46&Itemid=29.

———. 1994b. *Let Love In*. Mute Records.

———. 1996. *Murder Ballads*. Mute Records.

———. 1997a. *The Boatman's Call*. Mute Records.

———. 1997b. *King Ink II*. London: Black Spring.

———. 1998. An Introduction to the Gospel According to Mark. Pages 1–8 in *The Gospel According to Mark*. Edinburgh: Canongate.

———. 2000. *The Secret Life of the Love Song and The Flesh Made Word: Two Lectures by Nick Cave*. Mute Records.

———. 2001. *No More Shall We Part*. Mute Records.

———. 2003a. Interview with Jim Pascoe. Jim Pascoe Writing, 2005. Online: http://www.jimpascoe.com/writing/nickcave.html.

———. 2003b. *Nocturama*. Mute Records.

———. 2004a. *Abattoir Blues/The Lyre of Orpheus*. Mute Records.

———. 2004b. The Love Song. *Another Magazine* 7: 397–400.

———. 2008. *Dig!!! Lazarus Dig!!!* Mute Records.

Dax, Maximilian, and Johannes Beck. 1999. *The Life and Music of Nick Cave: An Illustrated Biography*. Translated by I. Minock. Berlin: Gestalten.

Goldman, Marlene. 1998. *The Gospel According to Nick Cave*. Rolling Stone, September 17. Online: http://www.rollingstone.com/artists/nickcave/articles/story/5919887/the_gospel_according_to_nick_cave.

Gracyk, Theodore. 1996. *Rhythm and Noise: An Aesthetics of Rock*. Durham, N.C.: Duke University Press.

Grinderman. 2007. *Grinderman*. Anti-.

Hadewijch. 1980. *Hadewijch: The Complete Works*. Translated by C. Hart. Classics of Western Spirituality. New York: Paulist.

Hattenstone, Simon. 2008. Old Nick. *Guardian*, February 28. Online: http://www.guardian.co.uk/music/2008/feb/23/popandrock.features.

Johnston, Ian. 1996. *Bad Seed: The Biography of Nick Cave*. London: Abacus.

Maume, Chris. 2006. *Nick Cave: The Devil's Advocate*. Independent, March 11. Online: http://www.independent.co.uk/news/people/profiles/nick-cave-devils-advocate-469418.html.

Paglia, Camille. 1992. *Sex, Art, and American Culture*. New York: Vintage.

Prophetic Voices in Graphic Novels: The "Comic and Tragic Vision" of Apocalyptic Rhetoric in *Kingdom Come* and *Watchmen*

Terry Ray Clark

This essay attempts to demonstrate that a graphic novel may function as a prophetic and religious voice in our society. Two graphic novels will be examined, each with an apocalyptic crisis at the center of its plot. Each corresponds in various ways to an ancient form of apocalyptic writing known as the "historical sketch," using this form to critique what its author perceives as inappropriate religious responses in modern Western culture—apocalyptic passivity and apocalyptic violence.

The apocalyptically passive individual views the world as irredeemably corrupt and ultimately destined for a destruction by which it will reap what it has sown. This perspective is often paired with a sense of powerlessness to change the outcome. The appropriate response is to wait patiently for destruction to come, either naturally or by divine intervention. In the latter case, God typically intervenes to rescue the faithful and condemn the wicked. Any effort to forestall the inevitable would merely delay the arrival of justice; thus, passivity is preferable to any endeavor aimed at redeeming the world. Instead, the emphasis is placed upon converting the repentant before the imminent end arrives and keeping the faithful remnant pure enough in the meantime not to lose their eternal, otherworldly salvation. Alternatively, apocalyptic violence is a response designed to speed up the arrival of the end, in which divine violence triumphs.

This essay argues that the graphic novels *Kingdom Come* and *Watchmen* represent and advocate a different kind of prophetic response to modern culture. Unlike passive apocalyptic thinking that affirms a disconnection from the current order of reality (politically, religiously, and/or socially), these works use various aspects of the apocalyptic genre and apocalyptic rhetoric to teach that humanity should not wait upon otherworldly salvation. Instead, the reader is implicitly encouraged to act heroically right now, in order to save this world or at least delay its destruction, but not by the use of apocalyptic violence. As such, the graphic novels, which on the surface appear to be secular modes of communication, actually offer a prophetic voice to modern society and seek to function, practically speaking, as sacred texts along the lines that Conrad Ostwalt elaborates in his book *Secular Steeples: Popular Culture and the Religious Imagination* (2003). Their ultimate purpose is to enlighten the reader to a new consciousness of individual and communal responsibility for transforming and saving the world.

OSTWALT'S THEORY OF SECULARIZATION AND SACRED TEXTS

As works of apocalyptic rhetoric, *Kingdom Come* and *Watchmen* demonstrate what Ostwalt has labeled a "shift" in the locus of religious authority in modern society (2003, 5). In this shift, a voice traditionally considered secular speaks authoritatively (or as one with authority) to a matter usually considered to be the exclusive domain of a more traditional religious authority (e.g., denomination, temple, bishop). This can be recognized in the graphic novels' teaching that: a) God exists, but he expects humanity to help themselves by rejecting egoism and fulfilling their duty to make the world a better place, even if it requires self-sacrifice (*Kingdom Come*); and b) a deity cannot be counted on to instill justice in the universe, and therefore it behooves humanity to solve the problem of personal evil itself (*Watchmen*).

In *Secular Steeples*, Ostwalt focuses upon the "functional authority of religion," rejecting the notion of a dichotomy between sacred and secular forces in society, which have traditionally been understood as locked in an endless struggle for superiority (2003, 5). Ostwalt argues that the social location of religious authority naturally shifts over time. There is an ebb and flow within society concerning which individuals, groups, or institutions wield authority to speak on religious matters and to influence behavior and values. This does not reflect a diminishment of religious sensibility or value per se over a given period of time. If religious behavior and/or sensibility is a "fundamental human characteristic" (35), as Ostwalt suggests, then "the religious impulse will not disappear with secularization" (5).

From this perspective, secularization is a two-way street, in which human culture is constantly evolving and constantly receiving an "infusion of ... new vehicles for the expression of the religious imagination" (Ostwalt 2003, 14). Religion is merely "a cultural form that is directed toward [some concept of] the sacred and that exists in dialectical relationship with other cultural forms that sometimes explore religious content" (23). Here, culture, including popular culture, is treated as a site of competitive values, a "contested landscape" that is always under negotiation by various individuals and groups (Storey 2009, 9). "When traditional religious institutions lose their power … religiosity will express itself in other parts of the culture, oftentimes in popular cultural forms," because "religious symbolism and questions … [become] dispersed throughout the cultural landscape" (Ostwalt 2003, 31). As a result, at any given time one may consider that not only is traditional religion becoming secularized, but secular culture is becoming "sacralized" (Ostwalt 2003, 31).

Ostwalt is equally critical of the way that both literalistic and historical-critical approaches to the Bible have led to a devaluing of the metaphorical and mythical "power" of sacred texts in western society (2003, 91–106, esp. 94). The one approach "renders" a sacred text as a "secularized instruction manual, barren and frightening in the wrong hands" (94). The other overemphasizes historical and scientific methods in order to limit the text to one appropriate, contextual (i.e., historical) interpretation, namely, a single message or meaning supposedly intended by an original author (93). The effect of both approaches is to demythologize or desacralize the text, thereby greatly limiting its usefulness for communicating sacred truth.

In such an environment, new cultural forms, including literary forms, will be created to take the place of those texts that become marginalized, practically speaking, because they have become devoid of sacred value. Religion will come to be, as Ostwalt puts it, "found elsewhere besides sacred literature and sacred spaces" as traditionally conceived (2003, 104). Ultimately, this void will be filled by new forms of religious expression. Because of "the power of secular literature to critique a culture's ideologies, religious institutions, and moral codes, … [s]ecular fiction can operate as myth to offer insight into … spiritual issues" (107). Thus, for Ostwalt, secular literature can function religiously, sometimes serving as a new vehicle to communicate timeless religious truth and values. In the following analysis of *Kingdom Come* and *Watchmen*, Ostwalt's theory, in conjunction with theories of apocalyptic literature and rhetoric, proves helpful for understanding the religious function of two popular literary texts normally classified as secular cultural products.

APOCALYPTIC GENRE AND APOCALYPTIC RHETORIC

Most academic studies of Jewish and Christian apocalyptic have focused on defining the genre of the apocalypse. In this regard, an important milestone was achieved by the publication of *Semeia* 14, a special issue on apocalyptic literature (Collins 1979) that sought to clarify "a significant cluster of traits that [would] distinguish it [the apocalypse] from other works" (Collins 1998, 4). Collins, building on this earlier work, defines an apocalypse as "revelatory literature with a narrative framework, in which a revelation is mediated by an otherworldly being to a human recipient, disclosing a transcendent reality which is both temporal, insofar as it envisages eschatological salvation, and spatial insofar as it involves another, supernatural world" (5).

Like other scholars, Collins treats the apocalypse as falling into one of two major categories: the historical apocalypse and the otherworldly journey (6–7). The former type is dominated by a revelation through which the prophet receives enlightenment about the way the current universe will be replaced or transcended by divine intervention. Here, the prophet receives a sketch of how the world will wind down. The latter type is dominated by an experience in which the prophet actually tours various realms of reality that lie beyond normal human perception (e.g., heaven, hell, the underworld).

In both types, a critical role is played by "discourse or dialogue" between the prophet, who receives the revelation, and an angelic figure, "who interprets the vision and serves as a guide" (Collins 1998, 5). The apocalypse also normally contains "both a temporal and spatial dimension" (6). Time travel and out-of-body experiences are common, and through the elaborate reporting of palpable, first-hand experiences, the prophet's audience gains insight and assurance about the culmination of history. This includes a "definitive eschatological judgment" by a transcendent power that "is directly relevant to human destiny" (8, 11). Unlike more traditional religious expression, which tends to lean upon preestablished sources of authority such as Scripture, the apocalypse derives its authority from new, direct, and divine revelation (Collins 1998, 40, citing Stone 1984, 429).

For Collins, the purpose of the apocalypse is to provide the reader with "a resolution in the imagination [that] shapes one's imaginative perception of a situation," thereby "lay[ing] the basis for whatever course of action it exhorts" (1998, 42). In this sense, the apocalypse expresses a twofold purpose. First, it provides a potential source of comfort to those dealing with a real-world crisis of suffering by promising an eventual and eventful resolution in which the forces of good conquer the forces of evil. In the historical sketch, the apocalyptic prophet and his audience receive a visual "down payment," by which the fulfillment of divine promises is witnessed in advance. By viewing or taking a tour of the future and/or otherworld, the divine plan of instituting justice is made more concrete and viable for those currently suffering oppression. This guarantees the faithful that God can be counted on to bring the divine plan to fruition.[1]

---

1. E.g., the tortures of divine punishment are quite vividly portrayed as having already begun

Secondly, the apocalypse provides a means of exhortation to righteous behavior for those who would survive upcoming judgment and reap the benefits of the faithful. Thus, in addition to providing solace and hope for those currently suffering as a result of evil, it provides inspiration for important this-worldly religious duties, which might include rescuing others from condemnation or transforming the world in an effort to delay or avert its destruction.

The apocalyptic tendency toward radical dualism, in which mundane realities are considered less potent, less reliable, and less valuable than supernatural ones, sometimes contributes to a decrease in "human initiative" (Collins 1998, 283). But alternatively, the "apocalyptic imagination" can sometimes have revolutionary consequences. Not only does apocalyptic contain "a powerful rhetoric for denouncing the deficiencies of this world," but it may also communicate "an appreciation of the great resource that lies in the human imagination to construct a symbolic world where the integrity of values can be maintained in the face of social and political powerlessness and even of the threat of death" (283). Therefore, exercising the imagination properly may inspire some to work for positive change in this life, rather than waiting for the next. Contained within the apocalyptic worldview are inspirational seeds of redemption and transformation that sometimes refuse to wait upon Armageddon to take root.

This two-edged nature of apocalyptic is highlighted by O'Leary's work on apocalyptic rhetoric, which emphasizes that apocalyptic argumentation "is a social practice of 'public, persuasive, constitutive, and socially constituted utterance'" (1998, 4, citing Zulick 1992, 126). As such, it is not limited to only one genre; it is adaptable to a number of different forms, including such popular cultural products as film, music, television, and even the combination of image and text found in graphic novels.

O'Leary describes apocalyptic as "a particular type of eschatology" or "discourse about the last things" that "reveals or makes manifest a vision of ultimate destiny, rendering immediate to human audiences the ultimate End of the cosmos" (1998, 5–6). He notes the similarity "between the apocalyptic mentality and that of the conspiracy theorist," the latter identifying the enemy as residing somewhere outside of the apocalyptic prophet's own "true community" (O'Leary 1998, 6, following Hofstader 1979, 29–30, and Creps 1980). This highlights the value of apocalyptic rhetoric for establishing and maintaining a sense of communal identity and solidarity. There is a universal human tendency "to develop foundational narratives that define the relationship of the social order to the per-

---

for sinners in hell in a number of apocalypses (cf., esp., the *Apocalypse of Paul* and the *Apocalypse of Peter*).

ceived evils of the universe," and apocalyptic rhetoric is one way that humans engage in such mythmaking behavior: "The story of the apocalyptic tradition is one of community building, in which human individuals and collectivities constitute their identities through shared mythic narratives that confront the problem of evil in time and history" (O'Leary 1998, 6).

Nothing builds identity for humans better than a shared perception of mutual threat, and one way to achieve this common perspective is through the vehicle of apocalyptic rhetoric, which identifies good and evil and elaborates how the former will ultimately annihilate the latter. The production of apocalyptic narratives, then, plays an important religious role in society not unlike the production of other metanarratives.[2]

O'Leary finds the enduring appeal of the apocalyptic mode of response in its versatility and effectiveness for dealing with the ongoing human struggle against three key challenges: time, authority, and evil (1998, 16). These represent perennial existential problems for human existence, to which apocalyptic rhetoric responds "as a symbolic theodicy, a mythical and rhetorical solution to the problem of evil ... accomplished through [a] discursive construction of temporality" (14). This means that apocalyptic discourse normally reconceives the current chaos in the universe as temporary and limited by a "divinely predetermined" plan that will soon manifest itself as the final solution to all prevailing forms of evil (O'Leary 1998, 16, building on McGinn 1979). "Mythic narratives of apocalypse function as temporal resolutions to the apparent contradiction created by the experience of evil within a framework of theistic belief" (O'Leary 1998, 18). They tend to argue that there is order in the universe as a result of a higher authority and power and that the limits of time itself are temporary, as are all other forms of evil.

But, as noted previously, apocalyptic discourse has been understood and responded to in radically different ways. From a rhetorical perspective, it may be interpreted deliberatively, "as a spur to action," or ethically, as an attempt to preserve a particular set of values or ethos. There is in fact a range of possible responses, because "ideologically it has been judged inherently radical, 'progressive,' and conservative" (O'Leary 1998, 12, citing Block 1985, xi–xii).

O'Leary turns to the work of Kenneth Burke on the tragic and comic "frames of acceptance" to explain these different modes of response (Burke 1984). The tragic frame understands human history primarily as a drama destined to end

---

2. However, it should be noted that challenges to social cohesion inevitably change over time, and as perceived threats change, so do the worldviews and the narratives that expound on them. Thus, as Ostwalt has recognized, the locus of authority for responding to such matters, as well as the medium of response, may also shift.

in tragedy for the mundane realm and requiring divine intervention to provide any hope whatsoever. It reflects a pessimistic attitude toward human achievement and typically elicits a social response that may be labeled passive-resistive. Its orientation is geared toward accepting an otherworldly authority and promoting the divinely revealed perspective that the world is irredeemably evil. It seeks to oppose the predominant values of the larger society, sometimes by actively resisting the reigning political powers and sometimes by resisting the urge to work for society's transformation, in order to avoid being tainted by evil in the process of interacting with it.

Alternatively, the comic frame emphasizes the human potential for goodness and wisdom, refusing to accept the idea that humanity's fate is predetermined. It reflects a hopeful attitude toward the future of this world, even in the midst of pain and suffering, typically eliciting a social response that may be described as active-transformative. Its orientation is more geared toward accepting and promoting a this-worldly authority in the form of human freedom and reason. Human destiny is limited primarily by human choice, and current problems may be solved by initiating transformational activity. Humanity's greatest problems and greatest solutions are therefore generated by humans themselves. Hope remains for this world as long as there are hopeful individuals willing to work for the greater good (see O'Leary 1998, 76–92).

O'Leary summarizes the tragic and comic frames in the following way:

> The comic reading of the Apocalypse addresses the topoi of time and evil by either postponing the End, or making its enactment a consequence of human choice and activity in the world, and conceiving of evil (to a limited extent) as something to be overcome by recognition, reform, and education. The tragic reading, in contrast, structures time by placing the End somewhere in the immediate future, and views this End as predestined and catastrophic; evil is depicted in demonic terms, and can only be overcome by divine intervention rather than human action. In the tragic interpretation, the predictive function of the apocalyptic myth is dominant; in the comic interpretation, the hortatory and allegorical functions are emphasized. (1998, 85–86)

Here it becomes apparent why the predominant orientation of the tragic vision is passive. Since the general "outcome of events" is predetermined, at least on a cosmic scale, the only work to be done is at the individual level, by which one may achieve a "proper [moral] alignment toward [the] cosmic forces" destined to win the so-called final conflict (O'Leary 1998, 88). Although the tragic mode reflects a primarily escapist mentality, the comic vision emphasizes the importance of this-worldly salvation. Since the evil that afflicts this world is predominantly understood in human terms, the solution must also have a human face. In the words of A. Cheree Carlson, "'Comedy' will recognize the 'evil' that exists in all humankind, and thus have charity for the enemy" (1986, 453).

In summation, O'Leary provides a perspective on apocalyptic prophecy that is rhetorical and therefore more broadly applicable than that which merely focuses on the written genre. This makes it especially useful for the student of religion and popular culture. By incorporating the tragic or comic frames of interpretation, apocalyptic rhetoric "enable[s] people to explain otherwise terrifying or anomalous events and incorporate[s] them into a structure of meaning" (O'Leary 1998, 92). Tragic interpretations are more literal, predictive, and ethos-oriented, emphasizing the predetermined nature of reality, and comic interpretations more often employ allegorical methods and deliberative rhetoric to teach the audience how to change the present course of events and avoid tragedy (76).

While popular cultural products may partake of either approach, or of some combination of the two, it is the comic vision that provides the best model for analyzing the apocalyptic and prophetic nature of *Kingdom Come* and *Watchmen* in the next section of this essay. Both reflect a number of characteristics of the genre of the apocalypse, both serve as historical sketches of what the future *might* hold in store, and each has its own unique approach to otherworldly realities, this-worldly salvation, and conspiracy theory.

Kingdom Come and Watchmen as Prophetic and Apocalyptic Texts

In the introduction to *Kingdom Come*, Elliot Maggin describes this graphic novel as a story in which superheroes serve as metaphors for "the way humans wish themselves to be; ought, in fact, to be" (1997, 6). Their struggles are the struggles of the entire human race, and in this story, "they learn that they are not gods ... [yet] despite their limitations they must be potent and responsible anyway. Now is the time in the life of the human race when all of us need to learn these same things" (7).

Kingdom Come draws heavily upon the ancient genre of the apocalypse to deliver this message. It opens with citations from the Apocalypse of John and the image of an eagle—whose body incorporates the stars and stripes of the American flag—confronting a red-eyed bat, the latter representing the forces of darkness with which America must (or feels it must) contend. The plot revolves around a washed-up preacher, Norman McCay, who is visited by a heavenly messenger named the Spectre, a character known in the world of DC Comics for instituting divine justice in the mundane realm.[3] Here, the Spectre comes not to institute God's judgment but merely to announce it, instead commanding McCay to determine the fate of humanity and the fate of all the supers, hero and villain alike.

The immediate and overt crisis facing all the residents of earth is their mutual annihilation in the escalating war among the supers, a war characterized by confusion over how to define heroism and villainy. *Kingdom Come* uses the character of Superman, the most powerful hero of all, to demonstrate the need to reflect deeply on the question of what makes one person morally superior to another. The morality of using force to resolve conflict is an important piece of this exploration. In the end, Superman learns that *might* alone does not make one *right*. This is especially noteworthy in light of the high value placed on redemptive violence in classical apocalyptic. The underlying crisis in the graphic novel is the "erosion" of "human initiative" that occurs when humanity "asked a new breed to face the future for them" (Waid and Ross 1997, 17). *Kingdom Come*, unlike traditional apocalyptic, considers it problematic for humanity to rely solely upon a "higher power" to solve their problems.

This suggests that *Kingdom Come* considers humanity's chief problem to be religious in nature—humans have a tendency to limit the realm of effective power to an otherworldly place, the result being an orientation of passivity that locates salvation entirely in the transcendent. At the other end of the spectrum is a radical this-worldly orientation that believes there is no otherworld or has lost all hope in it, which leads some to act irresponsibly, believing their actions have no eternal consequence. This seems to be the perspective of the ambiguous character Magog, who fully embraces violence as a legitimate means of destroying the enemy, as well as the world leaders at the United Nations, who decide to annihilate all the supers with nuclear weapons near the end of the graphic novel.

Kingdom Come rejects both extremes. It does so in a way that is at once generically apocalyptic and rhetorically unapocalyptic. Like most apocalyptic prophets, Pastor McCay is led by the Spectre on a tour of sights and sounds inaccessible to the average human. It is not unlike a form of astral travel. But while affirming the reality of a transcendent realm through McCay's interaction with God's messenger, the graphic novel does not explore the divine realm in a spatial or temporal way as in the typical otherworldly apocalyptic journey.

---

3. The DC Comics company was originally founded as National Allied Publications in 1934. In 1938, they introduced the first superhero story in *Action Comics* no. 1, which featured the character Superman. They are currently a subsidiary of Warner Bros. Entertainment. For more information, see the official DC Comics web site: http://www.dccomics.com/dccomics/.

Instead, McCay takes a miraculous tour of his own world in order to witness the rising conflict between superhero, super villain, and human, which is destined to end in Armageddon. Along the way, he is disappointed by heaven's unwillingness to offer any assurance for the future, an assurance typically received by the prophet on behalf of the faithful in an apocalyptic text:

> McCay: That's all? That's what you have to show me?
> Spectre: That disturbs you?
> McCay: Yes! You're an angel! That makes you a messenger of hope!
> Spectre: At no time did I promise you hope....
> McCay: A greater power sent you! Your very existence is a testimony to faith! You mean that all you have to tell me is that those who could save us won't?
> (49)

Later, the Spectre reveals to McCay that "long have these mortals suspected that they are no longer the captains of humanity's destiny," suggesting that the humans have, as a result of an outlook that makes them feel powerless to change their world, relinquished responsibility for even trying (70). Instead, they look to heaven or to the supers to dictate the future, not unlike McCay himself. Ironically, this passive response lies at the heart of the problem for which divine judgment is rapidly approaching. Not acting at all, in the belief that humans cannot make a difference, is treated here as an evil equal to acting irresponsibly and is worthy of divine judgment. But the judgment will come in the form of divine passivity, an unwillingness to intervene in order to let humanity and the supers reap what they have sown. This stands in direct contrast to the typical apocalyptic scenario, where the deity instigates Armageddon and personally enacts final judgment.

In the penultimate climax of the novel, with super fighting against super in a cataclysmic battle that threatens to engulf the planet, the humans act in concert to annihilate hero and villain alike for the sake of their own survival. Here, they briefly abandon passivity and embrace their own path of violence, launching a series of nuclear warheads into the melee. Captain Marvel, a so-called god-man (half-human, half-divine), sacrifices himself in order to find a "middle way," a path of nonviolence against others. He takes upon himself the brunt of a nuclear blast to prevent the annihilation of all the combatants, and in the process, enough supers die to thin their numbers and reduce their threat to humanity. At this point in the plot, apocalypticism is eclipsed by self-sacrificial messianism.

But this is not the end of the story. After the explosion, representing heaven's passive judgment on the supers, the Spectre prepares to depart the mundane realm as Superman speeds away to unleash reciprocal violence on his human attackers. McCay, foreseeing the next stage of destruction about to erupt, demands that the Spectre miraculously transport him, one last time, for an audience with Superman. Here, McCay fulfills an important prophetic role normally found outside the context of the apocalyptic genre, that of a human mediator who challenges the god(s) on behalf of humanity (see Muffs and Jacobsen 1995).[4] This initiative to change the natural or inevitable course of events is in opposition to apocalyptic passivity.

In *Kingdom Come*, the future is not predetermined; things end more comically than tragically. McCay convinces Superman to forgive himself for the prior failure of abandoning humanity and to resist the temptation to take his frustrations out on others.[5] McCay tells Superman, "Your instinctive knowledge ... of right ... and wrong ... was a gift of your own humanity.... [T]he minute you made the super more important than the man ... the day you decided to turn your back on mankind ... completely cost you your instinct. That took your judgment away. Take it back" (Maggin 1997, 193). Here, McCay counsels that it is the human part of Superman that should do the judging, not the superhuman.

Superman relents and goes on to condemn the "false division" between humans and superhumans (195).[6] Superman interprets Marvel's sacrifice as an attempt to expose this untruth "in the hope that your world and our world could be one world once again" (196). The story ends with McCay thinking that not every dream is necessarily a prophecy (in the sense of a dependable prediction of the future). Instead, "the future ... like so much else ... is open to interpretation" (203). This signals to the reader that the vision of the graphic novel is more comic than tragic. Its message of hope and responsibility is a call to action on the part of the reader. Once it is recognized that humanity wields an immense power to direct its own future, the reader is expected to respond appropriately.

To use O'Leary's categories of time, authority, and evil, the message of *Kingdom Come* is that humanity's awesome power is a potential evil, but so is the failure to recognize it and respond accordingly. Ignorance and passivity are equal,

---

4. Cf., e.g., Abraham advocating for Sodom in Gen 18 (he is referred to as a prophet in Gen 20:7), Moses advocating for Israel at Sinai in Exod 32, and Ezekiel advocating for the Judean remnant in Ezek 11:1–13. It should be noted that some scholars consider parts of Ezekiel "proto-apocalyptic" (e.g., chs. 38–39), but they do not classify this particular role of advocacy on behalf of humanity as an apocalyptic trait.

5. At the beginning of the graphic novel, Superman was in retirement, having given up on intervening in human affairs, thus contributing to a chaotic moral and power vacuum on the earth.

6. This perspective is shared by Maggin in the graphic novel's introduction, where he refers to today's human as yesterday's superhuman: "If a person from only a hundred years or so in the past could look in on our lives, that person would suppose that we were not mortals, but gods. He would be bowled over by what the most ordinary among us could do.... This is the way many of us have always looked upon our super-heroes—as though they were gods" (5).

if not greater, threats. Time is of the essence, since humanity holds the power for self-annihilation. But there is still hope if humanity will reject the temptation to despair or to embrace violence as the only solution to human conflict. Self-sacrifice and enlightenment about the false divisions that separate people are the way to move forward. Humans across the globe must acknowledge their commonality rather than focus on superficial differences.

WATCHMEN

Watchmen provides its own unique apocalyptic scenario, which also leans in a comic direction. It does not exalt the overt religious value of messianic self-sacrifice, although one of its main characters (Rorschach) is sacrificed (i.e., murdered) in order to preserve a newfound peace at the end of the story. The plot of *Watchmen* treats human morality, at least on the surface, in a very pessimistic way, depicting the world's moral sensibilities as being so dull that the only possible solution to self-annihilation is a secular, utilitarian strategy: create a common enemy large enough to unite all humanity as a species.

This strategy is dramatically revealed at the end of the work. The ambivalent hero/villain, Ozymandias, the world's most intelligent man, manufactures a common enemy in the form of an artificial alien, which is designed to simultaneously threaten and unite all races and nations on earth. The alien's supposedly sudden appearance from another dimension has both tragic and comic consequences. It explodes upon entering the earthly plane, resulting in its own death as well as the deaths of thousands of innocent New Yorkers. But the effect is to end the Cold War, since the threat of a possible future alien invasion, rather than the nuclear arms race, will now occupy humanity's attention.

Despite the graphic novel's dark, brooding tone and its undeniably tragic dimensions, Alan Moore's work ends on a comic note that reflects a hopeful rhetoric. In the climax, Dr. Manhattan, the most godlike character of all, whose knowledge and power are unfathomable, overcomes the temptation to recede permanently into the background like the transcendent god of the deists.[7] Being convinced that human life is a miraculous thing and worth preserving, he decides to intervene to prevent an all-out nuclear war between the United States and the Soviet Union. But he arrives too late to foil Ozymandias's plot and, ironically, chooses to ensure its success by killing the only potential whistle-blower,

---

7. The image of a deistic God, often referred to as a clock maker who winds up the universe and then "watches" it wind down, plays a major role in the imagery and rhetoric of the graphic novel.

Rorschach, a character committed to the principle of blind justice and making the truth known at any cost. However, in another ironic twist, the story ends with the likelihood that Rorschach's journal, which details Ozymandias's plot, will be discovered by a local newspaper reporter. Thus, future uncertainty persists.

Like *Kingdom Come*, *Watchmen* should be classified as an apocalyptic historical sketch with at least a comic rhetoric, if not a clearly comic vision. Generically speaking, *Watchmen* provides a more tragic assessment of human nature and a less hopeful ending, justifying, at least on the surface, the tragic label. But this is all placed in the service of deliberative rhetoric designed to undermine the tragic vision's fulfillment. The utilitarian ethic of uniting humanity against a common enemy persists, but, in the end, the real foe is implicitly revealed to be human ignorance—ignorance of our common humanity, our own power, and our own bent toward self-destruction. Thus, the common threat is more internal than external, and the purpose of the graphic novel is to convince the reader that a more comic conclusion to the human story can still be written.

Unlike *Kingdom Come*, *Watchmen* makes no explicit reference to the existence of a creator deity. However, through the godlike power of Dr. Manhattan and the godlike knowledge of Ozymandias, the author reveals his perspective on how a deity might respond to humanity's plight. Both characters get more directly involved in the human crisis than either God or the Spectre in *Kingdom Come*.[8] In the end, Manhattan acts in concert with Ozymandias; he kills Rorschach to cover up Ozymandias's plot. But a potential flaw in the plan remains as a result of Rorschach's journal. Will truth triumph over utility? Should it?

Watchmen's only trace of the otherworldly journey is found in the space travels of Manhattan and Laurie to the planet Mars (chs. 4 and 9). Here, there is an interesting temporal, as well as spatial, element, because Manhattan's perception is not bound to the present. While he cannot always see the future clearly (his perception can be temporarily clouded by electromagnetic static), he can replay the past, not unlike the way the graphic novel can temporally move backward and forward with its subject matter. But even as a historical sketch, Alan Moore's masterpiece purposely has an open-ended conclusion. It waits for humanity to decide its fate. Will we learn vicariously from the mistakes of others (including those in the author's story)? Will we learn from our own mistakes? Is the author's lesson clear?

Concerning O'Leary's categories of time, authority, and evil, we find a similar rhetorical strategy to that of *Kingdom Come*. Humanity is its own worst enemy,

---

8. In both works, the advocacy of a human character is critical to averting disaster, at least temporarily (McCay in *Kingdom Come* and Manhattan's girlfriend, Laurie, in *Watchmen*, the latter proving more precarious).

and violence, even strategically manufactured, is probably doomed to failure. A godlike mind and power may be persuaded to intervene, but there is no sure way to predict the nature or outcome of that intervention. It may be ideal, or it may be utilitarian. A more sure future may be attained only if humanity wields its own intellect and power in responsible ways. But again, time is running out.

Both graphic novels question the effectiveness of violence as a means to achieving a lasting peace. Both encourage readers to think and act as if we hold the power of God in our own hands. *Kingdom Come* seems to suggest the necessity of self-sacrifice for breaking the cycle of violence (see Girard 1977, 1987). It rejects the utility of violence against others most clearly through its depiction of the pathetic character Magog, who will go to any length to destroy villains, until he undermines his own purpose of protecting the innocent (see Waid and Ross 1997, 94–101). Like Ozymandias and, eventually, Manhattan, Magog believes the ends justify the means, until he accidentally kills a million people while attempting to fill the heroic void left by Superman's retirement. Coupled with the view that today's humans are yesterday's supers, this suggests that the only legitimate violent behavior is that which is self-inflicted for the sake of stopping the cycle of reciprocation.

Initially, one might interpret *Watchmen* as being more accepting of violence against others because its plot depicts the sacrifice of the few on behalf of the many as an acceptable trade-off for saving the human species. But the graphic novel does not encourage the reader to mimic the behaviors of Ozymandias and Manhattan, whose intentions may be foiled in spite of perhaps having silenced Rorschach. Instead, *Watchmen* contrasts humanity's technological evolution with human ignorance and brutality, the latter of which borders on sheer barbarism on the part of the world's most intelligent and powerful (i.e., godlike) men.

Here, the not-so-tangential nature of a parallel pirate comic ties into the larger plot of *Watchmen*.[9] In this story, an apparently civilized sailor reverts to his own form of brutality to save his family when he believes they are threatened by bloodthirsty pirates, in the process perpetrating his own crimes against humanity. His perception of reality is perverted by paranoia, and he descends into madness. The comic ends with him realizing that he has damned himself in the course of trying to save and/or avenge those he loves most. He becomes what he abhors—a savage—and the story ends with his wading out to join his new shipmates. The message is a version of "meeting the enemy," only to find that we should fear ourselves most of all!

---

9. Alan Moore weaves into the plot of *Watchmen* a parallel story from a purely fictional comic series, *Tales of the Black Freighter*.

The intended effect of this parallel tale is repulsion and revulsion. It highlights the fact that a purely utilitarian ethic of saving the many at the expense of the few does not properly question ends and means. As such, it provides a cipher for the central storyline. It holds up a mirror to the reader for the sake of self-enlightenment. But the conclusion of *Watchmen* is less clear about how the reader should proceed. Are there realistic alternatives? How should humanity emphasize the miraculous value of every individual life?

Conclusions

Both *Kingdom Come* and *Watchmen* should be understood as prophetic voices, because they provide the reader with crucial and timely apocalyptic rhetoric. They are adaptations of the apocalyptic historical sketch, and their tragic and comic visions of the end are designed to inspire a comic outcome for all humanity. Their authors assume the authority to speak on matters of supreme importance for their societies, not with reference to divine revelation, but because they consider themselves in possession of the charismatic gifts and insight necessary to produce an observant audience. Whether these gifts come from a divine source is unknown. Their sketches represent mythic narratives that uniquely address existential questions about time, authority, and evil.

Kingdom Come and *Watchmen* represent a shift in the locus of authority, in the sense that Ostwalt elaborates. They speak to matters of ultimate concern, in this case on the subject of humanity's survival in the face of potential self-annihilation. They respond with a predominantly comic rhetoric, implicitly assuming the moral authority and moral responsibility for staving off not an inevitable but, rather, an unnecessary self-destruction.

As apocalyptic rhetoric, the graphic novels do not teach their readers a tragic, divinely determined perspective on humanity's fate, but instead admonish their readers to avoid passivity and to exercise their freedom and power for constructive ends. In a practical and prophetic sense, they call their intended readers to repent, to turn from their current course of action, before it is too late for the species to survive. The authors of both works design a fictional future in order to stave off a potentially catastrophic non-fictional one. In a functional sense, *Kingdom Come* and *Watchmen* deserve to be labeled prophetic and religious texts.

Works Cited

Block, Ruth. 1985. *Visionary Republic: Millennial Themes in American Thought, 1756–*

1800. Cambridge: Cambridge University Press.

Burke, Kenneth. 1984. *Attitudes toward History*. Berkeley and Los Angeles: University of California Press.

Carlson, A. Cheree. 1986. Gandhi and the Comic Frame: "Ad Bellum Purificandum." *Quarterly Journal of Speech* 72: 446–55.

Collins, John J. 1998. *The Apocalyptic Imagination: An Introduction to Jewish Apocalyptic Literature*. 2nd ed. Grand Rapids, Mich.: Eerdmans.

———, ed. 1979. Apocalypse: The Morphology of a Genre. Special issue, *Semeia* 14.

Creps, Earl. 1980. The Conspiracy Argument as Rhetorical Genre. PhD diss., Northwestern University.

Girard, René. 1977. *Violence and the Sacred*. Translated by Patrick Gregory. Baltimore, Md.: Johns Hopkins University Press.

———. 1987. *Things Hidden since the Foundation of the World*. Translated by Stephen Bann and Michael Metteer. Stanford, Calif.: Stanford University Press.

Hofstadter, Richard. 1979. *The Paranoid Style in American Politics and Other Essays*. Chicago: University of Chicago Press.

Maggin, Elliot S. 1997. The New Bards. Pages 5–7 in *Kingdom Come*. Written by Mark Waid. Illustrated by Alex Ross. New York: DC Comics.

McGinn, Bernard. 1979. *Visions of the End: Apocalyptic Traditions in the Middle Ages*. New York: Columbia University Press.

Moore, Alan, and Dave Gibbons. 1987. *Watchmen*. New York: DC Comics.

Muffs, Yochanan, and Thorkild Jacobsen. 1995. Who Will Stand in the Breach? A Study of Prophetic Intercession. Pages 9–48 in *Love and Joy: Law, Language, and Religion in Ancient Israel*. Edited by Yochanan Muffs and Thorkild Jacobsen. Jewish Theological Seminary Series. Cambridge, Mass.: Harvard University Press.

O'Leary, Stephen D. 1998. *Arguing the Apocalypse*. New York: Oxford.

Ostwalt, Conrad. 2003. *Secular Steeples: Popular Culture and Religious Imagination*. New York: Trinity.

Stone, Michael E. 1984. Apocalyptic Literature. Pages 383–441 in *Jewish Writings of the Second Temple Period*. Edited by Michael E. Stone. CRINT 2/2. Assen: Van Gorcum; Philadelphia: Fortress.

Storey, John. 2009. *Cultural Theory and Popular Culture: An Introduction*. 5th ed. Essex, Eng.: Pearson.

Waid, Mark, and Alex Ross. 1997. *Kingdom Come*. New York: DC Comics.

Zulick, Margaret D. 1992. The Agon of Jeremiah: On the Dialogic Invention of Prophetic Ethos. *Quarterly Journal of Speech* 78: 125–48.

Reading "Pop-Wise": The Very Fine Art of "Making Do" When Reading the Bible in bro'Town

Steve Taylor

Karl Barth once commented that the task of preaching necessitated holding the Bible in one hand and the newspaper in the other.[1] One assumes that in today's world, Barth would applaud the replacing of the newspaper with a keyboard mouse or television remote. The task of this chapter is to apply that assumption, by holding the Bible in one hand and the remote in the other, with particular regard to *bro'Town*, a contemporary television prime-time animated cartoon series.

This will be made possible by employing a "pop-wise" hermeneutic of "making do," a method that seeks to engage popular culture by foregrounding the reader within culturally enmeshed acts of reading. The argument will be made that by reading *bro'Town* "pop-wise," we encounter a specific critique of the cultural captivity of contemporary Bible-reading practices in Pacific Island communities, while still maintaining an explicit theological framing for identity and ethics.

Written and performed by a four-man comedy group, the Naked Samoans (Oscar Kightley, Dave Fane, Shimpal Lelisi, and Mario Gaoa), *bro'Town* follows the lives of five teenage boys (Vale, Valea, Jeff da Māori, Sione, and Mack) who live in the Auckland suburb of Morningside. In exploring issues including identity, morality, land, and racism, the series provides a contemporary window on New Zealand culture, with specific reference to the experience of growing up as second-generation Pacific Island migrants, who are presently an ethnic minority in New Zealand culture.

---

1. The reality, as with most things pertaining to Karl Barth, is more complex (see Barth n.d.).

Currently in its fifth (and last) season, the television show has gained critical acclaim. In the *New Zealand Listener,* Nippert (2004) wrote that *"bro'Town* has made history; it's the first adult animated series produced in New Zealand." Initial episodes attracted up to 70 percent of the fifteen- to twenty-nine-year-old viewing audience, while AGB Nielsen's media research identified *bro'Town* as the most popular television series among school children (Earl 2008, 4). It has generated a DVD series and a hardcover book called *The "bro'Town" Annual.* An accompanying Web site offers clothing accessories, including street wear such as T-shirts, sweatshirts, hoodies, and beanies, along with figurines, plus toys, and postcards. Product placement is prevalent, including Coke, Vodafone, G-Force, Starburst Sucks, and L&P.

Special guests feature prominently, including regular cameos from prime-time newsreaders (John Campbell and Carol Hirschfeld), then–New Zealand Prime Minister Helen Clark, sports stars (including Michael Jones and Stacey Jones), film stars (Lucy Lawless and Sam Neill), and musicians (including rapper Scribe). Overseas guests have included Prince Charles and Australian television host Rove McManus. Each *bro'Town* episode is littered with literary and pop-cultural references, including novels and short stories by New Zealand's Witi Ihimaera, and numerous film references.[2]

The series has strong religious references, with most episodes starting in heaven and including a dialogue between God, Jesus Christ, and other historical figures. These "heaven" scenes introduce the themes of each episode. This presents avenues, in both the themes and explicitly religious material, for a reading of the Bible in *bro'Town.*

But first, the methodological terrain demands consideration. To read the Bible in *bro'Town* is to risk dismissal on many scholarly fronts—theological, biblical, and cultural. A methodology is required by which one might undertake a reading of the Bible in *bro'Town* that is "pop-wise" and is a demonstration of the very fine art of "making do."

---

2. Some episode titles are a parody of movies, e.g., "Zeelander," a parody of the film *Zoolander;* "Morningside Story," of the musical *West Side Story;* and "In My Mother's Den," of novelist Maurice Gee's *In My Father's Den.*

METHODOLOGY: READING "POP-WISE"

Whakapapa: (Maori) [Fah-kah-pa-pa] Ancestry. (*The "bro'Town" Annual*, 7)

Theological engagement with culture is nothing new. David Ford (1997, 1–3) surveyed twentieth-century theology by positing a continuum between two poles—content and context—on which various theologies and theologians might be sited. These include:

- Repetition, a stance that primarily refutes culture.
- Engagement, a stance in which Christian revelation remains the primary resource, yet a need for continual rethinking is considered as a basis on which to engage contemporary culture.
- Correlation, a stance that seems to correlate human questions and longings with Christian revelation in order to articulate Christian beliefs and practices.
- Reinterpretation (or accommodation), a stance that accepts that cultural philosophies or worldviews can be a basis for reinterpreting Christian beliefs and practices.
- Capitulation, a stance that might commence by investigating Christianity on the basis of another worldview but results in a capitulation to that worldview.

What is helpful in Ford's schema is the realization that culture (according to Tanner: what is made "of the world, of the practices and beliefs of the wider society" [1997, 61]) is essential to the task of doing theology. Talk of God is always conditioned and shaped by social realities. To be otherwise makes no sense of the Christian understanding of a Word made flesh, incarnationally embodied in a specific (Jewish) reality.

What is problematic in Ford's scheme is what is implied: that Christian beliefs and practices can be constructed on a continuum as an entity in isolation from context. In reality, for Ward, the "concrete Church lives in the shifting and changing world and it is in particular contexts that it performs its tasks of witness and discipleship" (2008, 42).

Kathryn Tanner, drawing on changing notions of culture in the field of human anthropology, warns against "assumptions about culture as a summary of human universals" and instead urges "theologians to develop a primary interest in the particular" (1997, 65–66, 67). Tanner's approach would encourage an exploration of the particularities of a culture-specific activity, including an animated television cartoon series such as *bro'Town*. Her method is one of intuition and bricolage: "Transforming the use of shared ideas from a non-Christian to a Christian one is a piecemeal process, in short; the items of another culture are not taken up all at once but one by one or block by block" (117). Such a method allows the scholar to hold a Bible and to use a remote control for channel surfing through pop-cultural artifacts.

Three caveats are needed. First, a focus on the particular need not be at the expense of the universal. Rather, universality and particularity can work as two sides of a coin, enriching rather than assuming exclusive dualities. For Terry Veling,

> we only attain a sense of the "whole" through our participation in what is "particular" to our specific situations and places of belonging … a journey of intensification into the concreteness of each particular reality—*this* body, *this* people, *this* community, *this* tradition, *this* tree, *this* place, *this* moment, *this* neighbour—until the very concreteness in any particularity releases us to sense the concreteness of the whole as an internally related reality through and through.[3] (1996, xvii)

Second, such an exercise encourages conversation between both the particular and the universal. For Tanner, an essential task of the academic theologian is both "operations found in everyday theological investigation, [and] a searching for clarity, coherence and comprehensiveness" (1997, 86–87). Third, a focus on the particular in no way assumes that theology will end up being culturally captive. Rather, the focus is on the shape of witness and discipleship in particular contexts that proceed in ways that leave open the space for scholarly conversations with, and within, embedded contexts to remain both critical and creative.

Tanner's argument for a scholarly conversation among everyday pop-cultural practices finds echoes in the work of Gerald West (2007), who argues that the biblical scholar and the ordinary, non-scholarly readers read differently, yet a mutually respectful collaboration can be creatively beneficial. For West, this does not mean educating the non-scholarly (bro'Reader) to read the Bible in a trained, scholarly way. Rather, for Kahl, the aim is a research methodology that creates "a community of intuitive and critical interpreters both of whom understand and appreciate that they come to the biblical texts from different perspectives that are equally valid" (Kahl 2007, 154).

West argues that there is a primary task: that of reading in "particular social sites where there are already substantial local interpretive resources" (2007, 2). This can then be followed by a secondary task (peculiar to the academic reader rather than the pop reader) of reflecting on the reading process in a dialogue with already-existing and historic tools, including literary and historical ones. This

---

3. In the latter part of the quote, Veling is citing Tracy 1981, 382.

is similar to Tanner's notion of the academic theologian both reading culture-specific activities and conducting a search that is critical and creative, for clarity, coherence, and comprehensiveness, among already existing theological resources.

West (2007) advances the notion of "particular social sites," which is a helpful way to frame a reading of *bro'Town*. The research is conducted by scholars listening to readers in "particular social sites," including prisons in the United States and women's Bible studies in Brazil. Yet surely an animated pop-culture, prime-time cartoon such as *bro'Town* is also a "particular social site"? Although animated, it nevertheless remains a reading by four Polynesian men growing up within a minority culture.[4] As a pop-culture artifact, it requires specific skills in interpretation, yet so does the act of listening to any voice, human or animated, artistic or ordinary.

Hence, this chapter will embark on a pop-wise reading, in which reading the Bible in *bro'Town* (or any pop-cultural artifact) is a way for scholars, biblical and theological, to collaborate with non-scholarly, pop-cultural readers of the Bible, in particular in socially enmeshed sites (in this case, migrant Pasifika cultures), as a method that leaves open the space for critical theological reflection using already-existing and historic tools. This pop-wise method allows a collaboration between the bro'Reader and the academy, based on the understanding that all readers, bro' or scholarly, come to the biblical texts from different perspectives and need to be willing to embark in a mutually critical and creative conversation.

This section has considered a method that might preserve the integrity of both the theologian and the social context. What remains to be clarified is the involvement of the ordinary bro'Reader—in relation to production, to text, and to audience—as pop-cultural artifacts are read.[5] For that, we need to consider Michel de Certeau's method of "making do."

METHODOLOGY: READING "POP-WISE" BY "MAKING DO"

Bro: Short for brother. A term of endearment, roughly equivalent to mate or pal. (*The "bro'Town" Annual*, 6)

Michel de Certeau, a French Jesuit trained in historiography, advanced a research method that sought to avoid the imposition of a term like "popular culture" as

---

4. This is not to assume that the voice heard in *bro'Town* is not shaped by other voices, including editorial and commercial pressures. For detailed discussion, see du Gay et al. 1997.

5. For a detailed discussion of these concepts of production, text, and audience, see du Gay et al. 1997.

an external hermeneutical apparatus. He argued, most clearly in *The Practice of Everyday Life* (1984), for the need to read popular culture through the tactics of everyday practices—acts of window shopping, the way people dress, the practices of graffiti, advertising, purchasing, and cooking—as a way of respecting that ordinary people are "making do," engaging in creative, adaptive, and subversive processes in relation to the cultural world in which they are enmeshed.

This was "a practical science of the singular" (Certeau, Giard, and Mayol 1998, 256) that explored the scattered fragments of popular culture, listening for the absent voice from which new questions and, thus, new interpretive treatments could emerge:

> The purpose of this work is to make explicit the systems of operational combination which also comprise a "culture," and to bring to light the models of action characteristic of users whose status as the dominated element in society (a status that does not mean that they are either passive or docile) is concealed by the euphemistic term "consumers." Everyday life invents itself by poaching in countless ways on the property of others. (xi)

Hence, people are never passive in the face of popular culture. "The central thrust of *The Practice of Everyday Life* is thus to affirm the resilience and inventiveness of 'ordinary men and women' against the analyses which present them as entirely informed or crushed by the economic and cultural apparatuses which set the terms of social life" (Certeau 1984, xiii–xiv). Tasks of reading, interpretation, and meaning-making are being enacted in everyday practices, and by researching these often-overlooked artifacts, we are making them intelligible, or pop-wise.

A key framework behind Certeau's "making do" was the notion of the difference between strategies and tactics. Strategies involve the power relationships that institutions use to seek stability and to organize reality, while tactics are what people actually do with these strategies in everyday life.

Certeau called these tactics acts of "making do," everyday transformative processes in which individuals "poach," creatively subverting, in countless ways, the influence of popular culture.[6] This allowed a reading of the reader, their practices, and their social contexts, what Ahearne applauds as "a close linguistic analysis ... [that also shows] how their reinstrumentation of this material points to a general sociohistorical set of circumstances" (1995, 31). Employing

---

6. "Making do" was a "category of 're-employment' ... a conceptual tool which enables [Certeau] to organize and to interpret the material he collects ... [to focus on] mutating elements 'within' different systems [and] the specific uses and trajectories of formal elements as they are taken up and trans-formed in different practices" (Ahearne 1995, 29).

Certeau allows us to respect bro'Readers and their "particular social site."[7] In the ironic humor of their animated cartooning, they are "making do," mimicking and repeating, taking language and using it in new ways, engaging in subtle acts of resistance.

The theory applied in this way is to nuance the work of Certeau. For Certeau, "once the images broadcast by television and the time spent in front of the TV set have been analysed, it remains to be asked what the consumer makes of these images and during these hours" (1984, 31). Certeau sought to focus not on the reader in production but on the reader as audience. Nevertheless, without in any way sidelining the place of the audience—those who watch *bro'Town*—(simply leaving it for another research project), the reality remains that *bro'Town* as a production is a form of "making do." It is a tactic, a reading by four "readers"—their response to growing up as a minority—amid the strategies of both a dominant New Zealand culture and the Pasifika (including religious) culture of their parents. As the boys from *bro'Town* animate how they experience the Bible being read, as they cartoon God in heaven, dressed in a lavalava, so begins a pop-wise reading at a "particular social site."

Reading Animated Cartoons "Pop-Wisely"

Morningside 4 Life! The Boys' territorial expression of solidarity. (*The "bro'Town" Annual*, 7)

In order to undertake any reading, the genre must be appreciated. For *bro'Town*, this involves working with the genre of animated cartoon (a genre rare in theological and biblical scholarship, although widespread in contemporary popular culture).

In *Understanding Comics*, Scott McCloud defines a comic as "sequential visual art" (1993, 7). While aware that at times comics have been considered "at best a diversion for the masses, at worst a product of crass commercialism," McCloud notes a range of features he considers essential to the very fine art of interpreting comics (140).

First, for McCloud, cartooning is based on the techniques of "amplification through simplification, allowing [both the comic creator and the reader] to

---

7. Certeau applied his methodology not only to Western popular culture, but also in analysis of how Amerindians responded to processes of European colonization. (See Certeau and Giard 1997, 226–28; Certeau et al. 1998, 17–18. For a critique of Certeau, see Frow 1991; Schirato 1992).

focus on specific details" (1993, 30). Hence, "[s]implifying characters and images toward a purpose can be an effective tool for storytelling in any medium. Cartooning isn't just a way of drawing, it's a way of seeing" (31).

Second, cartoons function for McCloud as a way of seeing ourselves, as a "vacuum into which our identity and awareness are pulled" (1993, 36). While all art does this to some degree, McCloud argues that the "amplification through simplification" techniques inherent in the comic genre, in which nearly every line has a meaning, are highly significant:

> The comics creator asks us to join in a silent dance of the seen and the unseen. The visible and the invisible. This dance is unique to comics. No other art form gives so much to its audience while asking so much from them as well. This is why I think it's a mistake to see comics as a mere hybrid of the graphic arts and prose fiction. What happens between these [comic] panels is a kind of magic only comics can create … All I [as a comic creator] can do is make assumptions about you and hope that they're correct. (92–93)

Thus a feature of comics is that "amplification through simplification" is a genre that, because of its minimalism, demands an above-average set of shared assumptions between the creator and the readers' experiences.

Third, McCloud underlines the need to be aware of the genre of storytelling when approaching comics. Despite the mix of words and pictures, the comic is a sight-based mode of storytelling, and thus interpretive appreciation of plot, character, and setting are essential.

Finally, McCloud applauds the way that comics work as a form of art, defined as "the way we assert our identities as individuals and break out of the narrow roles nature casts us in" (1993, 166). Comic as a genre enhances the search for identity, for "making choices choice!" (a theme we return to in the section on "Reading God in *bro'Town*").

For McCloud, animation is a particular subset within a genre of cartoons. Both are "sequential visual art" and both require an interpretive strategy of "amplification through simplification." Katherine Sarafian argues that the interpretive key for reading digital animation is that "story rules" (2005, 222) . She writes that "computer animation may be a different kind of moviemaking, but it is rooted in the most traditional of storytelling and motion-picture-production techniques … Digital moviemakers use new and evolving tools to tell their stories, but however new the tools, the techniques still must be rooted in effective storytelling" (211).

Thus we now turn to *bro'Town* (and any cartoon animation), attentive to the way that cartooning works by "amplification through simplification," and to the place of plot, character, and setting in reading *bro'Town* pop-wise.

READING THE BIBLE IN *BRO'TOWN*

Morningside: The suburb where the Boys live (also an actual suburb in Auckland, New Zealand). (*The "bro'Town" Annual*, 7)

Given permission by Tanner for piecemeal and bricolage, the obvious place to commence a pop-wise reading of the Bible in *bro'Town* is to fast-forward, with the remote in one hand, to the one place in which the Bible is being visibly read.

This occurs in series 1, episode 2, entitled "Sionerella" (Bro'town 2004–2006). According to *The "bro'Town" Annual*, "Sionerella" was "the first script ever written" (Firehorse Films 2005, 62). The plot builds toward the Morningside school ball, held annually between St. Sylvester's School (for boys) and St. Cardinal's School for General Knowledge (for girls). The main character in this episode of *bro'Town* is named Sione, one of the "bro's."

The opening sequences of the episode sketch the tension needing to be resolved. The headmaster (Brother Ken) presides over a school assembly, during which he announces to Sione and the boys of St. Sylvester's School that entry to the annual ball will require parental permission. Further, to prepare the boys, the school will host a "Making Choices" sex-education workshop, led by special guest Lucy Lawless.

Sione wishes to invite Mila Jizovich and embarks on the process of gaining consent from his highly religious mother, Mrs. Tapili. As Mrs. Tapili prepares to sign the consent form, the television is playing in the lounge. News presenters (special guests) John Campbell and Carol Hirschfeld describe the upcoming school ball as "Morningside madness," sensationalizing it as "an annual all-night wanton sexual rampage [about which] parents have no idea," and note a 400 percent increase in unplanned teenage pregnancies as a result of previous school balls.

On hearing the news, Mrs. Tapili refuses permission. Despite personal intercession from one of Sione's school teachers (Lynn Grey), Sione is grounded for the night of the school ball. His dreams are shattered, and his prayer, prayed in the (second) opening scene—"Please God, make Mum let me go to the ball so that I can go with Mila Jizovich, the most beautiful girl in Morningside"—seems unanswered.

On the night of the ball, Mrs. Tapili reads to Sione from the Bible. The scene opens with the Bible, portrayed as big and black, and the voice of Mrs. Tapili saying "and all the evil people—celebrities, next-door neighbors, liars, school teachers and people who never go to church—all died happily ever after. Amen." Mrs. Tapili closes the Bible and announces that she is now going to the church women's fundraising committee and will return at midnight.

Given that cartoons demand appreciation of interpretative processes of "amplification through simplification, allowing [both the comic creator and the reader] to focus on specific details" (McCloud 1993, 30), it is worth noting that the Bible in this scene is depicted as big, black, and dominant. Further, the only voice, the only interpretation heard in this scene, is that of Mrs. Tapili. Thus, the act of biblical interpretation resides only with this parental authority figure.

Applying Certeau's method to this "particular [Morningside] social site," one can begin to ponder the very fine art of "making do." Since no biblical text literally names the presence of either "celebrities" or "school teachers," the reading by Mrs. Tapili is clearly an act of "making do." She has inserted characters—celebrities, next-door neighbors, liars, school teachers, and people who never go to church, all of whom appear in this episode of *bro'Town*—into this bro'Reading of the Bible.

Given the need to interpret animated cartoon as story, it is worth considering these characters one by one, for together they in fact form a range of "choices," offering an alternative identity code to the bro'Reading code being enacted by Mrs. Tapili.

In "Sionerella," the celebrities include Lucy Lawless, who hosts the "Making Choices" workshop and encourages safe sex. They also include news presenters John Campbell and Carol Hirschfeld, seen on TV as promoters of the school ball. The next-door neighbors include Pepelo Pepelo, father of Vale and Valea Pepelo, who narrates the ball as an opportunity for partying and sexual conquest. The school teachers include Lynn Grey (Ms.), who visits Mrs. Tapili, encouraging her to attend, with Sione, the "Making Choices" workshop. Including the category of those who don't go to church is a way of reinforcing difference, aligning the church with Mrs. Tapili's act of interpretation and placing that in opposition to cultural factors, including media and school.

Each of these characters thus offers Sione a choice. By inserting these categories into her bro'Reading, Mrs. Tapili is "making do": co-opting the Bible, visually big and black, to reinforce her moral code, labeling as "evil" those people who are offering Sione alternative choices. The Bible has already made an appearance, named but not depicted, earlier in this episode of *bro'Town*. In order to gain his mother's permission to attend the ball, Sione has undertaken a range of chores around the house. They earn praise from Mrs. Tapili: "Sione, you have changed Sampson's nappy, painted the house, cleaned the church, scrubbed the footpath, read the Bible to Sampson. What do you want?" This dialogue suggests that acts of Bible reading between family members are commonplace. A broader commentary is being made. Given that a hermeneutic of "making do" allows "a close linguistic analysis ... and also ... show[s] how their reinstrumentation of this material points to a general sociohistorical set of circumstances" (Ahearne 1995,

31), then reading the Bible to family members is a family custom that, when practiced, suggests reward and reinforces family values. Hence, underpinning this bro'Reading is an image of God as judge and the Bible as the weapon of choice, used to maintain a certain familial and religious ethic.

Religion as a means of judgment runs throughout "Sionerella." In the opening sequences, we see Brother Ken addressing the school assembly with the line: "Hush, or you will all burn in hell." A church scene includes the Reverend Minister preaching: "God is good. Of course, we all know what happens at school balls. Just look at the first five rows of sluts, sitting in this church." These acts of "amplification by simplification"—of how parents use the Bible, of ministers that judge, of religion as judgmental—become a critique of the way that the Bible is being read within contemporary Pasifika cultures.

Reading the Bible in *bro'Town* points to practices in which the Bible becomes an instrument of adult and ecclesial power, to create a judgmental and oppositional stance between "the world" and the "religion/familial system."

It should be noted that neither *bro'Town* nor this chapter is making a normative claim as to the accuracy of this reading. That is not the point of the cartoon genre and the technique of "amplification through simplification." The methodology section drew attention to the work of Ward (2008), who describes the layers at work in a pop-cultural text: of production, text, and audience. The act of "making do" described above is a production (by the Naked Samoans) placed in a text (*bro'Town*). One could test the "universality" of this reading by researching the audience. Is this really how the Bible is used in Pacific Island communities? Whatever the result of such research, this act of "making do" remains. It highlights the substantial local interpretive resources at work in this context, holding a mirror to practices of Bible reading in "particular social sites." Does the reading serve the intentions of the local power group? How open are the readers to their own acts of eisegesis? Are multiple voices allowed in the reading?

At this point, the academy might be interested not just in the first bro'Reading, but in the second task, that of dialogue with existing and historic tools, including the literary and the historical. In particular, it is noteworthy that the list, as composed by Mrs. Tapili, has echoes of the "vice lists" that are common in the New Testament. A scholarly question then becomes: in what ways do these New Testament vice lists need to be reexamined in light of the questions of power and eisegesis that are raised by the bro'Reading.

One such vice list occurs in Rev 21:7–8. It is worth considering, given that, as with Mrs. Tapili, Revelation is a book fascinated with judgment and with endings. Further, for Michaels, Rev 21:3–8 "captures in a nutshell the meaning of the entire book" (1997, 235). Yet commentators conclude that this "vice list" should "be read as invitations to all who read" (Michaels 1997, 238–39). Further, the "key is to realize [that the vice list] ... is addressed to the reader" (Osborne 2002, 239–40). As such, the world or wider scholarship would wish to offer a critical reflection on the bro'Reading of Mrs. Tapili, the minister, and Brother Ken. In Revelation, "vice lists" critique the church, inviting the church "to decide where we wish to stand at the last judgment" (Michaels 1997, 239–40).

It is tempting to stop at this juncture, aware of the critique of Bible-reading practices being offered by *bro'Town*. However, to stop would be to overlook the fact that these images of judgment, while maintained by the church and its adherents, are not the only images of God. Each episode of *bro'Town* opens and closes with a "God in heaven" scene, and thus there are further layers that need to be considered in a pop-wise reading of the Bible in *bro'Town*.

READING GOD IN *BRO'TOWN*

Ho weh: An exclamation, roughly equivalent to "Wow!" (*The "bro'Town" Annual*, 7)

Alongside the very specific critique of Bible reading in *bro'Town* runs a continuing (theological) engagement with God. For Nippert, "In heaven, God wears a lavalava. He's an Islander with a chiseled chest and beard. His only begotten son sulks in his room listening to angst rock over Easter ... [This] depiction of the almighty—[is] probably the most inventive take on the divine since a giggling, mute Alanis Morissette played God in [the movie] *Dogma*" (2004).

Despite the claim that "God is dead," in the new millennium we find God opening and closing on prime-time popular culture television. If animated cartoons require interpretation as story, then these God scenes deserve attention. These will be explored under categories of God as creator, as active agent, and as ethical teacher.[8]

GOD AS CREATOR

The "bro'Town" Annual opens with a "Letter from God." This describes God's pleasure in creation: "After seven days, I thought, stuff this ... so I turned on the sun, sprinkled in some stars and a lovely moon, and thought to myself ... what a wonderful world! (oh yeah, there were trees of green, and red roses)" (*The "bro'Town" Annual*, 4–5). This theme of God as Creator introduces "Sionerella."

---

8. That these are deliberately Trinitarian, in line with God as Creator, Redeemer, and Sustainer, is an authorial assertion.

God speaks: "Hi. My name's God. I created birds and bees, flowers and the trees, and a crazy little thing called love. That's what this story is all about: Love, or amore, or alofa, or aroha."

God as creator is depicted as taking delight at the particular social site that is Morningside: "so I created Morningside … a town full of love and laughter, and people from lots of different ethnic groups … and somehow, I ended up introducing a television sitcom," and the people who live there, "that I have become rather fond of" (*The "bro'Town" Annual*, 4). A theology of incarnation is at work. To rephrase John 1:14, "The Word became flesh, dressed in a lavalava and moved into Pasifika culture."

The opening of "Sionerella" finds God in heaven, surrounded by palm trees. He is playing cards, specifically "Strip Jack Naked," with a bald-headed person, presumably Buddha. Whether this is playful or disrespectful might depend on where the viewer places him- or herself on the continuum (from repetition to capitulation) provided by Ford earlier. Given the need to respect genre, one clue regarding how to interpret this portrayal of God is provided by the presence of special guests on *bro'Town*. When a Prime Minister such as Helen Clark, or newsreaders like John Campbell or Carol Hirschfeld, present themselves to be cartoons, they declare a willingness to be subjected to the interpretive processes of cartooning and the humor created by "amplification through simplification."

GOD AS ACTIVE AGENT

God acts not only as creator in *bro'Town*, but also as active agent. An important scene in "Sionerella" takes place in a Pasifika church. We see the cars in a church parking lot, the congregants all dressed in white (typical Pacific Island church-going attire), and we hear the minister preaching. As Sione listens, his head starts to spin. He is surrounded by a variety of voices: the minister yelling "Sinners beware" and "Go to hell"; Mrs. Tapili's exclaiming "Praise the Lord" and "Thank the Lord"; Sione's friend Mack, offering an alternative voice, "I wouldn't put up with it" and "That's not fair."

In confusion, Sione cries out: "Why me, God?" The camera pans up toward heaven, where God is reading a newspaper. The cartoon genre allows humor to be created visually, even when not part of the verbal dialogue. Thus in this scene, the newspaper is the *Morningside Star* and the headlines include "Devil caught in a blue dress" and "Heaven 17; Hell 0." And God announces, in this episode and in response to Sione's cry for help, that God moves in mysterious ways.

As the episode concludes, Sione's prayer is answered. Through a set of mysterious circumstances, Sione does get to attend the ball and to dance with Mila.

Thematically, God has been portrayed as active, answering prayer and shaping circumstances in Morningside.

GOD AS ETHICAL TEACHER

God acts not only as creator and active agent in *bro'Town*, but also as ethical teacher. The episode of "Sionerella" concludes with a scene in heaven. Prayers have been answered in Morningside and God has the last word: "Well, if there's one thing that I know, and I know everything, it's all about choices. Me bless Morningside! Me bless me! Choice!"

Given that "choice" is a popular colloquial term to describe something positive, at one level this is simply a placing of colloquial words in the mouth of God. Yet the theme of making choices has been woven through this episode. It is the name of the sex education workshop offered by St. Sylvester's. It is central in the church scene and the spinning voices in Sione's head. As a teenager, Sione is making choices about his identity, how he treats women, and how he responds to the belief system of his family.

Indeed, Sione offers a nuanced reading of what it means to make choices with regard to gender relationships. In an early scene, Mila Jizovich, who is best friends with Sione's sister (Sina Tapili), is at Sione's house. The two teenage girls are comparing dresses in preparation for the ball.

Sione's friends arrive and crudely ask Sione if Mila is naked. This juvenile comment earns a rebuke from Sione: "She's not that kind of girl." Within this circle of teenage boys, Sione is refusing to pursue an understanding of relationships in exclusively sexual terms. Later, at the ball, the relationship between Sione and Mila is depicted as romantic, with Sione singing to Mila rather than acting sexual. Thus, in "Sionerella," Sione is making choices. And perhaps the choices he makes are the reason that God does answer prayer and, in the final heaven scene, blesses Morningside.

This argument could be pushed further. If God is creator and God is active agent, then is God also offering the last word regarding the very fine art of reading the Bible pop-wise in *bro'Town*? "Me bless Morningside! Me bless me!" can in fact be interpreted as offering two guidelines for ethical decision making and for biblical interpretation. First, it suggests a reading that blesses the whole community of Morningside and not simply the ethics of the religio/familial system. Second, a reading that blesses God would challenge any group that domesticates the Bible in acts of eisegesis (whether Mrs. Tapili, the Naked Samoans, or academic scholars). Thus, "making choices choice!" is in fact an alternative to the Bible practices being critiqued in *bro'Town* and stands against exclusive readings by dominant power groups.

Conclusion: "Making Choices Choice!"

Ow: A word or sound often used to end a sentence for emphasis." (*The "bro'Town" Annual*, 7)

Ward (2008, 191) argues that the mediation of theological expression in popular culture represents a vital and missiological challenge. This chapter has taken up this challenge with particular reference to the Bible in *bro'Town*. It has focused on only one episode, leaving many more episodes for further reflection and suggesting the richness of the pop-cultural terrain for theology and biblical studies.

A methodology has been advanced that might allow a scholar to read pop-wise, with the ordinary reader, within particular social sites, and in ways that preserve the integrity of the academy, the bro'Reader, the specific social context, and the genre (specifically that of animated cartoon).

This fine art of "making do" has then been applied to an episode of *bro'Town* to argue that by reading pop-wise, we encounter a specific critique of the cultural captivity of contemporary Bible-reading practices in Pacific Island communities.

This presents a challenge to the academy, the reader, and the church today. How might the Bible be read in ways that allow for critique of dominant power groups? How might we help people in cultural contexts that are fluid, migrant, and multicultural be part of "making choices choice!"?

Yet despite the critique of existing Bible-reading practices in "Sionerella," this episode in fact offers an answer to these questions, through the explicit theological framing of God as creator, as active agent, and as ethical teacher. Hence, *bro'Town* can be read as advancing an alternative hermeneutic for Bible reading, in ways that bless the community and maintain God's active agency.

Such are the possibilities when one practices reading *bro'Town* "pop-wise," utilizing the very fine art of "making do."

Works Cited

Ahearne, Jeremy. 1995. *Michel de Certeau: Interpretation and Its Other.* Cambridge: Polity.

Barth, Karl. n.d. Quotes by Karl Barth. Princeton Seminary Library. Online: http://libweb.ptsem.edu/collections/barth/faq/quotes.aspx?menu=296&subText=468.

Bro'town. 2004–2006. DVD. Written and performed by the Naked Samoans. Produced by Elizabeth Mitchell. Auckland, N.Z.: Firehorse Films.

Certeau, Michel de. 1984. *The Practice of Everyday Life.* Translated by Steven F. Rendell. Berkeley and Los Angeles: University of California Press.

———. 1986. *Heterologies: Discourse on the Other.* Minneapolis: University of Minnesota Press.

——, and Luce Giard. 1997. *The Capture of Speech and Other Political Writings*. Minneapolis: University of Minnesota Press.

——, Luce Giard, and Pierre Mayol. 1998. *The Practice of Everyday Life. Volume 2: Living and Cooking*. Minneapolis: University of Minnesota Press.

du Gay, Paul, et al. 1997. *Doing Cultural Studies: The Story of the Sony Walkman*. Thousand Oaks, Calif.: Sage.

Earl, Emma. 2008. Brand New Zealanders: The Commodification of Polynesian Youth Identity in *bro'Town*. MA thesis. University of Canterbury.

Firehorse Films. 2005. *The "bro'Town" Annual*. Auckland: Random House.

Ford, David F. 1997. Introduction to Modern Christian Theology. Pages 1–3 in *The Modern Theologians: An Introduction to Christian Theology in the Twentieth Century*. Edited by David F. Ford. 2nd ed. Oxford: Blackwell.

Frow, John. 1991. Michel de Certeau and the Practice of Representation. *Cultural Studies* 5, no. 1: 52–60.

Hall, Douglas J. 1982. "Who Tells the World's Story?" Theology's Quest for a Partner in Dialogue. *Interpretation* 36: 47–53.

Kahl, Werner. 2007. Growing Together: Challenges and Chances in the Encounter of Critical and Intuitive Interpreters of the Bible. Pages 147–58 in *Reading Other-Wise: Socially Engaged Biblical Scholars Reading with Their Local Communities*. Edited by Gerald O. West. SemeiaSt 62. Atlanta: Society of Biblical Literature.

McCloud, Scott. 1993. *Understanding Comics: The Invisible Art*. New York: Harper Collins.

Michaels, J. Ramsey. 1997. *Revelation*. Downers Grove, Ill.: InterVarsity.

Nippert, Matt. 2004. The Simpsons of the South Pacific. *New Zealand Listener* 195, no. 3359. Online: http://www.listener.co.nz/issue/3359/features/2630/the_simpsons_of_the_south_pacific.html.

Osborne, Grant R. 2002. *Revelation*. Grand Rapids, Mich.: Baker.

Sarafian, Katherine. 2005. Flashing Digital Animations: Pixar's Digital Aesthetic. Pages 209–23 in *Digital Matters: The Theory and Culture of the Matrix*. Edited by Paul A. Taylor and Jan Ll. Harris. New York: Routledge.

Schirato, Tony. 1992. My Space or Yours? De Certeau, Frow, and the Meanings of Popular Culture. *Cultural Studies* 7, no. 2: 282–91.

Tanner, Kathryn. 1997. *Theories of Culture: A New Agenda for Theology*. Minneapolis: Fortress.

Tracy, David. 1981. *The Analogical Imagination: Christian Theology and the Culture of Pluralism*. New York: Crossroad.

Veling, Terry A., and Thomas H. Groome. 1996. *Living in the Margins: Intentional Communities and the Art of Interpretation*. New York: Crossroad.

Ward, Pete. 2008. *Participation and Mediation: A Practical Theology for the Liquid Church*. London: SCM.

West, Gerald O. 2007. Reading Other-wise: Socially Engaged Biblical Scholars Reading with Their Local Communities: An Introduction. Pages 1–5 in *Reading Other-Wise: Socially Engaged Biblical Scholars Reading with Their Local Communities*. Edited by Gerald O. West. SemeiaSt 62. Atlanta: Society of Biblical Literature.

Texts and Their Afterlives in Literature Again: A Frame

Daemons and Angels: The End of the World according to Philip Pullman

Tina Pippin

"Children's stories ... these are children's stories! How can they help us?"
— woman bystander to Jesus in Martin Scorsese's *Last Temptation of Christ*

"The Bible: A Grim Fairy Tale"
— bumper sticker in Atlanta, Ga.

The Never-Ending Story

Once upon a time, in a land far away but very much like our own, there was a kingdom. There were seven cities in this kingdom, and all of them paid tribute to a king who lived far away in another realm and had always been absent from his land. In the cities dwelled many good people who remained loyal to this absent king. There were evil ones living among the good folks as well, and when an enemy nation conquered and reigned over the seven cities, there were many who gave allegiance to the new controlling power, headed by an evil queen who lived in a grand capital. Those who pledged obedience to and worshipped the enemy queen were promised great riches and power, as long as the ruling force remained victorious. After many years of longing for their king to return and defeat the queen and her armies, the good people began to lose hope that their king would fulfill his promise to return.

The queen had a magic cup in which she had extracted the essence of all those people in the cities who pledged loyalty to her. Her cup held their very souls. She promised eternal life and wealth. Her intentions were to build an empire organized around allegiance to imperial values. But to do so, she drained her subjects of their individuality and maturity; they remained zombielike[1] followers of the queen.

This sorry state of affairs went on for many years, until one day the king sent a great warrior to rescue the ones who remained obedient to him, both dead and alive. This supernatural fighter brought an angel army and set out to conquer the queen and her cohorts, powerful beasts, mighty armies, and many kings of other nations.

The nations fought in a great battle. The king's angel army poured out a fire that consumed the queen and her minions. The angel army sent the remnant of obedient subjects to the king's realm, where they lived out their days in a walled city, in a land that never knew night. And they all lived forever in the light of this king; whether or not it was happily, we will never know.

✱✱✱✱✱✱

This familiar fantasy tale takes us to numerous alternate universes. We can cut windows between worlds—our own and the various apocalyptic scenarios—to imagine the end of this world and the possibility of life after its death. The Apocalypse of John engages in a grand containment policy, reeling in women's sexuality and controlling all aspects of life and death. Not until later apocalypses, those of Peter and Paul, do the tours of hell begin. John leaves us staring into the abyss and the lake of fire and up to heaven where the good souls will eventually land. There is no ambiguity in the spatial binaries of the Apocalypse; the correct choice is clear. And the apocalyptic landscape is full of choices.

In my search for creative responses to the last book of the Bible, I am always looking for alternative visions in popular culture. About two years ago I finally got around to reading Philip Pullman's *His Dark Materials* trilogy. I had just finished reading to my seven-year-old daughter the entire Narnia series, subjecting her to my frequent rants about C. S. Lewis's theology. I needed to cleanse my palate, as it were, so I picked up Pullman's series, determined to bracket this reading not for some possible academic purpose but for pure pleasure, an attempt to relive the experience of reading Tolkien for the first time in middle school. The story and the characters in Pullman's trilogy drew me in, speaking loudly against the Apocalypse.

---

1. "A zombie is someone whose soul has been stolen, whose body has not exactly died but passed into the power of a magician or owner who uses it for his (rarely her) own purposes" (Warner 2006, 357).

Fantastic apocalyptic scenarios abound in recent fantasy fiction and film. The end of the world is imagined as an imminent possibility, and only the foolish would ignore the signs of the time. These stories, from *The Day After Tomorrow* to *The Road* to *2012*, focus on a singular universe in the present or near-present time. The line of history has unfortunately but reasonably led from creation to destruction, with only the residual survivors remaining. These stories usually evoke the uncanny, the more horrific edges of the fantastic.

Philip Pullman's *His Dark Materials* trilogy takes the reader through parallel universes and multiple apocalyptic fantasies, thus playing with the notion of human sin and culpability concerning the end time. Fantasy writers such as Tolkien, Lewis, and Le Guin evoke imaginative worlds that nonetheless face the same danger of extinction. The stories pull me in; they offer a journey into alternate apocalyptic worlds and a reimagination of the future. I want to know how Pullman reads the Apocalypse and how to read the Apocalypse through Pullman's series. In his redrafting of some of the main tenets of theology—cosmos, God, heaven, hell, apocalypse—how is he also redrafting (the) Apocalypse? In *His Dark Materials*, and especially the third book, *The Amber Spyglass*, the world almost—but not quite/does not—ends. The hera or shero, eleven-year-old Lyra (and later, her friend Will), is able to save the worlds through her (their) bold actions. There is hope, but not in the form of the biblical apocalypse. For Pullman, hope lies in brave young people who, through amazing courage and wisdom, are able to counter the destructive forces.

The basic plot of the *His Dark Materials* trilogy is as follows: Lyra, with her daemon-spirit Pantalaimon, grows up at Judson College at the Oxford University of an alternative universe. She has been left to the care of these scholars by her famous father, Lord Asriel. When Lord Asriel, whom Lyra believes is her uncle, visits, she hides in a wardrobe (a direct response to Lewis's wardrobe) to hear Lord Asriel's top-secret talk about the substance of "Dust." After the mysterious kidnapping of children begins in Oxford, Lyra seeks the truth. She is taken in by her evil mother, Mrs. Coulter, to be used as a lure for other children. Mrs. Coulter works for the Magisterium, a mysterious church council that is intent on experimenting on children to extract their Dust, a substance that comes from the separation of a child from its daemon, or companion animal spirit. Dust is the substance of original sin, and the Church wants to keep children in perpetual innocence. This separation results in the creation of zombielike children or, worse, death. Daemons shape-shift before puberty into a variety of animals and settle into one form only during puberty.

Lyra discovers a window into an alternate Oxford, where she meets a physicist, Mary Malone, and a boy, Will. In *The Subtle Knife* and *The Amber Spyglass*, Lyra and Will, and somewhat separately Mary, begin to cross the boundaries of universes to solve the mystery of Dust and stop the end of the world. They are pursued by Mrs. Coulter and by Lord Asriel, with a lot of plot twists and intervention (helpful and not) by magical creatures. They discover a magic knife, a subtle knife, that can cut windows into other worlds, and an amber spyglass that allows the viewer to see Dust.

ON THE TRAIL AGAIN

Most recent apocalyptic television, novels, and films are about "apocalypse as usual." After an Armageddon-like event, the survivors—and there are always survivors—engage in a continuing but downscaled battle of good versus evil. Amidst isolation, secrecy, and government conspiracies, the survivors attempt to rebuild the American nation ("Jericho," *The Day After Tomorrow* et al., *28 Days Later*, even *The Children of Men*, in a near-apocalypse Britain). The Left Behind series (plural) are based on this premise, although in much more cosmically divine ways. These dispensationalist, premillennialist Christian fantasies are a mirror image to our own world, but a world in which the Rapture has taken place and we are in the midst of the Tribulation. Since hell (or the dress-rehearsal for hell) is more interesting than heaven, Tribulation Trail and "Hell Houses" provided cathartic carnivals for living for the future and enduring the present.

Tribulation Trail enacts this alternate realm; you can pass through the gate (window) into this other universe—and back out again—all in about an hour. Tribulation Trail lulls us into acceptance of inevitability of (the) apocalypse. Inspired by Pullman's idea of journeying between worlds, I once again took a trip to the Tribulation Trail at Mount Vernon Baptist church in Stockbridge, Georgia. Since the trail is so popular and crowded, I brought P. D. James's *The Children of Men* in my coat pocket, just in case (of a delay in the Parousia). There were several additions to the trail: an enhanced Satan, two Jesuses, and a lot of noisy pyrotechnical heat. John of Patmos appeared first, on a beach complete with bonfire, palm trees, and gentle ocean sounds. Keeping the South Pacific theme, tiki torches lit the trail. There was death and screaming and machine-gun fire in the distance throughout. "Why didn't I listen?" was the constant mantra as relatives who were "left behind" searched for babies and raptured spouses. Those left behind were encouraged to die a martyr's death by refusing the mark of the beast (given by soldiers wearing United Nations armbands). At an instructional facility, the prisoners were ordered to receive the mark or die; if they refused the mark, then psychologists subjected the believers to their deepest fears, in an apocalyptic version of the television reality show "Fear Factor." And in a guest cameo appearance, Nicolai Carpathia, the Antichrist from LaHaye and Jenkins' series, appears, dressed in diplomatic garb.

The culminating experience on the trail is the Last Judgment. Jesus appears dressed in white on a high throne in a white room. The one to be judged that night is Reverend Jones, pastor of a ten-thousand-plus–member megachurch. Reverend Jones is so excited to see Jesus; it is what he's been waiting for all his life. He has worked hard for Jesus, building a church, leading countless people to Jesus, healing, and exorcising demons. He had a jet and a television ministry. He knows the Bible he waves in his right hand by heart. But his name is not in the Book of Life. Jesus tells him that being good and doing good were not enough: "All you had to do was believe!" Evidently, Rev. Jones had Jesus in his head and not his heart; he immediately begins praying the sinner's prayer, inviting Jesus into his heart. But it is too late. "There must be some mistake!" he moans as he is carried away to hell by the angel guards. An attending angel then hands Jesus a huge six-foot sword that he lifts up threateningly. I found myself wanting to defend this minister whose theology and politics are so opposite of my own.

By the time we got to the next (and last stop), the River of Life (with a hose spewing water in definite violation of the drought restrictions in Georgia), I could still hear the constant gunfire, the screams. Heaven was a bit disconcerting to me, as the sounds of suffering and death surrounded it. The description of the New Jerusalem fell flat for me amidst such constant violence.

At the end of the Trail, an evangelist gathered our group. She wore "higher the hair, the closer to God" blonde hair and a "got Jesus?" T-shirt, and related that she had gone "from the bar stool to the Bible." She told us that the actual Tribulation would be a hundred times worse than what we had just experienced. She wanted to lead us to certainty, as her mentor, a messianic Jew, had. "I want you to go to heaven with me," she pleaded, before leading us in prayer. She reminded us that although we are all creations of God, we are not all children of God—a definite warning to look back at the trail and see what fate awaits us if we are not certain of our salvation.

Many parts of the trail looked like scenes from *The Children of Men*—bleak, chaotic landscapes of suffering and death. But I realized that I should have instead brought *The Amber Spyglass* with me. Lyra's journey is apocalyptic; she lives in apocalyptic times. It is through her courage in fighting against the apocalyptic powers and Authority that she is able to save the universe/s. Lyra, a bit like Jesus in the Apostles' Creed, descends to the dead, but with different results. Or rather, she ascends to the dead-but-not-entirely-dead ghostly creatures in Pullman's vision of an afterlife controlled by a weak deity's minions. Marina Warner offers a more transparent description of heavenly bodies: "In a sense this is the apocalyptic condition: in the vision of the end, the flesh is resurrected not as flesh but as image-flesh, a form of angelic *apatheia*, or non-feeling, cyber-matter, which feels nothing and occupies nowhere but the screen, no time except the present unfolding through whatever medium of communication it is assuming as its vehicle" (2006, 352). Suddenly, heaven is less desirable. Such a grim vision of heaven leads Pullman to erase it altogether, collapsing heaven and hell into an eternal soul prison.

Lyra has to separate (painfully) from her daemon and in a certain sense die in order to enter the realm of the dead. She becomes a traveler in the most distant of lands, crossing by boat a terrifying, waterlike Styx. When they reach the island of death, they encounter all the dead from all the universes. Pullman describes the space of the dead through one of the dead: "Because the land of the dead isn't a place of reward or a place of punishment. The good come here as well as the wicked, and all of us languish in this gloom forever, with no hope of freedom, or joy, or sleep, or rest, or peace" (2000, 286). Lyra offers to lead the dead out into the world (if they can find an opening); she tells them, "You'll drift apart, it's true, but you'll be out in the open, part of everything alive again" (286). In a pantheistic move, Pullman puts the afterlife back into all creation in a form of ashes to ashes, dust to dust.

So Lyra and Will and all the dead/ghosts must scale the edge of the Abyss to find an opening out of the Authority's containment policy. But the windows they cut between universes are the openings for Dust to leak out and allow these specters to come from the Abyss; these evil creatures feed on Dust and humans. Without Dust, the universes, along with people, animals, and trees, will die. Dust is the creative substance of the created order, and the travelers between worlds are damaging the environments of the multiple worlds.

When Lyra and Will find the Authority, he is a feeble old man in a crystal coffin. Here's Pullman's description of his imagined God-figure:

> Between them they helped the ancient of days out of his crystal cell; it wasn't hard, for he was as light as paper, and he would have followed them anywhere, having no will of his own, and responding to simple kindness like a flower to the sun. But in the open air there was nothing to stop the wind from damaging him, and to their dismay his form began to loosen and dissolve. Only a few moments later he had vanished completely, and their last impression was of those eyes, blinking in wonder, and a sigh of the most profound and exhausted relief. Then he was gone: a mystery dissolving in mystery. (2000, 367)

Pullman is interested in children's literature that explores "the death of God and its consequences" (2001, 655). He summarizes: "Anyway, I take it that there really is no God anymore; the old assumptions have all withered away. That's my starting point: that the idea of God with which I was brought up is now perfectly incredible" (655). His main question relating to the afterlife is: "What happens to the Kingdom of Heaven when the King dies?" (655). For Pullman, God does not exist and even when God does make an appearance in fantasy, God has to be killed off. In this scene, God is words that crumble apart when lifted up.

In this regard, Pullman is vastly different from C. S. Lewis. Pullman has no kind word for Lewis's Narnia books. In the Narnia tales, the children can live out the ultimate fantasy of battling evil and ruling a kingdom, even witnessing the death and later resurrection of Jesus ... I mean, Aslan the lion. Pullman is especially opinionated about *The Last Battle* (Lewis 1984), in which the family dies. They all go to heaven, except for the eldest daughter, Susan, since "She's interested in nothing nowadays except nylons and lipstick and invitations. She always was a jolly sight too keen on being grown-up" (169). Pullman comments that Lewis is "a paranoid bigot" (Pullman 2001, 660) in killing off Susan and the others. He clearly takes Susan's side. He is more interested in this world with all its messiness—of puberty and nylons and growing up and old, of not everyone acting or looking alike (659). He believes that fantasy literature serves children best when it allows for their full development.

The Eve of the book of Genesis is rewritten through the character of Lyra and resurrected to come fully into the knowledge of good and evil, to find God, the Authority, to attempt to bring/haul him into the light, but when she does, he crumbles, shatters (into dust?). But he is useless anyway, an ineffectual but not harmless tyrant, a propped-up figurehead. And the universe/s are better off without him. He has confined the dead in a netherworld—into a perpetual hyper-zombielike state that mirrors the Magisterium's Dust experiments on children. Lyra, in a bit of a hospice-chaplain role, allows/affirms their death, and leads them into death. Pullman wants to lead his readers out of Narnia, even out of Middle Earth, into the Oxfords of his imagination. These worlds (continue to) hold apocalyptic potential, even after and because of the "final battle" in *The Amber Spyglass*. Thus we (readers) are pulled into possibilities—of life, our own maturity, a rejection of the mad apocalyptic deity.

The "sleep" of death (restless, unsettled) of our being stuck in endless apocalypses—of our own (biological, chemical, nuclear, etc.) or of God's making (or both)—is ended by an eleven-year-old girl who passes through apocalypse. We might be stuck in Left Behind's New Babylon, as one of the Tribulation Force, of course, or in one form or another of traditional theological thinking (or refusal to think) about the apocalypse. As Eve, Lyra gives us a new fruit to eat. Eat it and gain the knowledge of justice—antiapocalypse. Pullman takes great issue with the story of "the Fall" in Genesis. The choice is not immortality and not acceptance of death by apocalyptic means. For Pullman, the only choice is this world, the work to be done in the present.

When the dead in *The Amber Spyglass* emerge out of the underworld, they disperse into the universe, not into nothingness but back full-cycle into the very stuff of creation. Warner explains:

> So *His Dark Materials* resists apocalypse in favor of what Gerald Manley Hopkins called *haeccitas*, the thisness of things, the phenomenon of the here and now, the flesh you can pinch and that feels pain, the base, raw material of life. Pullman has in many ways dramatized—for children!—an epic claim that resounds to Blake's antinomian axiom, "Everything that lives is holy." This is to make large claims for Pullman, but it is important to note his swerves and soarings away from the usual apocalyptic script. (2006, 348)

In the trilogy, Lyra rejects the canonical "kingdom of God" and instead opts for working toward a "republic of heaven." For Pullman, "heaven" is "joy," as humans, not some transcendent God, create it in this world, individually and communally—not in some transcendent afterlife. Against Gnosticism and Lewis (and LaHaye), Pullman relates, drawing from William Blake: "it enables us to see this real world, our world, as a place of infinite delight, so intensely beautiful and intoxicating that if we saw it clearly then we would want nothing more, ever. We would know that this earth is our true home, and nowhere else is" (2001, 655).[2] LaHaye and the premillennialists are ironically quite gnostic in their assessment of the future of Earth. Pullman counters, "The Gnostic situation is a dramatic one to be in; it's intensely exciting; but it's the sort of paranoid excitement felt by those militia groups who collect guns and hide in the hills and watch out for the black helicopters of the evil New World Order as they prepare for Armageddon. It's nuts, basically" (2001, 658).

Good and evil battle it out on the field of Megiddo; this earth shall pass away for the new earth. Jerusalem is leveled for the New Jerusalem, all cleared of Jews, Muslims, and all non-premillennial Christians. Meanwhile, Pullman dreams of a democratic republic, without a vengeful, apocalyptic deity.

---

2. Pullman further explains his approach: "I'm an atheist. But we need heaven nonetheless, we need all the things that heaven meant, we need joy, we need a sense of meaning and purpose in our lives, we need a connection with the universe, we need all the things that the kingdom of heaven used to promise us but failed to deliver. And furthermore, we need it in this world where we do exist—not elsewhere, because there ain't no elsewhere" (Hatlen 2005, 92). [This doesn't seem like something from Pullman's The Amber Spyglass [= Pullman 2000]; do you mean that Pullman said this in 2000? If so, only the Hatlen reference is necessary. If not, just quote it from Pullman.]

Pullman also takes issue with J. R. R. Tolkien's more-distant orthodoxy in *The Lord of the Rings*. Good and evil are too clearly delineated in both these fantasy epics. Pullman likes the gray areas, the complexities of the spaces in and in between good and evil. For example, the characters are multifaceted, neither all good nor all evil. At the beginning of the trilogy Lyra saves Lord Asriel from being poisoned, and he in turn leads the opposition to the Church and the plot to kill the Authority (God). But he is also murderous (of Lyra's friend Roger) and consistently cruel. The harpies in the underworld appear evil at first but are able to assist in Lyra's liberation scheme. And most of all, childhood is the time of innocence but the real joy is the journey into adulthood.

Pullman is being anti-Nietzschean in his drawing of the kingdom of heaven for children (see Lenzen 1989, 69). Dieter Lenzen notes "that the erosion of the childlike is rooted in the doctrine of redemption" in which a child Jesus becomes an adult and then is "killed in order that we might become what He is: children of God" (73). For Lenzen, desire to return to childhood creates a "libidinous relationship to the apocalypse" (73–74) in which the fear of death must be replaced, since anxiety about death and the end of the world is a necessary component of adulthood (76–77). In Lenzen's view, our culture wants both eternal childhood and "a nasty End of the World, the contemplation of which might be well adapted to dissipate the boredom resulting, of necessity, from the first" (78).

Although Pullman's tale centers around children, he will not let us stay in some childlike state. Lyra and Will move toward and into puberty; their salvation is in becoming adults. They do not die or get eaten by daemon-separating machines. As Jack Zipes relates, the importance of fairy tales and why they "stick" is that they respond to the fears and dangers surrounding childhood:

> The only way that children (and adults) can be reared into tradition with stories that do not involve scaring them and encouraging them to submit to monsters and arbitrary deities is by transforming our notion of children, childhood, curiosity, and understanding more sensibly the conflictual nature of civilization and its discontents. (2006, 242)

So the Apocalypse also sticks, much as I wish it did not or had not over the centuries. If, as Burton Hatlen and many others relate, "Pullman's most distinctive contribution to the fantasy genre is his blurring of the line that separates the 'real' from the fantasy worlds" (Hatlen 2005, 75),[3] then the Apocalypse is just bad fantasy literature. Sure, it has its moments of spine-chilling horror and its lasting

---

3. Hatlen (2005, 93) calls the trilogy a "secular humanist fantasy" (the term secular humanism originated with John Dewey).

(and unfortunate) effect in religion and politics, but it fails to be good fantasy, at least if any ethical vision is required.

With Lyra in Apocalypse

Like Pullman's little follow-up book, *Lyra's Oxford*, I want to map Lyra in another, alternate universe. I want to create a narrative of Lyra entering, cutting a window with the subtle knife or finding an already-opened window (without, of course, the subsequent leaking of Dust!). I imagine Lyra entering through a window into the apocalyptic universe/s of the Bible. I say universe/s because the apocalyptic is always singular and plural in the biblical text. Creation begins, ends, and is renewed in an apocalypse (or multiple apocalypses—or the same one repeating itself over and over again). Creative chaos becomes equally creative abyss, Genesis to Revelation, apocalypse to apocalypse, amen. These bookends house a wealth of apocalyptic stories. The Bible, like some street preacher with a sign, shouts, "The End is near!" One cannot (should not?) separate the apocalyptic stuff from the Bible; any successful attempt would create Dust, resulting in a form of nuclear radiation. You would be contaminated on sight. Apocalypse is the swarthy companion of the Bible; like Pullman's daemons, it (he?) accompanies the stories everywhere, like Death in Ingmar Bergman's *The Seventh Seal*. We readers, like the medieval crusader knight in Bergman's film, cannot escape our fate, although we may trick Death into playing a lengthy, but stressful, game of chess. The plague has picked us out already. Chaos is patriarchalized, under lock and key, in the form of the abyss. Those biblical scholars who are apocalyptic deniers, who think they have separated the apocalyptic from the "good parts" or more sacred parts of the Bible, have a special glow about them. You'd better stay clear. On the other hand, there are those apocalyptic accepters who fail to question the sexist overthrow, fear, and subsequent containment of chaos.

I have been living in apocalypseland for years, well, maybe all my life. I grew up in the southern United States in the 1960s, with its inherent and ever-abiding racism, and now my country is immersed in the wars to begin all wars, wars without end, a possibly endless cycling of violence and terror. And this biblical text, the Apocalypse of John, continues to morph into bigger and more grotesque forms. When, as a reader, I enter the space of the textual world/s, I always lose my way, go down the wrong path, circle around, encountering the monsters that I know to avoid but that are at every turn anyway and unavoidable. They stalk my dreams and the political landscapes of war and destruction. Unlike my more-certain colleagues in biblical studies, I can never get a clear sense of the text; the historical tools fail me every time. "95 C.E. in the reign of Emperor Domitian!"

I shout at archangel Michael and the great beast (and at Tim LaHaye et al.). I hope those are the magic words to stop John's apocalyptic enactment. It is a feeble attempt to bring some historical sanity and proper placement to the narrative, but my cries are drowned out by the incessant noise of the text, the ever-whirling smoke and fire and thunder and heavenly choir. Useless. I need an alethiometer (the device Lyra has to predict the future) to read the Apocalypse, or an amber spyglass in order to see with a third eye or learn the intuitive skills to see through, in, and with this horrendous story of the endless end. The alethiometer would show me new possibilities in forming an ethical stance—and actions—against the nonsense and senselessness of violent apocalyptic desires. With practice and maturity, maybe I can become a more competent reader of the Apocalypse, but as yet the shadows remain, like the Spectres of Citagazze (a city in one of Pullman's parallel universes), threatening to devour my soul. The spyglass would allow me to see Dust, the original stuff of creation, the response of the Deep of Chaos before the prison house of language and patriarchy. Dust is the stuff of consciousness. This is a bit of what apocalypse as fantasy literature is about; we have to enter its fantastic universe, alternate but similar to our own, like Lyra and Will's Oxfords, parallel but altered. We have to close the window on this apocalyptic world and, like Lyra and Will, reenter our own world more fully empowered to create "the republic of heaven."

The Apocalypse of John leaves us in an extraordinary garden in an extra-worldly space (even if the New Jerusalem "comes down" to earth). Pullman pulls us out of our lives to wander with Lyra for a while but then go back home again. For him, real existence is here and to wish for another space is dangerous—that is why Lyra and Will must return to their respective worlds at the end. Do these stories need to exist so that the future of the future—the ultimate future—can be worked out? Does *His Dark Materials* leave us in an ordinary garden, in an ordinary (English academic) city on earth—where we are anyway? Pullman's garden is not enclosed; it is open to possibilities and imaginings, especially the idea that a girl child, a reincarnate Eve, will lead. That is the point—Lyra and Will avert the end, refuse apocalypse, choose a different way—not a kingdom but a republic of heaven. But is this republic better? Is it fair to compare or quantify Pullman's vision with the (multiple) biblical visions?

The Apocalypse is more than cathartic (for some) and more than just its horrors and posttraumatic aftertaste. It is an irresponsible story, even in the face of Roman imperialism of the late first century C.E. (still no excuse for the violence). To claim, as most biblical scholars (including me) do, that the Apocalypse of John is "a product of its time" is not just to ground it "historically," as much as that is even possible. It has another effect—to excuse it for its extremities, to explain it away. We cannot stop at the historical-critical method; for all its worth, since the

Enlightenment, the containers it provides are all full of holes (some tiny, some big). All theories are holey. The holes are not bad, since, after all, stories can never be fully contained. And I am not suggesting a metatheory here. I am suggesting companions, and the historical-critical method is one accompanist, although inadequate, to/with the apocalypse—the Apocalypse of John in particular, and even more, the tales of fantasy and horror that fly briefly alongside of and then away from the Apocalypse.

Pullman's trilogy opens a window for me to another universe, or set of universes, another way of understanding fantasy and apocalyptic as fantasy. There is a convergence of worlds, of alternate universes in apocalypse: the Apocalypses of John, Peter or Paul, Narnia, Dante, Milton, Blake, Dr. Strangelove, Left Behind. *His Dark Materials* is one of these spaces. We are travelers between these realms. With our subtle knives (if we are fortunate enough to possess one) we can cut a window in apocalypse, open the crystal coffin, returning all the nightmares and injustices to Dust, to star stuff.

WORKS CITED

Hatlen, Burton. 2005. Pullman's *His Dark Materials*, a Challenge to the Fantasies of J. R. R. Tolkien and C. S. Lewis, with an Epilogue on Pullman's New-Romantic Reading of *Paradise Lost*. Pages 75–94 in *His Dark Materials Illuminated: Critical Essays on Philip Pullman's Trilogy*. Edited by Millicent Lenz with Carole Scott. Detroit, Mich.: Wayne State University Press.

Kamper, Dietmar, and Christoph Wulf, eds. 1989. *Looking Back on the End of the World*. Translated by David Antal. New York: Semiotext(e).

Lenzen, Dieter. 1989. Disappearing Adulthood: Childhood as Redemption. Pages 64–78 in *Looking Back on the End of the World*. Edited by Dietmar Kamper and Christoph Wulf. Translated by David Antal. New York: Semiotext(e).

Lewis, C. S. 1984. *The Last Battle*. New York: HarperTrophy.

Pullman, Philip. 1995. *The Golden Compass*. New York: Ballantine. Originally published as *His Dark Materials I: Northern Lights*. New York: Scholastic, 1995.

———. 1997. *The Subtle Knife*. New York: Ballantine.

———. 2000. *The Amber Spyglass*. New York: Dell Laurel-Leaf.

———. 2001. The Republic of Heaven. *Horn Book Magazine* 77: 655–69.

———. 2005. *Lyra's Oxford*. New York: Knopf.

———, et al. 2004. *Darkness Illuminated: Platform Discussions on "His Dark Materials" at The National Theatre*. London: Oberon.

Warner, Marina. 2006. *Phantasmagoria*. Oxford: Oxford University Press.

Zipes, Jack. 2006. *Why Fairy Tales Stick: The Evolution and Relevance of a Genre*. New York: Routledge.

RESPONSES

Close Encounters:
The Bible as Pre-Text in Popular Culture

Laura Copier, Jaap Kooijman, and Caroline Vander Stichele

Compared to the Bible in art and the Bible in film, the Bible in popular culture is a relative newcomer in the field of biblical studies. A volume such as the present one can therefore be seen as a timely and useful contribution to a more systematic engagement of this fascinating theme. Moreover, the wide variety of topics addressed in this collection of essays gives one a sense of the virtually "omnipresent" nature of the Bible in (mostly Western) culture at large.

In our response, we adopt a bird's-eye perspective in order to discuss some of the overarching hermeneutical issues related to the close encounters between the Bible on the one hand and popular culture on the other, as documented in this volume. The point of departure for our analysis is the title of this collection: *The Bible in/and Popular Culture: A Creative Encounter*. Each element of this title gives rise to a number of reflections as to how it is dealt with in this volume.

The Bible

First of all, the Bible as a whole is seldom referred to in this volume. The focus, rather, is on particular texts, stories, characters, and themes. The choice is often that of the author, but the selection is also determined by the material under discussion. However, the Bible in question is almost always the Christian Bible and, more specifically, English translations of that Bible. Sometimes the translation used is relevant; for instance, the King James Version in the case of Bob Marley (Erskine). What these initial observations illustrate is that the Bible is always already part and parcel of culture at large, and, as such, it is not an entity somehow situated outside that culture to begin with.

A second point we want to address relates to the process of selectivity involved in almost all references to that Bible. Selectivity as such is, of course,

-189-

difficult to avoid and almost comes naturally in the case of the Bible, with its
wide range of views and literary genres. Moreover, some biblical texts have
played a major role in the course of its reception history, whereas others have
been obscured. As far as this volume is concerned, a more important question
is what choices are being made and if it is possible to determine why. A closer
look at the biblical texts that feature in this volume reveals that although both the
Hebrew Bible and the New Testament are mentioned, with a few exceptions, the
New Testament receives more attention than does the Hebrew Bible. Within the
Hebrew Bible, references are mostly made to the Pentateuch and the prophets,
especially Isaiah. As for the New Testament, the Gospels and the book of Revelation are mentioned more often. Some of these choices are informed by the
fact that a number of the essays focus more on biblical characters, such as God
(McEntire, Taylor), Jesus (Boer, Clanton), and Mary Magdalene (Culbertson), or
themes, such as the apocalypse (Pippin, Clark), than on biblical texts. Given the
importance of God and Jesus in Christian tradition, their presence in popular
culture is hardly surprising; that of Mary Magdalene is more intriguing and may
well be related to the renewed interest in her character since the second half of
the twentieth century, reaching a peak after the publication of Dan Brown's *The
Da Vinci Code* (2003). Something similar can also be observed with respect to the
popularity of apocalyptic scenarios in light of the end of the second millennium,
an event that strongly resonated in the Western, and especially the American,
imagination. Another trend worth noting here briefly is the increase of popular
interest in extracanonical writings. This is an aspect not covered in this volume,
which focuses more squarely on the Bible, but it is a phenomenon that is definitely worth exploring.

A third observation relates to the interpretive strategies used in this volume
to analyze the material under discussion—the biblical as well as the popular.
Here a wide range of methods can be noted, from a reception-historical approach
(Clanton, Culbertson, Erskine, Gilmour) to more literary-oriented (Clark, McEntire, Pippin) and theologically interested approaches (McEntire, Sample, Taylor),
but a combination of different methodological tools and theoretical lenses is also
used (Boer, Culbertson). Some contributors push the boundaries of more-estab-
lished approaches even further by developing approaches that seek to engage the
encounter between popular culture and the Bible in new ways. Thus, inspired by
Gerald West's notion of reading the Bible "other-wise," Taylor advocates reading
popular-cultural expressions "pop-wise." An even more intense fusion of popular
culture and the Bible is established by Perkinson, who employs a hip-hop hermeneutic of Holy Writ. Both contributions express a positive attitude toward
popular-cultural expressions as a valuable "medium" for biblical scholars. This
observation brings us to the other "side" of this volume—that of popular culture.

Popular Culture

What is popular culture? The answer to that question seems obvious, as we all recognize popular culture quite easily, both as consumers and as academics. Yet, when looking at the objects discussed in this volume, one cannot help noticing their wide range: pop music by Nick Cave, Emmylou Harris, and Kris Kristofferson (Boer, McEntire, Sample), television series like *South Park* and *bro'Town* (Taylor), graphic novels, hip-hop, reggae, books by Salman Rushdie and Philip Pullman, and even a bumper sticker (Pippin). Moreover, this wide range of objects forms only a relatively small segment of the broad realm of popular culture, which seems endless. The strength of popular culture is its inclusiveness and boundlessness and, perhaps most importantly, its ability to appropriate other forms of culture in a widely attractive way. Popular culture can be manipulative, turning culture into commodities that audiences are seduced into buying, yet it can also be remarkably democratic, opening up space for consumers to create meaning by making it part of their daily lives.

Instead of giving a strict definition, it might be more fruitful to recognize popular culture as a broad, almost arbitrary collection of cultural objects that are intertextually linked and open to a wide range of interpretations. Moreover, its triviality should be recognized as what makes popular culture a relevant object of study, rather than trying to reveal a hidden "serious" side that only an academic can detect. This is not to suggest that an informed reading cannot provide an additional value to a pop-cultural text. The presence of the Bible (or other religious texts) in popular culture is often implicit and one does not need to know the "original" biblical texts to understand and enjoy these objects of popular culture. Making this presence explicit may not necessarily lead to a "better" understanding of these objects, but it may provide an additional pleasure to those "in the know."

In/And

As the volume's title suggests, the Bible can be seen as both *outside* as well as *part of* (Western) popular culture. When perceived as *outside of* popular culture, the Bible becomes a source of inspiration for popular culture, providing scholars with the opportunity to analyze the ways in which the Bible has been appropriated and translated in forms of culture that have quite a different cultural function (most often, entertainment and pleasure) than the Bible itself. Even though these appropriations are often intended as "fun," they remain quite powerful in their triviality. The whorish image of Mary Magdalene as depicted in pop music (Culbertson), for instance, is so entrenched in popular culture that even a closer look at biblical texts cannot "correct" this dominant perception. As will be discussed in more detail below, this example also reveals that the trajectory from Bible to popular culture is a complex one. There is a long reception history situated between "then" and "now" that cannot be ignored when discussing interpretations of biblical texts, themes, and characters in popular culture.

However, the Bible can also be perceived as *part of* popular culture, as is effectively demonstrated by Jim Perkinson's hip-hop "mini-sample"—not a hip-hop translation of the Bible, or vice versa, but a creative interaction between the two realms, thereby showing their intertwinement. Perkinson thus challenges us to recognize that the Bible can be a dynamic part of popular culture, not simply open for new interpretations but in itself constantly changing.

The different ways in which the Bible is engaged in popular culture also raises the issue of its interpretation. In her introduction, Elaine Wainwright states that the present volume arose out of the "awareness that popular culture is a significant arena of contemporary biblical interpretation" (Wainwright, 3). Popular culture, in its clashes and interactions with the Bible, thus itself already performs a kind of exegesis—perhaps not the traditional exegesis as carried out by some biblical scholars but, rather, a popular form of exegesis. As such, this collection of essays underlines the divergent ways in which the Bible manifests itself as a key text in popular culture and functions as an apt reminder that "theologians … are not the only, and not the most important, persons who interpret the Bible" (Clanton, citing Luz, 6).

In the essays collected here, two different types of approaches/attitudes to a popular exegesis of the Bible can be discerned that differ in the amount of authority they give to the Bible as master text. Put differently, is the Bible simply one text among countless others, or does it have a special status? One way of dealing with this issue is by using the concept of intertextuality. The intertextual approach is familiar to both biblical scholars and popular culture scholars. A common view in the study of intertextuality is that an intertextual reading entails the investigation of sources and influences or, put differently, a work's relation to particular prior texts. Moreover, once an "original source" is identified, a definite meaning is often established, thereby closing off the process of signification. According to Jonathan Culler, however, intertextuality is a more complex phenomenon. In its nature rather lies the paradox of discursivity: "If one attempts to identify an utterance or text as a moment of origin, one finds that they depend upon prior codes" (Culler 2002, 103). Or, as Gilmour points out in his discussion of Salman Rushdie's *The Satanic Verses*, the relationship between biblical and extrabiblical texts is not so clear-cut or univocal. As Gilmour remarks, "narratives—even canonical, biblical narratives—do not stand alone and consequently do not gain preeminence over others" (24). One of Rushdie's metaphors, the countless streams that make up a river, is a good way to picture this.

Another illustration of the complex interaction between popular culture and the Bible is the representation of Mary Magdalene as discussed by Culbertson. In his article, he documents the numerous ways in which this figure has been appropriated in film, art, and popular music. As Culbertson remarks, these multiple appropriations lead to new interpretations of the underlying canonical texts yet do not necessarily express reverence/reference to the alleged "original" source (the exegesis-vs.-eisegesis debate). Culbertson's essay also shows that the divergent popular adaptations of Mary Magdalene are instrumental in shaping his students' interpretations, thereby eclipsing the influence and authority of the Bible as the key to understanding this figure. According to Culbertson, "no matter how well we teach the exegesis of Scripture and the hermeneutics of culture, there will still be people who actively resist what we are trying to teach because they have uniquely individual reasons for hanging on to *some alternative meaning* that better serves their personal needs, values, and life experience" (63, emphasis added).

The idea that the clash between the Bible and popular culture generates some alternative meaning is precisely the point: popular culture is not some form of wayward exegesis, performed by those who refuse to listen to the biblical experts. The confrontation between the Bible and popular culture irrevocably results in the transformation of both objects. Any attempt to "correct" popular culture's interpretation of biblical sources is a project that is destined to fail. Moreover, in our view, Culbertson's additional critique that popular culture's misguided appropriation of Mary Magdalene "makes it much more difficult for biblical scholars to reclaim ground for Mary Magdalene and reverse the damage done by centuries of institutional and ecclesiastical sexism" (71) points to an altogether different battle, which needs to be fought elsewhere.

In light of the preceding discussion, it is important to keep in mind that intertextuality is characterized by two basic traits: the nonautonomous status of texts and the absence or impossibility of defining origins. How then to use this potentially confusing tool? In the case of this volume, it would be useful to understand the Bible as "pre-text" in relation to its many different manifestations in popular culture. A pre-text in this case is what comes before, *but does not fully determine*, a later text. The main point here is that a pre-text can function as a source for the later text (because there are, for instance, thematic similarities), which means that the pre-text will initially be recognized as such, but, more importantly, this recognition will be followed by the observation of *differences* between the two texts.

An excellent example of an approach deploying the Bible as a pre-text, rather than as a master text, is the article by Clanton on images of Jesus in American pop culture. Here, one can find the most clear-cut example of the way that popular culture shapes our understanding of a biblical figure. Clanton persuasively argues that pop culture's interpretations of Jesus are to be valued and understood within the context in which they have emerged. Furthermore, the author demonstrates that popular renderings of Jesus shape the way that people understand and value this figure. Clanton thus shows that the Bible *informs*, yet never fully *determines*, the reading of popular manifestations of biblical themes, figures, motifs, etc.

The displacement of classical hermeneutical theories by popular "lenses" (note the emphatic difference between a theory and a lens) can be worrisome to biblical scholars. However, this gloomy scenario, which would imply that there is no longer room for exegesis in the classical sense of the word, is not altogether realistic. Perhaps (as Culbertson concedes and Clanton demonstrates) the two can coexist, in which case "popular culture not only influences biblical interpretation but also opens up new perspectives and challenges and confronts the conventional, stylized hermeneutical frameworks of the 'industry' of the academic study of biblical texts" (Culbertson, 71).

CREATIVE ENCOUNTERS

In contemporary audiovisual culture, the boundaries between information and entertainment, between politics and popular culture, are not as clearly drawn as they were in previous eras. All texts, including the Bible, are part of a dynamic intertextual process of meaning-making in which new meanings are created, whereas others may no longer be recognized. Moreover, as a culturally relevant text, the Bible can serve a wide range of functions, from a literal master text demanding religious authority to merely being one among many sources of inspiration. In the latter sense, the Bible is part of a cultural toolbox, supplying themes, stories, characters, and images that can be appropriated and reworked in popular culture, often popping up in new and unexpected places. Worth mentioning in this respect are popular "new" media such as the Internet, games, iPods, cell phones, and so forth, which deserve more attention than is given them in this volume.

In such an academic analysis, it is important to keep in mind that the use of the Bible in popular culture is not always meant to be taken (too) seriously, as (biblical) scholars are prone to do. Yet, simultaneously, we should also not underestimate the political workings and ideological implications of popular culture, particularly in these current "post-9/11" times, in which Western popular culture is often defined as "secular" in opposition to the "religious" cultures in Islamic countries. Recognizing the Bible in film, popular music, television series, graphic novels, and other forms of popular culture, as this volume does, opens up a space not only for exploring how the Bible as pre-text informs much of the culture we live in and consume every day, but also for critically engaging with the diffused and slippery boundaries that characterize contemporary audiovisual culture. Such an approach calls for creative encounters between the Bible and popular culture, thereby providing ever-new perspectives on this ancient book and revealing its continuous cultural relevance.

Works Cited

Culler, Jonathan. 2002. *The Pursuit of Signs: Semiotics, Literature, Deconstruction.* Ithaca, N.Y.: Cornell University Press.

Pop Scripture: Creating Small Spaces for Social Change

Erin Runions

This volume provokes a new way of thinking about biblical scripture and its contents. Together, these essays show how biblical "truths" are negotiated and modified in popular culture. Popularizations of scripture work for social change, redefine the idea of God, reconceptualize power as expressed in human relation to the divine, and reenvision community. They show us a very different kind of scripture than that enclosed in a single two-testamented, leather-bound book. As Elaine Wainwright suggests in her introduction, the volume foregrounds a kind of Scripture that stands outside of organized religion and that pushes against the analytic comfort zones of traditional biblical scholarship.

Right from its opening essay, the volume shows how the Bible's appearance in culture problematizes any notion of scripture as a fixed set of texts and truths. Michael Gilmour's essay on Salman Rushdie's *The Satanic Verses* explores Rushdie's manipulation of canon. Gilmour shows how Rushdie stretches the boundaries of canon, "flooding his stories with a seemingly endless mix of voices, reflecting religious and cultural diversity" (24). Rushdie reimagines the (already-expanded) "biblical" tradition of Lucifer's fall from heaven. Milton's *Paradise Lost*, the Qur'an, the Rolling Stones, and Shakespeare swirl together in the tale of the devilish transformation of Saladin Chamcha, who falls into an immigrant's experience of London from an exploding airplane. Chamcha's metamorphosis into a goaty devil symbolizes the dehumanizing racism experienced by south Asian immigrants in Britain. "In Rushdie's world, the fallen, devilish angel is a victim, not a villain" (15). Resculpting scriptures in this way, Rushdie imagines another world and another kind of community, which coexist and flourish and in which immigrants are not treated as though they have a pair of devilish horns. Gilmour shows how Rushdie treats biblical scripture as a malleable, flexible medium that can be shaped into a national or communal space that can handle more than one truth and, subsequently, more than one culture and ethnicity.

Several of the volume's other essays likewise take up the ways in which culture opens up scripture for the purposes of cultural change. Music, like fiction, seems to facilitate such an expansion. Noel Erskine shows how Bob Marley's use of the Bible in reggae, combined as it is with Rastafarianism, challenged colonial oppression in Jamaica and fostered Jamaican visibility, voice, and a sense of community-in-struggle. "Through reggae, Marley was able to help oppressed Jamaicans fashion their identity as they placed their oppressive history within the larger context of the narrative history of the biblical story" (105). Biblical narrative is fused with Jamaican history and Rastafarian beliefs, so that "as the people discover their story conjoined with the biblical story, they begin to leave Babylon; they begin to recognize that their sojourn in Babylon is temporary as they discover they are meant for Zion" (106). Perhaps echoing Marley's music in some capacity, Jim Perkinson's hip-hop improvisations rewrite and rerhyme "the writ of salvation ... sounding out the delirium below the doctrine, representing the tic-toc rip-rock inside the teaching" (83), in the pursuit of social and racial justice. Perkinson's hip-hop interpretations of biblical pericopes transform them so that Babel becomes, like hip-hop's best self, "the code of the clamor, the mode in which the city challenges its own meaning" (86); the Gospel of John's Jesus is "free to live inside a stigma, ally with the demonized ... suffer with the racialized" (91). In Perkinson's retelling, the Bible becomes its own hip-hop afterlife. Tex Sample takes his cue from country music, in particular Kris Kristofferson's tunes "Help Me Make It through the Night" and "Me and Bobby McGee." In conversation with these songs, Sample thinks about how to ameliorate the inequalities that mark the struggles of the working class. He argues that Kristofferson's songs speak to a working class "struggle for dignity . . . [while] surviving and coping are the order of the day" (119), as well as to a "dream of being free of bosses, released from sucking up, and no longer kissing ass" (120). The desire for freedom and release from subjection are themes that Sample also finds expressed in Paul's writing. Sample argues that Paul's vision of *ekklesia* provides a place for freedom, festival, community, and "an alternative to the dominations of class" (122).

The essays by Gilmour, Erskine, Perkinson, and Sample powerfully articulate the use of scripture in the demand for racial and economic justice and freedom from oppression. New communities are imagined. For Marley, as for Rushdie, scripture is freed from canon in order to work for change. In Perkinson's and Sample's reworkings of scripture, it is less canon that needs to be supplemented— for they both adhere to canon in many respects—than genre. Music, poetry, and rhythm give voice to scriptural themes in a cadence that may be better able to voice the particular injustices of racialized and class-segregated urban life and to inspire change. Significantly, each of these essays shows how culture crosses the (canonical and literary) boundaries of scripture in order to imagine communal struggles for justice and a world of equal freedoms.

But culture's rewriting of scripture is not always unambiguously for the purposes of social change, as several of the articles illustrate. Gender and sexuality seem to be a place where the push and pull on limits to change are felt most keenly, at least where scripture is involved. So for instance, Erskine shows how Marley is not able to chant down sexism in Babylon (105). Philip Culbertson insightfully explores the way that Mary Magdalene's sexuality persistently merges with readers' non-scriptural presuppositions about her, even in the face of textual evidence. Culbertson shows how the Bible disintegrates under the weight of the sex-negative theological tradition of Mary as the healed and reformed prostitute. He wonders whether perhaps this tradition has remained dominant because there are still, unfortunately, some social and emotional gains for women, as well as men, in upholding gender hierarchies. Yet Culbertson also shows that popular songs about Mary Magdalene, while sometimes holding in place an unnuanced and dichotomous view of women's sexuality, also create spaces for imagining a mutual sexual relationship between Jesus and Mary. In short, Mary becomes a testing ground in popular culture for exploring female sexuality, sometimes reaffirming misogyny and sometimes imagining more-equal sexual relations. Along similar lines, Dan Clanton's essay shows the way that cultural refashionings of Jesus in comic books, graphic novels, films, and music may be used to try to push norms of gender and sexuality and yet pull back from change at the same time. Clanton unearths a fascinating array of refashioned Jesuses (what he calls Jesus in "Elseworlds") that can sometimes modify gender and sexual norms (the "Hippie" Jesus) but that can also reify them (the "Manly" Jesus), sometimes doing both in the same production. So, for instance, the Jesus of *Jesus Christ Vampire Hunter* (2001) is cared for by a transvestite and refuses to categorize (non-vampiric) lesbian love as deviant (53), yet he still has to fight off evil deviant lesbian vampires. The film thus associates deviance and lesbianism, even as it disavows that it does so. Despite such limitations, what the Jesus(es) of the Elseworlds and the melodic Mary Magdalene make clear is that there is a push and pull between cultural and scriptural change, each informing the other. As culture changes, scripture does too, incrementally creating at least one form of moral permission for acceptance of gender and sexual difference.

One of pop scripture's chief interventions is to negotiate with an understanding of the divine. Several essays demonstrate the way that popular media self-consciously depict a culturally adapted God, rather than an ostensibly timeless and unchanging God. So for instance, as Erskine makes clear, Marley's Jah is particularly bound up with the Jamaican people's struggle. Steve Taylor shows how the New Zealand indigenous animated TV show, *bro'Town*, reenvisions God more optimistically, not as distant or dead but rather as an Islander wearing a lavalava, who delights in creation and laughter, and who is an ethical teacher (170). In so depicting God, the show works against the racial norms more usually upheld by images of a white deity. Roland Boer finds in the music of Nick Cave an appealing, queerly eroticized, and slightly heretical Jesus, "who has a peccadillo for threesomes" (135). These renditions of God—which imagine God as a way to work through pain, dysfunction, and cultural exclusion—reflect time- and culture-bound needs and desires.

Popular culture is not always so positively disposed toward God, however, and the apparent absence or death of God is also culturally productive. Mark McEntire shows that Emmylou Harris explores the absence of God in the face of pain in the album *Red Dirt Girl*. McEntire argues that the album as a whole tries to make meaning in the shadow of the absent God, which is felt as pain. Terry Ray Clark gives a compelling and complex reading of the graphic novels *Kingdom Come* and *Watchmen* as apocalyptic religious and prophetic texts that critique a tragic view of a controlling, distant, and violent God. The God of these graphic novels is not one who intervenes and brings salvation in a time of crisis: the "deity cannot be counted on to instill justice in the universe" (142). Tina Pippin illustrates how Philip Pullman similarly works against such an apocalyptic worldview, by exploring the death of God in the *His Dark Materials* trilogy. There Pullman imagines God as a shriveled-up puppet, with "no will of his own" (180), who turns into dust when extracted from his protective casing. The child-heroes of the story watch in dismay as he dissolves before their eyes. As Pippin puts it, "God is words that crumble apart when lifted up" (181). God may disintegrate, but these essays indicate that scripture does not; scripturalizing continues, even as it tries to handle the absence of God.

Pop culture's rethinking of God reveals a high value placed on human agency, both individual and communal. Boer suggests that beneath Cave's idiosyncratic and personalized Jesus lies the liberal "Enlightenment ideology of the sacrosanct and inviolable individual" (137). For Boer, such a reaffirmation of the status quo, although perhaps appealing, is ultimately not iconoclastic enough (137). McEntire suggests that, for Harris, what emerges is a sense of human agency and persistence in the face of pain. He writes, "*Red Dirt Girl* ... introduces this haunting divine silence then dives into the pain and struggle of human existence that fills the resulting space," in which "a thing of beauty [is] created from a life of pain" (38). In McEntire's reading of Harris, human agency is more powerful than God in dealing with pain. Clark similarly shows that *Kingdom Come* and *Watchmen* value human agency; in a comic apocalyptic mode, they "admonish their readers to avoid passivity and to exercise their freedom and power for constructive ends" (155). One might read both Harris and the authors of these graphic novels as being informed by the same liberal ideology as Cave (indeed, who isn't?). But as both Boer and McEntire point out, Cave and Harris work out their respective theologies relationally, and the kinds of relationships they envision go beyond the usual solipsistic familial formations. They point toward differently modeled communities. *Bro'Town* is more explicit in rethinking community. As Taylor points out, in *bro'Town* God's agency is shown through teaching humans to make ethical choices that benefit the community. Moreover, the view of scripture and of God in *bro'Town* rethinks community by "stand[ing] against exclusive readings by dominant power groups." Further, it is oriented toward a communal ethics, and "not simply the ethics of the religio/familial system" (170).

Ultimately, pop scripture's emphasis on human agency—whether individual, relational, or communal—reflects and enables a shift in power from the top down to the bottom up. Drawing on the work of Conrad Ostwalt, Clark diagnoses popular culture's interest in human agency as a shift in religious authority (142). But in many ways, such a shift in religious authority also marks the more general shift in authority and power, as elucidated by Michel Foucault in his many writings. Post-Enlightenment, power is no longer a simple top-down affair but rather is produced betwixt and between, in the disciplining of bodies and in the everyday actions of humans. As Pippin importantly points out in her reading of Pullman, this shift in power is the movement from monarchy to republic, from the kingdom of heaven to the republic of heaven. Pullman and Pippin argue for the more compelling ideal of collective cooperation that is grounded in the beauty and possibility of this world, rather than in the future glory of a long-absent king. Certainly pop scripture's new conceptualization of power is ideologically conscribed (i.e., through liberal ideology, as Boer implies) and limited (often with respect to gender and sexuality, as demonstrated by Culbertson and Clanton). Nonetheless, these "pop-wise" renditions of scripture (to borrow a term from Taylor) at least create spaces for change in the very movement from hierarchy to community.

Taken together, these essays implicitly argue that popular culture is more than simply entertaining; it not only reflects but also engages philosophical, theological, and political concerns in its own rewriting of scripture. The volume illumines the multiple ways in which popular culture reads, modifies, inspires, and expands our notion of scripture, rescripting traditional ideas about God, human agency, and community. It shows how pop scripture insists on social change, or at least inches toward it. Wisely, these papers show that change is not automatic or uncomplicated by existing power structures, ideologies, or norms. But as a whole, the volume shows that as culture changes, so does scripture; as scripture changes, so can culture. Pop scripture is, at the end of the day, far more complex in its dynamism and engagement with important issues of contemporary justice than is any notion of a fixed, unchanging, canonically bound Word of God.

Contributors

Roland Boer is a faculty research professor at the University of Newcastle, Australia. Apart from voyages by ship and cycling as far as he can, he has also published a few books. The most recent are *Political Myth* (2009), *Political Grace* (2009), and *Criticism of Religion* (2009).

Dan W. Clanton Jr. is assistant professor of religious studies at Doane College in Crete, Nebraska. He regularly presents and publishes on the intersection of Bible, religion, and popular culture, including the NBC drama *Law & Order*; the presentation of Hanukkah in *Friends* and *South Park*; and the Jewish identities of musicians such as Matisyahu and the Hip Hop Hoodios. His new book, *Daring, Disreputable, and Devout: Interpreting the Hebrew Bible's Women in the Arts and Music* (2009), focuses on aesthetic and scholarly interpretations of biblical women.

Terry Ray Clark holds the joint PhD in biblical interpretation from the Iliff School of Theology and the University of Denver. He is currently assistant professor of religion at Georgetown College (Kentucky), specializing in Hebrew Bible and religion and popular culture. He has written two articles on the Bible and graphic novels for the *SBL Forum*, an online journal of the Society of Biblical Literature dedicated to the study of the Bible and popular culture. He is currently coediting an introductory textbook on religion and popular culture for Routledge.

Laura Copier studied film and television studies at the University of Amsterdam. She completed her PhD at the Amsterdam School for Cultural Analysis (ASCA). Her dissertation, entitled "Preposterous Revelations: Visions of Apocalypse and Martyrdom in Hollywood Cinema 1980–2000," focused on representations of the apocalypse and notions of martyrdom in contemporary Hollywood cinema. Currently, she is a lecturer in both the Media and Culture Department and the Department of Religion Studies at the University of Amsterdam.

Philip Culbertson is an adjunct faculty member on the theology faculty at the University of Auckland, New Zealand, and in the Philosophy Department at College of the Desert in Palm Desert, California. With Elaine Wainwright and

Susan Smith, he recently coedited *Spirit Possession, Theology, and Identity: A Pacific Exploration* (2010).

Noel Leo Erskine is professor of theology and ethics at Candler School of Theology and the Graduate School of Arts and Sciences, Emory University. He is the author of *Black People and the Reformed Church in America* (1978), *Decolonizing Theology* (1981, 1998), *King among the Theologians* (1994), *From Garvey to Marley* (2005), and *Black Theology and Pedagogy* (2008). His research interests include the history and development of the black church, black theology, and pedagogy and theological method in the works of James Cone, Karl Barth, Dietrich Bonhoeffer, and Martin Luther King Jr.

Michael J. Gilmour is associate professor of New Testament and English literature at Providence College (Canada). His publications include *Tangled Up in the Bible: Bob Dylan and Scripture* (2004) and *Gods and Guitars: Seeking the Sacred in Post-1960s Popular Music* (2009).

Jaap Kooijman is associate professor of media and culture and American studies at the University of Amsterdam, the Netherlands. His latest book is *Fabricating the Absolute Fake: America in Contemporary Pop Culture* (2008). For more information, see: www.jaapkooijman.nl.

Mark McEntire is professor of religion at Belmont University in Nashville, Tennessee, where he teaches courses in Old Testament and Hebrew language. He is the author of several books, including *Struggling with God: An Introduction to the Pentateuch* (2008) and *Raising Cain, Fleeing Egypt, and Fighting Philistines: The Old Testament in Popular Music* (2006).

Jim Perkinson is an activist/educator from inner-city Detroit, teaching as professor of social ethics at the Ecumenical Theological Seminary and lecturing in intercultural communication studies at the University of Oakland (Michigan). He holds a PhD in theology from the University of Chicago, is the author of *White Theology: Outing Supremacy in Modernity* (2004) and *Shamanism, Racism, and Hip-Hop Culture: Essays on White Supremacy and Black Subversion* (2004) and is a recognized artist on the spoken-word poetry scene in the city.

Tina Pippin is professor and chair of the Department of Religious Studies at Agnes Scott College in Decatur, Georgia, and an activist educator and scholar of apocalyptic cultures, postmodern religion, and human rights. She is a coeditor with Cheryl Kirk-Duggan of *Mother Goose, Mother Jones, Mommie Dearest: Biblical Mothers and Their Children* (2009).

Erin Runions is assistant professor in the Department of Religious Studies at Pomona College. Her work brings together politics, culture, and the reading of the biblical text. She is the author of *Changing Subjects: Gender, Nation, Future in Micah* (2001) and *How Hysterical: Identification and Resistance in the Bible and Film* (2003).

Tex Sample, the Robert B. and Kathleen Rogers Professor Emeritus of Church and Society at the Saint Paul School of Theology, is ordained in the United Methodist Church. A freelance lecturer and preacher, he lives in Goodyear, Arizona. His recent books on the working class include *Blue Collar Resistance and the Politics of Jesus* (2006), *White Soul* (1996), *Ministry in an Oral Culture* (1994), and *Hard Living People and Mainstream Christians* (1993). Early on he worked as a cab driver, a laborer, and a roust-about in the oil field.

Steve Taylor is a New Zealand Baptist minister. Currently he serves in South Australia as director of missiology at Uniting College of Leadership and Theology and as senior lecturer at Flinders University. He is author of *The Out of Bounds Church? Learning to Create a Community of Faith in a Culture of Change* (2005) and writes regularly on theology and pop culture, including being a monthly film reviewer for *Touchstone* magazine since 2005.

Caroline Vander Stichele is lecturer in religious studies at the University of Amsterdam, the Netherlands. Her research and publications focus on hermeneutics and the reception history of biblical texts and characters, representations of gender in Early Christian literature, and the Bible in modern media. She is the coauthor of *Contextualizing Gender in Early Christian Discourse: Thinking Beyond Thecla* (with Todd Penner; 2009) and has coedited several volumes, including *Creation & Creativity: From Genesis to Genetics and Back* (with A. G. Hunter; 2006).

Elaine M. Wainwright is professor and head of the School of Theology at the University of Auckland, where she introduced and cotaught The Bible in Popular Culture with Dr. Philip Culbertson. She is a New Testament scholar and author of *Women Healing/Healing Women: The Genderization of Healing in Early Christianity* (2006) and *Shall We Look for Another: A Feminist Rereading of the Matthean Jesus* (1998). She has recently coedited *Eco-Theology* (Concilium 2009/3) and *Land Conflicts, Land Utopias* (Concilium 2007/2) as a member of the editorial board of Concilium.

INDEX

CPSIA information can be obtained
at www.ICGtesting.com
Printed in the USA
FFOW03n2044280115
10686FF